ACHIEVE

Secrets from Successful Entrepreneurs

Bogdan Marzewski
Robert G. Allen
Sunil Tulsiani
and Leading Experts Around North America

LEADERS IN GLOBAL PUBLISHING

PRIVATE INVESTMENT CLUB
THE LARGEST REAL ESTATE CLUB IN CANADA

Published in association with:
Private Investment Club
21 Queen Street East, Suite 200, Brampton, Ontario L6W 3P1
PrivateInvestmentClub.com

Published by Motivational Press, Inc.
7777 N Wickham Rd, # 12-247
Melbourne, FL 32940
www.MotivationalPress.com

Manufactured in the United States of America.

ISBN: 978-1-62865-138-6

CONTENTS

WELCOME LETTER FROM SUNIL AND ROBERT

Dear Friend,

Welcome to *ACHIEVE: Secrets from Successful Entrepreneurs*, and congratulations on your decision to step up and take your business to the next level. First, we want to express how much we respect your decision to invest in yourself and your business. There are plenty of people who talk about creating success and achieving greater results, but few people actually do, and we commend you for taking the bold and committed action to pick up this book!

Our ability to achieve top level results is what separates those who reach success in their business from those who will spend their lives struggling. Contrary to common belief, the skills and abilities to achieve are not inherent qualities, but are learned qualities. *ACHIEVE: Secrets from Successful Entrepreneurs* is all about that learning. It's about learning the top tools, strategies, principles, and skill-sets that today's top entrepreneurs use in achieving results and creating success in their businesses. The best part is, you aren't just going to learn from us, you're going to learn from a collection of the foremost business experts in North America. Not those who spend all their time teaching about success, but those who are actually on the ground, implementing, day in and day out.

So let's get started! It's certainly up to you to decide how you want to approach this book, but if you are truly looking to maximize your results, we recommend these three tips:

1. Use this book as a guide and get creative about how to implement these strategies. Not every strategy in the book will be a fit for you, and some of them will have to be adjusted to meet your business.

2. Stay Committed. It's easy to pick up a book, read a chapter or two, implement a few good ideas and put the book down. True commitment lies in your ability to pick up the book day after day and consistently look for what's next in building your business and growing your ability to achieve results.

3. Have Fun. The concepts in this book, while serious, are also designed for you to extrapolate, innovate, and play in various ways to see what works for you. As we're sure you know, there's no "one size fits all" strategy to business success or life success. Be willing to adapt, adjust and overcome the hiccups that come up along the way.

We hope you enjoy this book and thank you for allowing us to share it with you as you create new opportunities for extraordinary success in your business and throughout your life.

To Your Success --

Sunil Tulsiani and Robert Allen

How I Doubled My Income With Real Estate Investments—Part Time

By Bogdan Marzewski

I'm commonly known as the full-time math teacher and part-time real estate millionaire in the Toronto area—but I don't think I'm so different from you or anyone reading this book, for that matter. I have a regular "day job," a family, and a desire to live a long, rich and fulfilling life.

What I do know, however, is that my life *is* very different from most of my peers. And the primary reason for that is because I knew I wanted something more, and I actually took the necessary steps to ensure my future prosperity. In order to do this, though, I had to first overcome my *fears*. I also had to be willing to do what it took to create my future. And to do that, I had to find the right person to help me figure out what those proper steps should be.

Sound too easy? Well, I assure you that success can be yours as well if: (a) you commit yourself to finding it, and (b) you find the right mentor to help with the search. These truly are the two keys to creating the life you want. And I hope that I, like my mentors, can help you to take the steps you need to take to ensure your financial success and freedom.

This is my success story. It can be yours, too.

Creating a Life in Canada

My wife and I graduated university in our home country of Poland in June of 1989. One month later, we landed in Montreal. We made our way to Toronto, where we applied for a visa to stay in the country. The good news is that, at the time, the Canadian government had implemented a program to assist Eastern Europeans such as ourselves, and we were allowed to stay on a temporary visa until they reviewed our application.

The bad news— it would take two-and-a-half years for them to decide. In the interim, we had no work permits, which meant we could not hold a "real" job for 30 months while we waited to hear our fate.

Because our home country's government was in such flux, we were determined to stay in Canada. That meant, in order to survive, we had to take a lot of simple labour jobs, which paid in cash and had no official records.

While not ideally what we had expected, I was able to learn some invaluable trade skills. For example, I did a lot of interior installations in a chain of shoe stores where I learned how to work with my hands.

As you might have guessed by now, we were allowed to stay in Canada. I became a math teacher in1994. I made a decent, stable living. Like many families, we worked hard and saved hard, so we were finally able to buy our first home. I used my new restoration skills to fix up the basement so we could rent it out to a tenant. We became landlords. And thanks to those rental payments, we were able to pay off the mortgage on our home within six years. We found ourselves happily mortgage-free.

So, what to do with that all that extra money? My wife said we should invest it and watch it grow. Because I had seen how powerful buying real estate could be in the terms of equity, investment and providing positive cash-flow, we decided to look at real estate investing. It worked once, Why not a second time? So we bought another low-priced property that needed a little tender loving care. Once again, the skills I learned during my earlier years paid off in spades, and we fixed the property up and sold it for a good profit. What was amazing is that even though we decided to flip this property instead of rent it, I could see that with the equity I had in my home and the money we just made from the flip, we could literally do this as many times as we wanted!

The Problem

Yes, it was profitable, but it was an *awful* lot of work! My wife and I now wondered if there was a way to make money in real estate without having to endure the hard work required to remodel and upgrade a home—every single weekend.

So I decided to find out. I read books, I researched the Internet, I talked to people, and then, in the local newspaper, I finally found what I was looking for—an ad for an investment real estate seminar. It seemed perfect. Not only could I learn how to invest in real estate without breaking our backs, but more importantly, become financially free.

In 2006, at a weekend workshop held by the Robert G. Allen Institute, I met my soon-to-be real-estate mentor, Sunil Tulsiani, aka "The Wealthy Cop," who left his job as a police officer to pursue real estate investing full-time. This, of course, intrigued me—especially after Sunil told me he did virtually none of the work on his investment properties himself—and he had about 77 properties at the time I approached him.

Eventually, Sunil put together an elite real estate club called Private Investment Club (PIC) and invited other people interested in pursuing real estate profits to join. I was very excited to become a part of this wonderful group so I could learn everything I needed to learn about the options available for a regular guy like me. I certainly didn't have the capital and resources he did. I was, and still am, a high school math teacher. I understood, however, one important thing—in order to succeed, you need to learn from somebody who has already done it and follow in their footsteps.

Investing in a New Beginning

As I began attending Sunil's investment meetings, other members would share stories about the deals they were making. As a mathematician, I instinctively look at numbers in an analytical way, and probably more closely than the average person. I saw how Sunil and other members in the club were making investments that made absolute sense from a numbers standpoint. My mindset began to change completely.

Just like the majority of people I know, I was skeptical at first. As much as I knew on an intellectual level that investing in real estate was a great idea, I was still very afraid of buying and holding onto properties. I worked hard for my salary, and the thought of not making an immediate profit on our sizeable investment, was scary. I worried about something going wrong, that we might get stuck with an unsellable home. I treasured the huge relief I felt when a property was sold and the closing period was over.

But with my new mentor's guidance and the stories of other investors in the group, I realized I was allowing my fear to get in the way of my future. I was, indeed, a regular guy, and my mindset proved it.

Changing Your Mindset

At the PIC meetings, I discovered that, he and other successful members were reading personal growth books by people like Robert G. "One Minute Millionaire" Allen, Robert "Rich Dad" Kiyosaki and Napoleon "Think and Grow Rich" Hill. These inspirational people actually had mentors in their lives who helped them to overcome their fears and empowered them to move ahead with plans that proved to be profitable.

So I read these books, too, and they helped me to change my perspective and my perceptions about fear in general. More importantly, they helped me to think DIFFERENTLY. I learned how to work from an "achievement-oriented mindset" instead of a "fear-based" one. With this new thought process in play, I put my name on the list of people in the group who wanted to "get in" on a real estate deal. I decided to take *action* when I came across lucrative positive cash flow properties or properties that were below market value.

Still, I have to admit, when my wife and I made our first deal on a rental investment property, I was very nervous. Still, I remembered my mentor's advice, and I put my $5000 down and moved forward. Through the club, I found an excellent real estate lawyer as well as a mortgage broker that would help find the best loan terms to fit our needs. The support and resources my mentor made available to us was crucial to our efforts. As I said, numbers are important to me—they make sense. In theory, you can make many things work. The trick with real life is in the *application* of those theories. For example, once I invested in the property, I needed to figure out who I would rent it to. At that time, I discovered Craigslist. Today, I use Kijiji and a Realtor who also invests in real estate.

When I did find an appropriate tenant, it was one of the best days of my life. The tenant was in our property the first week it became available. Then, when the rent cheques started coming in consistently, month after month, and when I still had something left in my pocket after I paid all the expenses, I finally saw for my own eyes that you could rent out your real estate at a profit and make it work. That, in turn, gave me the confidence to make the next deal.

Now, every time I make a new deal, I still find I'm nervous—you have to line up your financing and your tenant again. The difference, of course, is it's no longer the first time, and I have the experience to know how to make it work. It's a process I can now repeat over and over—because I have systems in place that I trust—and this is a key to my massive success.

Creating and Enjoying Success

My wife and I are much happier with our "new" system of real estate investments. We no longer have to work all week long and then every weekend. I spend only a few hours a month on our properties, and that's mainly on paperwork. We are able to sustain many properties at once. We've made 25 deals and still own 13 investment properties, including rental properties and investment land across Canada and the US. My real estate holding portfolio is worth $3.5 million. Not every deal I made was profitable, but I kept going and continued learning from the experience, which allowed me to grow and become more successful.

I personally manage my properties that are within 90 minutes of my home. As I expanded my real estate portfolio to properties outside Ontario and even Canada, I used a trusted management company and an experienced individual to take care of these properties.

If you're wondering how much money we make on the properties, the gross income is over $90,000, the equivalent of my yearly salary. In other words, I have been able to double my salary through my real estate holdings. This is, of course, an incredibly valuable feat to accomplish at any time. Moreover, in an era when teachers and other public employees find their salaries being frozen and even their pensions threatened, it's actually a Godsend.

Every day I watch as my teaching colleagues grow more disappointed and nervous that they will be just a few pay cheques away from disaster. Many who relied on government jobs and other private sector positions, where everything seemed guaranteed when they started, now face the prospect of having those promises broken. The rules are changing faster than anyone thought they could—and I believe the outcome for many won't be a happy one.

I believe you should put yourself in the driver's seat and focus on achieving your goals in life NOW, rather than stressing each and every day and letting your employer take the wheel. The more you can take control, the better off you'll be.

And more importantly, taking control includes seeking out mentors, building your power team and connecting with like-minded people to help you navigate the road. We use maps and a GPS to find places we have never been. Why should it be any different when jumping into a situation–like real estate investing–we are not familiar with?

How Mentors Can Change Your Life

With the help of a mentor, I was able to buy positive cash-flow and investment properties below market value in the Greater Toronto Area—sometimes *with little or no money down*. Prior to having a mentor, I would never have even dreamed this was possible. At the very least, I thought it to be a risky venture, but I was able to do this because there was an investor interested in the deal who was willing to put up the entire down payment and the closing costs. You are probably wondering why anybody would do this. How can they benefit?

Every situation must be 'win-win' for both parties. On one side, you have a solid deal, and there is a need for a down payment in order to be able to make the purchase. On the other side, another investor wants to invest his or her money in a great deal without having to do the work. So both parties prosper. My investor paid the down payment, and I did the work—Win-Win.

You can go only so far on your own, no matter what you do. In order to grow, you need other like-minded people and a mentor in your life.

It All Comes Back to the Numbers

This investment property has a mortgage of $ 136,000 with a monthly payment of $594. The property taxes are $136 per month. The management fee is $304 per month, and the insurance is $25 per month. The monthly rent collected is $1275. Our tenant pays for the hydro (electricity) plus other standard utilities: cable TV, Internet and so on. So the net monthly cash flow from that property is $216, which is $2592 per year. When you also consider that every year there is a mortgage pay down equivalent to $3000, this property generates about $6000 per year—with $0 down. What do you think the return on the investment (ROI) is?

Since that first deal we have bought three more properties together and all with no money down on my part! We simply split the profits 50-50. I find the deal, and he provides the down payment.

You might be wondering, if I am making the same income from my investments as my teaching salary, why I continue to teach. The simple answer is that I still love my job. I am passionate about working with my students, and I try to teach them more than math. What I really want to do is inspire them to follow their dreams, even though those dreams may not generate a lot of income. You can always find other ways of making money, as I did.

Unfortunately, most people are brought up, generation after generation, to believe that in order to be successful you must become a doctor, an engineer, or a lawyer or some other profession that makes you a lot of money—even if you are not passionate about your work. I obviously disagree. I am proud that I am able, thanks to my mentors and now my extra income, to help my daughters finance their futures. One of my two daughters was studying outside of Canada at a cost of over $35,000 a year, but I was able to refinance one of my properties and make $60,000 in one fell swoop, which covers not only one child's education, but our other daughter's as well.

Now, It's Your Turn!

So what is my point? I'm not that unique. I just made the commitment to change my mindset and ultimately my life.

So can you. One of my fellow teachers heard about my real estate investments and said, "So…I hear you spend all your weekends fixing toilets?" I replied, "Actually, no. I was afraid of that, because that's what I thought landlords had to do. But, it turns out, they don't!" I told him my time commitment is just a few hours of bookkeeping a month.

He was surprised and intrigued. I, like many others love my job and I am proof that you can still do what you love and make extra income in your spare time.

And I am proof that you can still do what you love and make extra income in your spare time.

When you are ready to change your mindset, you can achieve results beyond your wildest dreams. You just need to be willing to learn and to put into action a new set of skills— and, of course, continue learning while you're doing.

There is absolutely no reason you not to try!

Once you know WHY you want to make changes in your life, the HOW will follow, especially when you are coached by someone who already has what you want. Follow the individual who can show you real life experience, as I followed my mentor, Sunil.

It's easy, it's doable, and it brings you two very big benefits:

1. You can have the lifestyle you desire.

Thanks to our extra investment income, I am able to afford a quality education for my children. We are also able to afford to travel at least twice a year—during my school breaks, of course. We've gone on trips to Europe and throughout North America— trips that wouldn't have happened without our positive cash-flow properties. Whatever you want to do— but currently can't afford— can suddenly become possible!

2. You can literally make money while you sleep.

When you invest in real estate, you not only realize positive cash-flow on your properties from your tenants' rent payments, but those properties are also appreciating in value as time goes on. For example, we bought one property in 2008 in the greater Toronto Area for $200,000 (with a $10,000 down payment). Over five years, the positive cash-flow equals roughly $2600 per year, adding up to $13,000 over those five years. Return on investment (ROI), including the down payment? Approximately 28 percent per year. Meanwhile, the value of the property over those five years has increased by roughly $70,000.

As I said, I am a numbers person— and I like those numbers very much.

Anybody, regardless of your educational background, skillset, age, or gender, can design a real estate business that provides this kind of income. Whether you want this extra money to help augment an existing source of income from a job or to eventually replace it entirely is up to you.

Just imagine that you have two, four, ten properties or even more. Imagine the numbers I shared with you times the number of those properties. Imagine achieving that kind of return on investment with very little extra work required on your part. Do not let average people distract you from your desires, and always follow your dream.

Are you ready to do things differently than most people? Are you ready to define your dream, set your clear goals, and surround yourself with like-minded people? Are you willing to follow and copy someone who has what you want? Once you make a decision to change, you will be ready to take action—immediately. And I want to be there to help you to create the lifestyle you crave.

And for this reason, I spent months writing my book called *Your Dream, Your Life—on Your Terms*. And I want to give it to you for free. Just visit www.bogdanmarzewski.com/yourdream for your print copy or an eBook.

About Bogdan Marzewski

Bogdan Marzewski is a public speaker, mentor, author and mathematics teacher at Mary Ward Catholic Secondary School in Toronto, Ontario. He is also a successful real estate investor looking to mentor motivated individuals who want to follow in his footsteps and invest in cash-flow properties in Canada and the US. Bogdan also mentors his students and inspires them to succeed. His business skills, coupled with his real estate experience, gives him firsthand knowledge that he uses to advise these young people on life and education. Bogdan was featured in *Real Estate Magazine CRE* December 2013 and has been showcased on PIC blogtalkradio.

For more information, visit http://www.bogdanmarzewski.com or visit his blog at: bogdanmarzewski.wordpress.com, where he provides financial literacy and innovative strategies for investing in real estate.

FAST CASH WITH REAL ESTATE
7 WAYS TO EARN $10,000 CASH IN 90 DAYS OR LESS

By #1 New York Times Bestselling author
By Robert G. Allen

Real estate is an amazing and versatile investment vehicle as long as you are flexible and creative enough to try different approaches. No matter what you read in the newspaper about the ups and downs of real estate values, real estate will always be a powerful investment. Bargains can always be found. Find great deals and either flip them to people who need them or keep them and rent them out. This formula will never change.

1. Wholesale Real Estate Strategy

One of the most obvious ways of playing the real estate game is to search for bargains. Don't get caught up in the way most people buy real estate—by paying full price. If you pay full price for your property, then you're speculating that the property will appreciate in value. That's a fool's game--a speculator's folly. I challenge you to make money the day you buy each property. Why? So you can turn around and rent that property out for a positive cash flow or flip that property for some short term cash—like a quick ten thousand dollars. This requires some bargain hunting—sifting through hundreds of shiny cubic zirconium fake diamonds to find the real diamonds in your market.

What kind of discount can you expect? Let's assume it's possible to buy a property twenty percent below market or more. It won't be easy. It will require some serious sifting. But a twenty percent discount is certainly possible, and sometimes even more. A typical $200,000 single family home could be purchased for $160,000.

I bought a home during the Great Recession in the Los Angeles area that sold a year earlier for $850,000. My purchase price was $465,000. Almost half off.

Buying low and selling high is the most basic form of entrepreneurship there is. So using your money to buy real estate at below market prices and sell it at full value is the first and most basic real estate strategy. You can always buy fix-up and flip real estate. This formula is as old as the hills and will NEVER change.

So real estate strategy #1 is to be a wholesale buyer. I'm not just talking foreclosures, by the way. Smart investors have a wholesale mindset. They're looking for bargains no matter who owns them. You're always looking for the "highly motivated seller" because they are much more flexible.

But I can just hear you complain, "But I don't have any money! I can't afford deals like these."

That's when you employ the next strategy.

(My first and most famous real estate book is called *Nothing Down: A Proven Program that shows you how to buy real estate using little or none of your own money.* It contains a list of dozens of ways to buy real estate using NONE of your own money. If you'd like a summary list of 50 Nothing Down Techniques, just send me an email to robertgrantallen@gmail.com and I'll send it to you.)

2. The Bird Dog Strategy.

If you try to borrow money from a bank, the banker will ask you to qualify for the load by asking you about your Four C's: Cash, Cash Flow, Credit or Collateral. What if you don't have ANY cash? Your credit is shot. You lost your job last week. And the bank just repossessed your house. What can you do?

You tap into your Inner Four C's: Courage, conviction, *chutzpah* and creativity.

You don't need cash—you just need a deal that is incredible. Money flows to a great deal. It doesn't need to be your money. It could be another investor's cash. You just need the courage to tie up the deal and offer it to another investor for a finder's fee.

I've always taught that the three great skills you need to be a real estate investor are:

You've got to learn how to FIND great deals, FUND those great deals, and then, FARM those great deals. Find it. Fund it. Farm it.

Most people assume that they can't go looking to FIND a deal until they can afford to FUND a deal. Not so. Nothing stops you from looking. You can have the worst credit rating in history, and it doesn't stop you from talking to Realtors, calling on ads in the newspaper or the Internet and then looking at properties. After my bankruptcy many years ago, I was out there looking for deals the next week. You're always looking for deals.

Before you launch your Bird Dog Strategy, my first advice would be for you to create some stability in your life. Find a stable place to live, even it's a small apartment, and try to figure out how to earn a steady stream of income that you can count on for the next six months. Keep your creditors at bay, hunker down, and turn on your cash engines. It's time to make some money.

You'll be a bird dog for people with cash looking for great deals. You don't need 50% of the profit at first. You just want a finder's fee for finding hot deals. Join the local real estate investor's club in your city. Be on the lookout for deep pockets willing to pounce on once-in-a-lifetime deals. How do you find people like that? You find an unbelievable deal that you can't afford and you run a cheap ad in the local newspaper—or online. Advertise like a desperate seller. Suppose you've located a $250,000 house. The seller is spooked by the real estate market and needs cash for an emergency. His loan is $150,000. He wants out. You ask him if he'll take $30,000 cash for his equity for a quick cash deal. You don't have to have ANY money to be having a conversation like this with a seller. He doesn't need to know that you're broke and your credit stinks. You're just asking hypothetical questions: "Would you consider selling if I could cash you out for thirty grand?"

Suppose he says yes. Now, you've got a potential deal on the line. You bounce it off one of your cash partners. You tell them you've found a deal valued in the $250,000 price range that can be had for $180,000-

-$70,000 below the market. It will take maybe $5,000 to fix it up. It could also be rented out for $2,000 a month with a positive cash flow of $250 per month. That's about $3,000 a year. Thus, the total cash investment would be about $35,000. Your partner would have a positive cash flow of around $3,000 a year….so they'd be earning just under 10% on their money. Plus, they'd have over $70,000 in immediate equity. Given time, this equity could be converted to cash. So the investor would get over 200% return on their investment when the property sells. You've packaged the deal so the investor get excited. Why should they leave their cash in the bank at 1% when they can be earning 10% in cash flow and over 200% eventually?

And what is your fee for packaging this deal? $10,000. A very reasonable profit to you to find, fund and farm a deal like this. Do this once every 90 days and you might replace your income from that job you don't like. Do this twice every 90 days and you're starting to make some REAL money.

3. The Angel Strategy.

In the Broadway business, an angel is someone who funds a Broadway play. In real estate investing, an "Angel" is someone with deep pockets who is looking for a great deal. Most often, they have cash, but don't have the time to find the deals. The Bird Dog has plenty of time, but no money. They make perfect partners and solve each other's needs.

The angel partner provides the capital. The bird dog becomes the catalyst.

As I described previously, a Bird Dog learns the ropes of real estate investing and markets himself as the bird dog.

Your motto is: If you've got the cash, I've got the deals.

It'll be your job to find the bargains, negotiate the transactions, do the fix-up when necessary, manage the property, handle the tenants, etc. But for this "active" effort, you expect your "passive" partner to share up to 50% of the profit. Take a smaller share of the profit at first until you prove yourself, and then you can move up to full partner. The angel puts up the cash for 50% of the profit … and you put up everything else for your 50%.

If you've got some extra cash lying around, why don't you become a real estate investment angel? You don't want to actually DO the work, but you might be willing to put up the money. What you need is a "bird dog"—someone who doesn't have a lot of money, but who does have the time to ferret out a good deal or two. You form a partnership. You provide the cash, and your partner provides the sweat equity. You split profits. Just make sure that you have an attorney draw up an iron-clad partnership agreement.

4. The Fix-Up Strategy

Is there a person in North America who hasn't heard of ordinary investors buying a property, applying a coat of paint or other cosmetic improvement, some new carpet, some kitchen shelves … and dramatically increasing the value of a property? This may not be your specialty … it certainly isn't mine (I've often said that golf clubs fit my hands, but hammers just don't seem to fit.) But just because you're not good with tools doesn't mean that you can't hire an expert to do these tasks for you. The yellow pages are filled with contractors and specialists who are more than willing to give you a "non-binding bid." They'll tell you what, in their expert opinion, you would need to invest to bring a property up to snuff. You can make your purchase of the property contingent upon having these estimates completed to your satisfaction.

But there is also a risk associated with the fix-up game. Before you get too excited, you might check out a copy of the 1986 movie *The Money Pit*, starring Tom Hanks and Shelley Long. It demonstrates how a dream fix-up project can quickly turn into a nightmare.

But a reasonable investor can expect to earn at least a dollar in equity profit for every dollar of fix up investment.

Right now, as you read this, tens of thousands of investors are buying, fixing and flipping amazing real estate deals. It's entirely feasible to turn a five to ten thousand dollar profit in 90 days. One of my books is called *The Road to Wealth*. It tells the story of a trip to the unemployment lines of St. Louis, Missouri. I selected three broke, discouraged, unemployed individuals and showed them how to make at least $5,000 in cash starting with absolutely nothing–no job, no cash, no credit.

One of the couples found a run-down property, spent several weeks cleaning the junk out of it, and then flipped it for a $5,000 cash profit in 90 days. They went on to earn $100,000 in the next 12 months. This stuff works!

If an unemployed person can do it, with some minimal training, then so can you.

(By the way, if you'd like a digital copy of my book *The Road to Wealth*, just send an email to robertgrantallen@gmail.com.

5. The Cash Back Strategy

What if there were actually a way to get cash back every time you bought a property? Well, it doesn't happen every time, but it certainly is possible under the right circumstances. Here's a true story.

Bob and Kitty Kokott saw an ad in their local Wisconsin newspaper for a ten-unit apartment building. The property was free and clear of any mortgages and was owed by a senior gentleman who wanted to move to Florida. The property was listed for $600,000. The Kokotts felt that the price was a bit low, so they made him a very creative offer.

Purchase price:	$600,000
Seller gets	$480,000 in cash at closing
Seller agrees to carry	$120,000 second mortgage with an attractive interest rate

Since this was the only offer the seller had received at full price, he was willing to be more flexible with his terms. After all, he was going to get huge amount of cash at closing ($480,000) and his remaining equity would be carried in the form of a second mortgage ($120,000) on the property with an interest rate substantially higher than he could get anywhere else. For him it was a win/win offer—lots of cash and a high-interest-bearing note.

For the Kokotts, it was a dream come true. The property was appraised at $675,000, and because of this, their banker (with whom they already had a great relationship) was willing to lend them $480,000 on a first mortgage even though he was aware that the Kokotts would be putting up NONE OF THEIR OWN MONEY. The seller's mortgage of $120,000 was secondary to the bank's first mortgage ... so, in essence, there were two loans on the property totaling $600,000. The Kokotts didn't put up a dime of their own money to close this transaction.

But it gets better. At the closing, with rent deposits and credits, the Kokotts actually walked away with over $6,000. To this was added the rent collect from each of the 10 tenants. Therefore, the Kokott's pocketed over $12,000 in cash within a few days of the closing. To repeat: Not only was this not nothing down ... it was cash back at the closing.

There are approximately 60 million mortgages on homes in North America. We hear a lot of talk these days of the ten to twelve million properties that lost value during the Great Recession and were worth less than their existing mortgages—"under water," as they say. But there are always about 25% of the real estate inventory that are FREE and CLEAR of mortgages. These properties are prime for this cash-back technique. Why? Because there is so much equity in the property.

Are these deals easy to do? Of course not. They were much easier to arrange a few years ago, but banks have been extremely "gun shy." So why not arrange this type of "mortgage" with the seller directly? Many sellers are having major difficulty selling their properties, but some sellers NEED to sell and will be much more flexible in negotiating more creative terms for a buyer.

For example, in the above example, let's suppose the owner is desperate to move to Florida, but is "handcuffed" to his Wisconsin apartment building. The market is soft. He can imagine his retirement nest egg cracking. Along YOU come to the rescue.

Rather than beating the seller down to the lowest price with hard negotiating, you use just the opposite strategy. Since the 10 unit building is fully rented with excellent cash flows, you agree to buy the property for almost full value. The seller will receive NO CASH down payment ... but will carry a first mortgage that will generate a steady monthly income for the next 25 years. The problem is now solved, and he can look for another great deal in Florida. He could even trade his cash-generating note for another free and clear property.

What do you get? You end up owning a cash-generating apartment building with a small positive cash flow. You'll also get the same $12,000 in rents and deposits that the Kokotts received at closing.

This is the ideal scenario. You put cash in your pocket the day you buy.

6. The Conversion Strategy

When is a house not a house? It depends upon where it is located. Have you ever driven by a residential-looking house on a busy street occupied by a commercial establishment—an insurance broker, a dry cleaner, a florist? How did such a normal house get built on such a busy street? At one time it was in a sleepy residential neighborhood that slowly became a busy business thoroughfare.

By going down to your city planning commission, you can find out exactly where the new streets are going to be for ten years into the future. One day, those residential homes will be instantly worth double their value simply because the city leaders will rezone the property from residential to commercial.

Sometimes, by just doing a bit of homework you can plan your investments to have a dramatically improved value in the future just by selecting properties in the path of progress.

One of my favorite conversion experiences was transforming a run-down 12 unit apartment building just off of Center Street in my city into a well-appointed office space. The conversion costs were about double what I had originally anticipated, but I was rewarded with a value quadruple what I had paid for the building.

Whenever you look at a piece of property to buy, put on your profit glasses and be willing to dream about what might be done with the property. Perhaps you can reap a huge conversion profit. But rather than going through the hassle of doing the conversion construction, which requires, time, cash and expertise, just look for properties that are ripe to be rezoned. Follow through on the paperwork for rezoning and then "flip" the property to a conversion specialist—a general contractor who will do the hard work of conversion. Your cash profits will be smaller, but more immediate. It's entirely feasible to flip the right deal for a quick $10,000 in cash.

7. Flip for Cash Flow strategy

One of the students of my Wealth Training in the early 1990s came up with an ingenious strategy. If you remember, the deals were aplenty in the early 1990s. It was very similar to today's investing climate. Foreclosures were everywhere. He searched out government HUD foreclosures in Arizona. His target property was valued at $100,000. He was able to buy each property at about $80,000 with less than $5,000 down payment, often using "angel" investor money. But rather than selling the property for cash, each property was sold at FULL price ($100,000) with NOTHING DOWN. In other words, the profit was in the form of a $20,000 note with an interest rate of 10%.

The note generate yearly interest payments of $2,000 ($20,000 note earning 10% = $2,000 yearly interest only). The total investment to acquire this note was $5,000. So what is their rate of return?

$$\frac{\$2,000 \text{ yearly cash flow}}{\$5,000 \text{ initial down payment}} = 40\% \text{ first year rate of return}$$

That's right. Forty percent!

If you don't have cash, there is plenty of interest rate profit to entice an investor (your father-in-law or your buddy in the car pool) to come up with the cash to buy into a few of these deals. That's exactly what my student did. In the next five years he acquired 800 houses using this strategy. Cash flow profits were staggering, and he generated MILLIONS of equity profits. Then, the market for foreclosures dried up.

Well, those times are BACK!

Your local Realtor probably won't know about a lot of these "alternative" ways to make quick cash in real estate. But now YOU know.

Hopefully, you can generate multiple streams of income using these ideas.

Robert G. Allen

#1 New York Times bestselling author of the mega-bestsellers,
Nothing Down
Creating Wealth
Multiple Streams of Income
The One Minute Millionaire
www.robertallen.com
robertgrantallen@gmail.com.

Robert G. Allen is one of America's most famous and most influential financial advisors. After graduating with an MBA from Brigham Young University in 1974, Allen began his real estate investment career and turned his successful experiences into the #1 bestselling book *Nothing Down*, with fifty-eight weeks on the *New York Times* national bestseller list. He followed that success with four other major New York Times bestsellers: *Creating Wealth, Multiple Streams of Income, The One Minute Millionaire* and *Cracking the Millionaire Code: Your Key to Enlightened Wealth.* His latest book is *Cash in a Flash: Fast Money in Slow Times.* He has appeared on hundreds of programs including *Good Morning America, Larry King* and *Your World with Neil Cavuto.* He has also been featured in such national publications as *The Wall Street Journal, Newsweek, Barron's, Money Magazine, Redbook,* and *Reader's Digest.* His most important achievement is his 37-year marriage to Daryl Elyse Lieurance Allen. Together they have three incredible adult children, Aimee, Aaron and Hunter.

SECRETS TO RAISING ALL THE MONEY YOU NEED TO INVEST IN REAL ESTATE

By Sunil Tulsiani
Award Winning #1 Best-Selling Author and Founder
of Private Investment Club

Put yourself in my shoes: I was a cop ... with a goal. I was granted permission to take a leave of absence from the police force, and in that year I intended to become a real estate investing millionaire.

How would I achieve such a lofty goal?

Did I receive a wealthy inheritance from a long-lost uncle?

Did I pick a winning lottery ticket?

That's what some people think when they first come to Private Investment Club and meet me. When they talk about getting on the deal-making fast-track themselves, they consider similar options.

But I did none of those things. And although I did use bank's money, I quickly tapped out and realized I had to move beyond that option.

That's when I discovered four stunning money-magnetizing secrets that totally changed the game for me.

In fact, these four secrets were so powerful, they allowed me to start from scratch and, without begging or borrowing from my family or friends, I did 77 deals in those 12 short months.

And I *almost* achieved my millionaire goal.

That was just the beginning. Today, I've bought and sold about 500 properties using some of these secrets. And now I'm going to show you exactly what I did to tap into money sources to do deals.

#1: The Secret That the Gurus Use to do Deals

I want to you to close your eyes and imagine that you are an investor who has money, and you are approached by two people who are each asking for money to do a real estate deal.

One investor is positive and confident, with a track record of deals, and other people look to him or her for investing advice. The other investor doesn't have any track record of deals, and no one really goes to him or her for help. In fact, it's hard to know if the second one is an investor at all.

Whom would you likely give your money to?

There is one major difference between the first and the second person, and it has absolutely nothing to do with how many deals they've done.

The key difference is credibility. Credibility is so important. It's like a magnet that attracts the right people to you.

So how can you build credibility? Here are several ideas.

Build a kick-butt LinkedIn profile

Work on building a top-notch LinkedIn profile. LinkedIn is the professional's social network, and people who want to do a deal will check out your LinkedIn. What does your LinkedIn profile say about you? Would you give your money to an investor if that person had a LinkedIn profile like yours?

Add a professional-looking picture and fill out all the relevant areas of your profile *including contact information.* Be sure to mention that you are a real estate investor. Even if you do something else for your career right now, add "real estate investor" to your profile.

Point out any successes you've had and include them even if they weren't specifically real estate investing successes.

For more great ideas about improving your LinkedIn profile, you're welcome to check out *my* LinkedIn profile.

Get amazing testimonials

You can say anything you want about yourself, but nothing speaks louder than a testimonial from someone else. The most credible testimonials are those on video, so after every deal, ask the other person to record a brief video testimonial for you. If you cannot get a video testimonial, the next most credible testimonials are those on LinkedIn (because LinkedIn has verification functionality to prove that the person providing the testimonial is a real person).

Become a mentor

Train others and help *them* do deals. Take on two to four people and coach them through a deal. Then use *their* success stories as a case history for *you*. Get them to give you a video testimonial where they explain how your coaching helped them.

Here's how you can become a mentor: Go to a real estate investing club, connect with people who are starting out, and offer to mentor them for free in exchange for their testimonial.

Publish newsletters and articles

Publishing content shows that you are an expert in the area. You don't have to be the best writer. You just need to write regularly to show that you are thinking about investing and sharing your knowledge with them.

Now, I know what you are thinking. "How do I get access to content?" I've got you covered!

All you need to do is go to Google and search for "real estate investing" or "Mortgage rates." Then set up Google Alerts: They will search the web for the latest information on the topics you chose, and they'll email those topics to you so you always have a flow of current information coming to you.

Become a speaker

Better than writing, becoming a public speaker on the topic of real estate investing puts you into a credible position because people get to connect with you immediately.

Here's how to become a speaker: Use networking and free advertising to invite about 10 people to your seminar. Offer a topic that is interesting to real estate investors, such as:

"How to Become Wealthy in Real Estate"

"How to make $5,000 Cash Flow"

"Where to buy properties"

Then use your experience and training from live events and reading of books/articles to formulate your lesson.

Interviews on TV, radio, in magazines

What else do credible experts do? They're interviewed by others, and those interviews may appear in TV, on radio, or in magazines.

In my case, I've been lucky enough to be on the front cover of *Profiles of Success Magazine* and *Real Estate Wealth Magazine* as well as *Book a Speaker Magazine*. I've also been featured in the *Toronto Star* and *USA Today*, and I've appeared on *CP24 Breakfast Television*.

Now, you might not get into these large publications and TV shows right away. That's okay. Start small by contacting small local radio and newspapers and letting them know that you're available to discuss real estate investing.

Write a book

I can't stress the value of this credibility-builder enough. Use the platform that most people think is credible:

Now, I have to admit, writing a book is hard. You do need to make sure you are giving a great value to the readers.

Here's how to write a book: Schedule 30 to 60 minutes into your calendar every day. Start by writing your table of contents and then work through it.

But here's an important tip (I should know! I've written several best-selling books.): You **must** stick to your schedule and write daily.

Most printed books are about 200 pages long. If you don't want to write a full book yourself, you can write an ebook, which is usually about 30 to 40 pages.

After writing the book, you need to hire an editor, designer, and a publisher to help you bring your book to market. You can find these people by searching online for these professionals in your area.

Build a business

Remember that real estate investing is a business. Even if you don't think of yourself as a business person, that's okay. You're more likely to attract other people's money if you take a businesslike approach. Set up a logo, tagline, website, and business cards. It doesn't have to be expensive, but a professional look will demonstrate significant credibility.

Tie them all together

As you complete each of these powerful credibility-building activities, you should tie them altogether–for example, by adding your logo to your LinkedIn page and linking to your book to the different TV or radio interviews you've done.

#2: Use This Powerful Leverage Secret to Tap into Other People's Hard Work

You can start this right away, but you'll have even more success if you start doing this after you've built up some of those credibility-enhancing activities I revealed above.

What makes this secret so powerful is that it uses the power of leverage to make your networking so much easier. Even though you might be starting from scratch, you'll almost instantly skyrocket to a higher level of networking because of leverage.

Instead of building relationships one-by-one with individual investors, you connect with COIs (Centers of Influence)–people who know many investors. Centers of Influence are the reason I was able to buy 77 properties in the first year.

Because I connected with so many people at once, the deals came together quickly. I connected with those Centers of Influence and offered a win/win/win deal: They won, their investors won, and I won. That's a powerful equation, and Centers of Influence love to do deals when everyone wins.

One Center of Influence can bring all the money and the deals you need to become financially free. Remember: It's not what you know; it's not even who you know, but it's who knows you!

Who are some ideal Centers of Influence?

There are many different Centers of Influence–anyone who potentially knows many real estate investors or people with money who might be interested in doing deals. They include:

Attorneys

Accountants

Real estate investors

Public speakers

Mentors

Authors

Private Lenders

That's just scratching the surface. There are many more, and I'll show you a couple of others next ....

List owners

Find someone with a big list of real estate investors. Perhaps they have a website or a club of real estate investors that they communicate with regularly. People who read real estate magazines, for example, are interested in real estate investing, so find a real estate magazine and ask for the cost to email their list.

Contact these list owners and ask them about how you can work together. Some of them might place an advertisement on their website or in their email newsletter, or they might even communicate with their list for free if you offer something that they and/or their members will find extremely valuable. They might also be interested in doing a joint venture with you.

Join elite clubs

A Center of Influence might not be a person: It might be a group, such as a real estate investing club, so tap into that group of eager real estate investors by joining one or more real estate investing clubs in your area.

Don't just look for *any* real estate investing club. Choose an elite club. Find a club that gives you access to money, resources, and deals, whose membership is full of serious investors and whose founder actually invests in real estate.

Aim for quality and raise the bar on your investing by joining the best investing club in the country–don't settle. This automatically puts you in touch with a big group of people who are eager to do deals and who share the same desire for win/win deals that you do.

Find a club that has a paid membership, since you can be sure that the members are more serious about doing deals because you know they are willing to invest in themselves.

Here's one area where I would caution you when looking for a club, and it surprised me as a former cop when I first discovered it: You should check to make sure the founder of the club actually does deals!

Of course, you can join any club you want, but most real estate clubs are set up by people who don't actually do any deals. When I learned this, it wasn't acceptable to me, and that's one of the reasons I founded Private Investment Club. I invest in real estate; it's how I make most of my money, and I even provide funding to my members. To learn more about Private Investment Club, visit www.PrivateInvestmentClub.com or www.SunilTulsiani.com.

Never stop building your credibility

Building credibility is a key step in connecting with Centers of Influence. The more credibility you have, the easier it will be to connect with these Centers of Influence, so always ask yourself, "What am I doing today to build my credibility?"

#3: The Unbelievably Easy Way to Find Money AND Close Deals at the Same Time

You're building credibility and you're connecting with Centers of Influence. Now it's time to build a bridge to yourself and start attracting some of that money your way.

With the credibility you've built and the Center of Influence connections you've built, people who have money will get to know and trust you, and they'll bring you their money; together you'll close deals.

This money-attracting secret is critical: Start building your own list of potential buyers and joint venture partners. Collect names and contact information and start putting them into your database.

Every time you meet someone who is a potential buyer or joint venture partner, gather that person's contact information and enter that information into your database.

Every time.

Without fail.

Build that list every single day.

My exact secret list-building ads: REVEALED!

Here are the exact ads I used to build my list at lightning-fast speed. Once I had a deal, I'd place these exact ads in the real estate sections of newspapers:

Dirt cheap. Must sell. Motivated seller. (email address)

And my other ad was:

Desperate seller. Way below market. Must sell. Respond now. (email address)

These ads were like a magnet for real estate investors. They'd see the ad, it would hit all the hot buttons that they were interested in, and they would get in touch with me.

But here's the one extra trick I did that you need to do, too, if you want to grow your list as lightning-fast as I did: I included my email address–not my phone number–in the ad. There were fewer responses than if my phone number was in the ad, but I ended up with two great results:

The people who were motivated enough to email me were more likely to do deals.

With their permission, I added their email address to my database to contact them for future deals.

Adding names is only the first step

Once you have a name in your database, there's something else you need to do. You guessed it: Build credibility with the people on your list. Credibility means that someone likes you and trusts you.

That's why I'm such a strong advocate not only of constantly building the *quantity* of names on your list, but also building the *quality* of the relationships in your list. Share with your list. Help them. Work with them. Talk to them. Listen to them. When you do these things for your list, you'll develop a powerful bond of trust and loyalty with them–so much credibility that they wouldn't even dream of giving their money to anyone else!

#4: This Is the Secret that Most Investors Forget

I'm going to remind you of a weird truth about the universe, and I want you to stick this into your brain and remember it from now on: The more you give, the more you get. I don't know why it happens, but it ALWAYS works that way.

When you give a little, you get a little in return. When you give a lot, you get a lot in return.

Give to get

When I took a leave of absence from the police force and did 77 deals in one year, I got a lot … but I also gave a lot. When I built up Private Investment Club into the largest elite real estate investing club in Canada, one that has exploded beyond Canadian borders and is now in many countries worldwide, it's not because I only get, get, get. It's because I also give.

I'm always helping and educating our members. If you follow my emails, you'll know that I'm putting my "cop hat" on and doing my due diligence on any deal I think the Private Investment Club members would benefit from. In other words, I get a lot … but it's because I'm giving a lot.

And you should do the same. As you connect with your investors, give to them by offering win/win deals that benefit them and you.

Value them and care for them

When you do that, it comes back full circle: You do those deals AND get great testimonials and case studies, which gives you greater credibility, which helps you connect with even more Centers of Influence, which helps you build an even bigger list, which helps you do even more deals.

Here's What Happens When You Apply These Four Secrets

Something powerful happens when you apply these four secrets.

Have you ever rolled a stone down a hill? Perhaps you did as a child. It takes a bit of effort at the top of the hill to get the stone moving, just as it might take a bit of effort at the beginning of your money-attracting journey to start building credibility.

As the stone starts moving, though, gravity takes over, and that stone starts rolling on its own, building momentum and energy as it rolls. In the same way, your credibility will build and build; you'll meet more and more Centers of Influence; you'll build a bigger and bigger list, and you'll add greater and greater value. And as your efforts build on one another, you'll build momentum, doing more and more deals.

Put yourself in my shoes again: Imagine what it felt like at the beginning of my year's absence from the police force. All I had were my goals.

Now imagine what it felt like at the end of the year when I crossed those achieved goals off my list–77 deals and a real estate millionaire!–and I resigned from the police force.

Now open your eyes and realize that you are at exactly the same point. It doesn't matter how many deals you've done. If you want to do more deals and achieve your goals of financial freedom, these four secrets are the ones that can get you there.

Before signing off, I would like to gift you a DVD which was recorded live in front of over 400 people. You can grab it right now by going to: http://privateinvestmentclubdvd.com/

I wish you all the best and hope you take immediate action!

About Sunil Tulsiani

Sunil Tulsiani fulfilled his dream in life by becoming a police officer and serving on the force for 15 years, achieving the rank of Platoon Commander.

But something was wrong: His dream job had become a burden; it had taken over his life. He was spending too much time away from his family, and he was afraid that his children would grow up and barely recognize him.

So Sunil formulated a new plan … a bold plan!

He asked for a one-year leave of absence from the police force, and in that year he changed his life forever.

During his 12-month leave of absence in 2005 and 2006, Sunil did 77 real estate deals, achieving another lifelong goal of becoming a millionaire.

Today, he is, first and foremost, a real estate investor. But if you ask any of the thousands of members of the elite Private Investment Club he founded, they would tell you that he is not only one of the most successful investors they've ever met, he's also a great mentor who believes in helping others.

Sunil is also an award-winning best-selling author who has written books with Jack Canfield, Dr. Deepak Chopra and Brian Tracy. He's a popular public speaker and has shared the stage with Robert G. Allen, Jack Canfield, Ron LeGrand, Don Campbell and many others.

For more information about the Private Investment Club and how you can gain access to massive amounts of money, cash flowing properties, and a huge network of investors, visit www.PrivateInvestment-Club.com or www.SunilTulsiani.com .

How to Create Your Own Blue Print for Wealth

By Shahzad Ahmed

"Fortune sides with him who dares."
-Virgil, Ancient Roman Poet

"I've failed more times than I can count."

"I'm too tired to even try anymore."

"I can't seem to do anything right."

"I feel like I am letting my family down."

Strong words, indeed. Sadly, they are more than just words. This is how one of my students described his life as he slumped in a chair across from me in my office one day. I could see the despair in his eyes even before he opened his mouth. He, like so many others, tries every day to make more of his life. He works hard. He saves his money. Like so many others, though, he simply doesn't have the financial know-how or resources to create a consistent and seamless source of income that will allow him to retire comfortably. And, as I said, he is not alone.

Let me explain . . . .

I am an associate mechanical engineer by profession. I worked in the automotive industry for almost 20 years. I started my career with Toyota, and by the time I quit my job, I had dealt with practically all the major automakers in the world.

Born to an average family, I immigrated to Canada in 1995. I started my Canadian journey as a sanding operator. I worked hard, and yes, I struggled at times, but I never gave up. I continued to educate myself, and with a lot of determination and self-confidence, I went from a sanding operator to a quality manager.

I always wanted to be an entrepreneur, and in pursuit of that dream, I opened several businesses, including a dollar store, pizza store, carpet cleaning business, Forex, and an Internet business; I traded and bought stocks, and I even opened a mortgage business. And I failed at all of them—successfully. The one thing I can safely say I did not do was to surrender my dreams. I never gave up.

Then, in 2007, I decided to look at real estate. Why not? I had tried everything else up to this point. I dabbled a little, and as I could see the potential, I started to invest more until, finally, in April 2009, I quit my full-time job as a quality manager. This was one of the biggest leaps of faith I had ever taken because if you remember, 2009 was one of the world's worst recessions. Hundreds of thousands of people were laid off. Businesses were going bankrupt, and everyone was glued to their job.

But I knew I had to make a decision—and I did. I quit. Nothing is scarier than the day you realize you no longer have a steady pay cheque every week. But I had a dream. I wanted to build a strong real estate business and help as many people as I could by providing them with the opportunity to invest in positive cash-flow properties to create passive income for themselves and their families.

And now, I am going to teach you the keys to building a solid foundation in the real estate investment business.

Wealth Building 101

Building wealth is like building a house. When building your house, you need certain materials that will be used to secure a stable foundation so your house will last for many decades, if not centuries. The same is true when you are building your real estate investment business.

There are four things I consider to be your foundation in your new money-building blueprint. These elements are key to securing the necessary ingredients that will allow both you and your new business to succeed right from the get-go. Without these foundational elements, you can probably succeed, but it will take you years longer, a lot of headache, and there is no guarantee you will actually succeed long term. And isn't that really what it's all about?

So, make sure you have these four things in place before jumping into your first investment, and I guarantee you will experience a much easier, faster and more lucrative deal.

The 4 Keys to Successful Real Estate Investing

There are many variables when investing in real estate. Often people think it's just about the money—the down payment you can come up with. Don't get me wrong: Having a strong down payment is often essential, but there is something that's even more important—credit.

You can have $20K or $50K saved up, but if your credit isn't good, then what? How are you going to get the mortgage to finance the property? One of the tricks to good investing is being able to jump on deals when you find them—they don't call them *deals* for nothing. If you find an excellent property at a great price, the reality is, someone else also found this great deal. In order to beat them to the punch, as they say, you will need to act fast. If you do not have the resources to do that, you will lose the deal and your chance at an excellent investment property. Some of the best deals I have ever made needed to be acted upon quickly. If I had not had access to money, there is no way I would have gotten the property. Someone with better credit would have simply gobbled it up before I could even consulted the bank.

So the first key to successful investing is having good credit. You MUST be able to have access to lots of money at all times.

1. Money—Have access to money, Good Credit

When I say you need good credit, what that really entails is actually having readily available money (money already in your bank accounts or other savings or financial accounts of some sort) when you need it or having access to money through a lender.

If you do not have access to money because you don't have good to even stellar credit, do not give up. There are ways you can improve your credit in as little as six months. This is crucial, however, so if you are serious about investing in real estate, I suggest you start building or rebuilding your credit as soon as you finish reading this chapter. And to get you started, I am going to give you the best credit building tips I know.

7 Tips to Help Build or Rebuild Your Credit Score

i.   **Check your credit score:** If you have ever purchased something with a credit card or applied for a bank loan, you already know what a credit score is. But are you aware of how your credit score is arrived at? Credit report agencies such as Equifax or Trans Union (that work with about 24-million Canadians) pull data from other companies such as your utility companies, cell phone providers, banks, credit card companies, etc. (essentially any company you repay debt on regularly). They then base your score on a number scale from 0 -850 where 0 means there is simply no information on your credit at all and 850 means you have the best credit there is. In reality, banks look at anything over 700 as good. There are many variables, however, besides just paying your bills on time, and these include: Balance to limit ratio (your credit card balances should be below 75 percent of your available credit. Ideally they should be below 50 percent or they will affect your credit negatively.) As well, the majority of credit reports have errors that often go undetected for years because people never take the time to review their reports. You can dispute any errors by calling the company.

ii. **Make regular payments.** Make sure you pay at least the minimum payment on all debt. This will show other lenders you are responsible and will at the very least make the required payments.

iii. **Pay your bills on time.** This is just common sense as it will also save you money on expensive late-fees and other unnecessary charges.

iv. **Never go over your credit limits.** Although companies will often honour a charge that exceeds the limit, it does still affect your score negatively. It can also allow credit card companies to increase the interest rate on your cards. Always check the fine print when accepting a credit card and know your balances at all times.

v.   **Don't accept credit cards just because they are offered.** Having too many cards can also affect your credit negatively. It can also affect your ability to keep track of all the due date for payments. Do not accept more credit cards just because they are offered.

vi. **Avoid collections.** Stay on top of your finances. If you are behind or you fall behind, don't ignore calls or reminder letters. If your account is sent to a collection agency, it will stick with you on your credit history for six years in some cases.

vii. **Always communicate with your creditors.** Often creditors have easy solutions and will work with you to make payment arrangements. They don't want you to default on your accounts, so they will do what they can in many cases, even lower your interest rate for a time or permanently. Whatever you do, do not jeopardize your credit history.

2. Have Access to Potential Opportunities and the Knowledge to Evaluate a Deal

If you are just starting out in the real estate investing business, you will likely not have all the resources you will need to start. Like anything in life, you need to have the know-how to do it successfully. Would you walk onto the golf course your first time out and expect to hit under par on an 18-hole course? Unless you are Tiger Woods, I highly doubt it. How do you think professional golfers became successful? They studied, practiced and listened to people who had the knowledge and experience they needed. If you do not have access to this kind of expertise, then find it. There are many real estate investors who are willing to work with new investors and help them achieve the success they have. They can offer you a wealth of knowledge and access to all the resources you will need.

So what should you look for in a good real estate investor mentor or coach?

7 Qualities you Should Look for in a Real Estate Investor Mentor

i. **Is the prospective mentor qualified?** How many successful deals has he or she made in the last 5 years? How many properties does the prospective mentor currently own? Are the properties owned currently being rented for positive cash-flow? If the mentor you are looking for does not have a verifiable track record, he or she likely will not be able to provide you with one. Look for someone who is active in the business and who is successful. Ask him about his past, what properties he currently owns, where and how they are doing. A real investor will gladly answer these questions and in fact, would be surprised if you didn't.

ii. **How long has your prospective mentor been in the real estate investing business?** While success is a good indicator of having some know-how, nothing beats years of experience. A good real estate investor will not only have experienced the good part of investing—making money. He will also know the bad parts—losing deals, dealing with bad tenants, dealing with deals that go south, etc. This is all part and parcel of the business, and unless someone has actually experienced it all, he or she will not be able to impart this same information on you. And isn't that why you are looking for a mentor in the first place—experience?

iii. **Is this investor close to you?** One-on-one and face-to-face training is the best way to learn from someone. You can also get to meet the mentor in person, which can tell you volumes about someone. You can watch his reaction to your questions, i.e., does he squirm a lot or avoid eye contact? This can be a red flag. So meet your potential mentor in person and make sure you connect on a personal level as well on a business level. If you are not comfortable with this person during your first visit, imagine how working with him or her will be long term.

iv. **Do the prospective mentor have the time to work with you?** Just because someone measures up on quantifiable deals and properties does not mean he will actually have the time to teach you how to do what he does Often, the more successful a person is, the busier he or she is, so unless the prospective mentor is also good at time management, he may not be the perfect fit for you.

v. **Is the prospect respected in the community and by their colleagues and peers?** Again, someone may have all the qualities you are looking for on paper, but if he or she has a bad reputation or is not liked or respected by the industry, by former clients or colleagues, there has to be a reason for this. Investigate the prospect before investing with him.

vi. **Does the prospective mentor sincerely want to help you or is he just looking to pad his pockets?** You will obviously want to find someone who is sincere in his wish to help you achieve your goals. If that person is only looking to get money from you, that is not the person for you. Talking to the prospect is the first start. Ask him why he wants to mentor someone when he is already successful himself. Ask him what mentoring means to him. What does he get out of helping other people? A face-to-face connection can usually give you a good idea of his intentions, so ask for names of other clients. If the prospective mentor cannot give you a name for confidentiality reasons, do a little research into the company or the person. You must also learn to trust your gut feelings. If you don't have a good feeling about someone, it's usually a good indication he or she is not the person you should be working with anyway.

vii. **Is this someone you can trust long term?** Again, this is something you may have to do a little research into, but your initial impression is usually a good indicator. Don't, however, just judge a book by its cover. Do not take one look at someone and make up your mind based on appearance alone. Yes, appearance has a lot to do with how a person lives his or her life, but some of the most successful people are or were a little odd at first glance. Take Howard Hughes, for example. He was highly eccentric, and at first glance, his behavior would probably seem odd to others. So, you need to also look at other qualities to determine the entire package. We do not always necessarily agree with everything our friends and family do, but that does not mean we can't trust them.

3. Pay off your mortgage faster than the traditional 25-year term

If you have any idea of finances, I probably don't have to go into why paying off your mortgage faster is a good idea. You may not know how to do this, however, so here are five tips to pay down your mortgage quickly.

i. **Accelerate your payment schedule:** If you are currently paying your mortgage monthly, an easy way to pay it down faster is to change your payments to bi-weekly instead of every month. You will shave close to three years off of the amortization schedule and save thousands of dollars in interest.

ii. **Round up your mortgage payments:** Rounding up your payments is relatively painless, and you may not even notice those few extra dollars coming out of your account, but they can really make a difference. Here is an example. If your bi-weekly mortgage payments are $550, round your payment up to $600. The extra $50 will help decrease your mortgage faster, and in the big scheme of things, you probably spend $50 every few weeks on things you really don't need anyway. So put that money to good use.

iii. **Use your tax refunds to pay down your mortgage.** Any refund on your tax returns is really found money anyway. If you put this toward the principal of your mortgage, it can make a big difference not only in the pay down, but also the interest you will have to pay.

iv. **Every year make one lump sum payment**. Even if it's a small amount like $60, it can help decrease the number of years to pay off your mortgage. This money can be applied directly to your principle.

v. **Stay informed.** Keep on top of your mortgage. Don't forget about it because it simply comes out of your account automatically. If you are constantly thinking of ways to decrease it (keep on top of interest rate), you will be more likely to actually do it.

4. Build a Real Estate Investing Power Team

This is probably the most important factor to consider when investing in real estate. You MUST have good and knowledgeable people on your team. You can't do everything yourself–at least well–so you need honest and trustworthy professionals who are experienced at what they do best, to help and guide you as you build your real estate portfolio. People like Realtors, mortgage agents, bankers, lawyers, home inspectors, contractors, etc., are a necessary part of the business. The trick is to find them. This is where your mentor can help.

People always say that knowledge is power, but I say knowledge is not power, but *proper and right* knowledge is power. Even more powerful is the ability to put that knowledge into action.

Plan, Plan, Plan

Just like any other business or investment, real estate investments should be well planned out. Ask yourself the following questions before jumping on a potential deal.

- What is my goal?

- Am I looking for a long-term or short-term investment?

- Do I need cash-flow now, or am I looking to secure a future for my kids?

- Am I being realistic, or am I just attracted to shiny objects?

- Am I a steady and patient person, or do I want to be a millionaire in the next six months?

- Can I thoroughly evaluate an investment opportunity, or do I need help?

- What kind of minimum return on investment (ROI) am I looking for?

- Do I know what *not* to do when investing in real estate for the first time?

These are basically just a few questions of hundreds of questions you should have as a potential real estate investor. But if you follow the above four steps, these questions should not intimidate you—they should empower you! So do your due diligence. If done correctly, you will quickly find yourself living your dreams and retiring sooner than you ever thought possible. Happy investing!

Are you still thirsty? Get my free eBook, *Secrets of Successful Real Estate Investment* at: www.secretsofrealestateinvestment.com

To your success

Shahzad Ahmed

About Shahzad Ahmed

Shahzad Ahmed has a passion for helping as many people as he can. He knows that our lives on this planet are finite, so he wants to leave behind a legacy of as many people as he can that he has helped make positive changes in their lives.

Shahzad began his professional career as an associated mechanical engineer working in the automotive industry for over 20 years in the field of Quality Assurance. His engineering and Quality Assurance background allowed him to become a very detail-oriented individual. He has worked across the globe in countries such as Japan, the Philippines, Pakistan, the US and Canada.

In 2009, his entrepreneurial spirit coupled with a desire to make more money and help as many people as he can led him to become a professional real estate investment expert. Shahzad is committed to three basic principles in his real estate business: *honesty, integrity* and *professionalism*. He further believes in continually exploring innovative ideas and technology to make real estate transactions as fast and easy as possible.

This, as well as his passion and commitment to his clients, has afforded him much success. He can help individuals and families looking to buy, sell or lease a home, invest in real estate, or simply learn about the real estate market and investment opportunities.

Shahzad is the co-founder of Elite Training Pros, a company designed to educate and help real estate investors.

You can reach him at: Shahzad@elitetrainingpros.com or at: www.elitetrainingpros.com

DINING ON REAL ESTATE—WHY REAL ESTATE IS LIKE A THREE-COURSE MEAL

By Rinay Chand

"Real estate investing, even on a very small scale, remains a tried and true means of building an individual's cash flow and wealth."

—Robert Kiyosaki, Investor, real Estate Entrepreneur and Author *Rich Dad, Poor Dad.*

I think we can all agree that Robert Kiyosaki knows a thing or two about investing. His name is synonymous with wealth. In fact, I am willing to bet there isn't a household in North America that doesn't know his name. You may also know that real estate investments are a huge part of his portfolio, and the simple reason for this is that there is no better investment than real estate.

Ask Donald Trump, another indisputable real estate tycoon.

"It's tangible, it's solid, it's beautiful. It's artistic, from my standpoint, and I just love real estate."
—Donald Trump

So what do these two multi-millionaires (and even billionaires) know that the rest of us don't? I'm about to tell you. It's the SECRET of wealth building in real estate.

What Makes Real Estate Investing Superior To Other Investments?

Real estate is a physical investment—it's tangible, meaning it's real, you can touch it. You can see it, feel it and visit it when you want. This is important for some people.

People are often more comfortable investing in real estate compared to bonds or stocks. Why? Because most of us have been conditioned to believe we need to own a home. I'm not sure how many people are told they need to own stocks or bonds when they were growing up. For this reason they are likely more open to looking at real estate investing.

In this day and age where there are so many scams and fraudulent investment opportunities, real estate provides a safe way to invest your money and an excellent return … for the most part. If you do your due diligence, and actually show up to inspect the property, assure it has the proper titles, make sure it is free from any liens, taxes, and encumbrances and it has had the proper and appropriate inspections, etc., it can be a safe investment.

You can grow your investment tax free until you sell it. And you can reinvest on the equity in your property to buy more investment properties. In fact, you don't have to pay tax (Capital Gains Tax) until you actually sell the property. Essentially it is a tax-free investment.

Real estate investments can be safely used as an inflation hedge to protect against a declining dollar.

You can write off many of your expenses with rental properties. Owning real estate is a business, which means you can write off many expenses such as repairs, costs associated with buying the property, closing costs, travel expenses to check on your properties, property manager expenses etc. Essentially, you must treat your real estate portfolio like a business.

You can use any debt in a property to your advantage, which is not the case in many other investments.

Real estate is as good as a forced retirement plan. Unfortunately, most people are not good at saving money. Many are even up to their noses in credit card debt and other debt. Purchasing a property you will rent out can not only pay off the mortgage, but also provide you with guaranteed equity you can either reinvest or sell to cash out on your rewards.

As far as I am concerned, there is no other better investment. Other investment opportunities are not nearly as safe or as profitable, and with a little education you can even purchase properties for little or in some cases even no money down. What do you have to lose?

I equate real estate investing to eating a three-course meal. It's an odd analogy, but it works. The appetizer of real estate investing is the cash flow the property produces; the main course is the mortgage pay down that happens over time, and the dessert is the appreciation on the property. You can make a lot of money on mortgage paydown alone, i.e., in flat markets with little cash-flow—but a good meal has all three.

The Appetizer: Cash Flow

Rental homes and apartment buildings produce money each month through rental income. Each door or unit that you own generates rental income on a monthly basis. That income, if the property was purchased properly, with all due diligence, and is well managed, should far exceed any and all expenses (like your mortgage payment taxes and maintenance costs etc.) What's left over after all expenses are paid is what is called "**POSITIVE CASH FLOW.**"

Unlike stocks or GICS, which simply sit in an account and hopefully go up in value, rental properties generate positive cash-flow each and every month. When an asset puts money into your pocket each month and you can use that money to further increase the value of the asset, it's a truly powerful, wealth-building cycle.

Main Course: Pay Off Your Mortgage In 10-12 Years!

Each month, as your tenants pay rent, you in turn can use that money to pay down your mortgage. Depending on interest rates, a large portion of your mortgage payment actually goes toward the principle. As such, before you know it, you will have built a ton of equity in the property. Typically, paying off a mortgage can take up to 25 years. But you don't have to be typical. There are ways and techniques to pay off that same mortgage in 10-12 years, which, of course, means you will have more equity in the property in a shorter period of time. To learn more about how to pay off your mortgage in 10-12 years, visit: http://www.elitetrainingpros.com/mortgage-freedom.php

Dessert: The Appreciation On Your Property

Investment properties tend to follow inflation when it comes to appreciating in value. So on top of your mortgage being paid off by your tenants, you can expect the value of your property to increase a little every year.

Depending on the size, location and condition of the property, appreciation may vary; however, a 3 percent appreciation is a safe and conservative number for the purposes of calculation. If you have a good property, then appreciation is just a bonus in the equation.

The stocks or the mutual funds you own, on the other hand, may fluctuate wildly over the same period of time. That's yet another reason we prefer the slow and steady uptick that real estate offers us as investors.

As you can see, investing in real estate is essentially a gift. It can provide you with positive cash-flow; if you rent it out, your tenants can pay the mortgage down for you, and over time, your investment will continue to appreciate. What other investment does all of this?

Where Should You Invest?

Now that you know *why* you should invest in real estate, you are probably wondering *where* you should invest in real estate? It is the *where* that separates the great investor from the average investor.

Purchasing real estate is based on several criteria, such as income levels of possible renters, housing market values, the economic climate of a particular area, etc.

In order to invest properly and with confidence, you need to get to know the area in which you want to invest. Unfortunately, many investors are caught in the past when looking for the best area to invest. While it may have been a great city or area to invest in years ago, that does not mean it is still a good investment. This type of investment is called "speculative," as the investor is always *chasing the market.* You might as well be rolling the dice. Effective investing is all about managing your potential risk and, obviously, increasing your returns on investment (ROI.) In my eyes, speculating is not real or at least effective investing. When you discover how to determine the best area to invest in, and how you can implement this one tactic, you will discover how you can reach the top of the real estate investing ladder fairly quickly and confidently.

How Do you Determine Where to Invest?

When looking at an area to invest in, there are 5 areas you should examine:

Population: Is the area's population growing faster than the state or provincial average? Does the area meet with the lifestyle needs of key purchasers— affordable downtown shopping areas, malls, theatres, etc.?

Infrastructure: Are new infrastructures being built to handle growth?

Employment: Is the area creating new jobs? Is it working to keep stable employment levels? Is there more than one major employer in the area?

Transportation: Are there major transportation improvements slated? Are new roads scheduled or is there ease of access to key areas?

Political Climate: Do current political leaders support economic growth? Is the majority of the population pro-growth?

Okay, now that you know "what" to look for, let's look at "how" to find a suitable positive cash-flow property.

Resources To Help Locate Good Investment Areas

There are several ways to research a good rental property investment. We just discussed what you should be looking for. Now let's figure out how you can go about this.

Specific Neighbourhoods: It should come as no surprise the area in which you invest will determine the type of tenants you will attract. If you pick an area near a University, students will be your bread and butter. Older couples with children or seniors will likely not want to rent in the area for obvious reasons—students can be loud, and they are not always good at keeping a property neat (i.e. lawns mowed, weeds removed etc.). The trade-off is a steady flow of guaranteed income because students typically have student loans, their parents pay their expenses or they work. You must also be prepared that you may incur vacancies while the students are off school. To determine the type of neighbourhood to invest in, you can talk to a real estate agent and people in the area. Even drive through and look at the homes, the cars in the driveways, the manner in which the homes are kept etc. This should give you a good idea of what types of tenants occupy the area.

Employment: There are several ways to determine the employers in an area. You can visit the area in person and see the local businesses. You can talk to people and ask who the major employer is. You can also visit http://canadabusiness.ca/eng/page/2828/, which offers statistics and trends on Canada's Labour and Employment market.

Crime rate: Whether or not an area has a high crime rate will be a huge consideration for renters. Go to the local police stations. Do a drive-by (no pun intended) and look at the homes, businesses etc. Do you see any gang-related graffiti or obvious vandalism? You can also check with Statistics Canada, but a face-to-face inquiry with police is probably the best way to determine what you are buying into.

Property Taxes: Look at the area's property taxes as this is something that can eat into your profits. Visit the area's assessment office for first-hand knowledge.

Education: Schools are always a big concern for renters with children or those who are thinking about having children. Find out what schools are in the area. Are they good schools? Are they close by? Visit the area and/or call the school board. Find out how many children graduate and go onto college or university for example. How many students have been expelled? How does the school rank on a provincial level, etc.? If you don't do this homework, be assured your prospective tenants will, and you don't want any surprises.

Local Amenities: Does the area have malls, access to public transportation, theatres, a variety of grocery stress, skate parks, recreations centers, etc.? Are there any future plans for such things? A quick trip to the local planning office, as well as a drive through the city, will give you an idea of what renters can expect.

Vacancy rate: A high vacancy rate can be a big red flag. On the other hand, a low vacancy rate can only bode well for potential investors. Canada Housing and Mortgage Corporation (CMHC) can provide you with these statistics. A quick drive through the area will also be helpful. Are there a lot of "For Rent" signs? Are there a lot of empty businesses?

Rental rates: You will have to be competitive if you want to rent your property, so look at what similar houses, apartments or condos are renting for in that area. Make sure the rent will cover your costs and more. One good place to see the average rental costs for a particular area is http://www.rentboard.ca. You can also talk to a real estate agent or rental company.

There are obviously many other factors to consider when choosing the perfect location to invest in a rental property, but this should be a good start. If you are serious about investing, you can also speak with other investors and find out what they know. They can give you some good, first-hand knowledge or even help you with your investing needs, even doing much of the necessary research.

How To Build Wealth—Simply

Now that I have told you "why" real estate is the best possible investment opportunity and "what" to look for when investing in positive cash-flow properties, you are probably thinking, "Great . . . but I don't have the resources to actually get into real estate investing."

Not to worry. Life does not have to be complicated. Neither do the real estate investments. Many of the most successful people in the world started out with little to nothing. And some of the most prosperous companies ever started began as a simple idea in a dorm room (Facebook), a basement or garage (Disney, Harley Davidson, Mattel, and Google) or at a kitchen table (IKEA). While these founders may not have had many resources to start, they had plenty of determination, imagination and initiative. If you can muster these qualities and do what it takes to see your dream come to fruition, then there really is NOTHING that can stop you.

I thrive on helping other people bring their dreams into reality. For me, this is the best part of what I do. Here are just a few quick and easy tips that you can start implementing in your life now, so you can start earning the "big bucks" faster—and see your dream of financial freedom come true.

Know What You Are Worth—NOW

It is simply impossible to figure out where you are going if you do not have a destination. So, until you figure out what your "Net Worth" is (your total assets such as your current home, other investments like RRSPs, stocks, bonds, mutual funds, etc. minus your liabilities such as your mortgage, any lines of credit or credit cards debt and other debts you owe to creditors.)

In order to reach your goal of financial freedom, you need to start with smaller goals that will eventually help you achieve your bigger goals. Every year, you need to set a "mini-goal" to increase your net worth. As logic would have it, there are only two ways to increase your net worth—increase your assets by investing more or reduce your debt. And how do you do this? Read on.

Get Rid of or Reduce Your "Non-deductible" Debt First'

There are many kinds of debt—some necessary and some better than others. The goal should always be to pay off any debt that is not deductible on your income tax returns first. The obvious one is credit card debt, which can have as high an interest rate as 21 percent in some cases! I think anyone will agree this is insane. As you learned earlier, if you also pay down your mortgage, you can actually increase your equity and reduce the interest you pay. This alone is one of the best investments you will ever make for you and your "shareholders."

Spend Your Money Wisely

There has never been a time when so many people simply want what they want NOW. With the Internet and "one-click" everything, we are bringing up a generation of people who can cope only when they receive "immediate gratification." While the Internet and all it offers has essentially made our life easier and more efficient, it has also wiped out some of the core values that old-time millionaires and billionaires were instilled with—such as patience, determination, long-term vision. That's not to say that today people do not have these same qualities; it just means they probably had to work that much harder to maintain them. For example, as a society, we have so much more access to consumer goods that are "depreciable assets," meaning they may fulfill a need for more immediate gratification, but they are not assets that will ultimately BUILD your wealth. That amazing $70,000 car, $50,000 boat, and house full of high-end furniture are never going to grow in value (for the most part they depreciate as the years go by.) In order to build wealth, you need to concentrate on investing your money into appreciable assets such as real estate. So to build your asset column, you need to invest only in things that will grow in value.

Don't Overspend

The ONLY way you will ever increase your net worth is to spend only what you actually make in a way that will propel your net worth in a positive direction. Today, far too many people live on credit, whether that is credit cards, lines of credit or other forms of money that is not actually there. Remember, it is not how much you make, but what you do with that money that is going to determine whether you build or deplete your net worth.

If you want to increase your net worth, you will have to start treating your household income like it is a business, and as part of that business, you have shareholders to be accountable to. Your shareholders in this case can be your family members, since how you spend your money also affects them both in the short and long term. The next time a "shiny object" finds its way into your path, simply ask yourself a) Do I need this now? 2) If I buy this, how will it affect my net worth? And c) Will this object benefit my shareholders (family members) in the long term?

The next step will help you see how your past and present spending habits are affecting your bottom line.

Keep Track of What You Buy

If you are running your household income as if it were a company with shareholders, then it will become a natural reflex to track all expenditures. You can do this easily with simple paper ledgers, bookkeeping ledgers like Excel, and online programs like Mint.com, software such as Quick Books or Quicken. The point is not what you use, but to make sure you use *something*. Once you are able to see exactly what you are spending and where, you can then make the necessary adjustments to improve your spending habits.

Forced Savings

If you don't see it, you won't miss it. That is my theory, and it should be yours as well. Have the bank automatically take a certain percentage of your paycheque, and deposit it directly into a Tax Free Savings Account (TFSA.) This will not only begin to build your net worth, but you will also avoid paying taxes on up to $5,500 of this money.

So, are you still hungry after this three-course meal? If so, visit www.mistakesofrealestateinvestment.com to get my free eBook, *How to avoid the 7 Costly Mistakes in real Estate Investing.*

To Your Success
Rinay Chand

About The Author

Rinay Chand has a passion for helping as many people as possible. He knows that God has put us here for a reason—to help Mankind and leave behind a legacy to be cherished forever!

In 1995, at a very young age, Rinay immigrated to Toronto from the Fiji Islands. After graduating from high School, he decided to go to George Brown College in the Toronto area. Rinay began his professional life as a Dental Assistant. He quickly realized this wasn't for him since most people associate dentistry with pain and he wanted to bring happiness to people.

When his parents bought their first dream home in Canada, they insisted he and his brother's name also appear on the title to the property. So, at 19, Rinay got his first taste of owning real estate. His family further owned farm land in Fiji so Rinay was able to see the benefits of land and home ownership first-hand.

In 2000, Rinay, through his Father's guidance, became involved in negotiating the sale of his family home, which made money in property appreciation and through the mortgage pay down. This allowed them to buy another, bigger home.

Sadly, Rinay lost his Father. Being the eldest son, this was a huge blow to his Grandfather, who also passed away within the same year. Both Men were not only very monumental but also the backbone and foundation of their Family. But with the help from his Mother, brother and sisters, Rinay was able to go through these challenging times.

They both understood the massive potential that lies in Real Estate and had encouraged Rinay to pursue this path. So he pursued it to make their dream come true. And in 2005, he jumped into the real estate industry. He even bought investment land in Saskatchewan with a JV Partner. Rinay began to attend numerous courses on positive thinking, personal growth development, real estate investments and financial freedom. He also began to network with the Robert G. Allen

Group and now he not only helps Real Estate Investors make profitable investments designed to bring in monthly positive cash-flow, but he also helps them to achieve their financial goals.

Rinay actively gives back to the community. In order to help people become healthier, he donates his time as a volunteer yoga instructor. He is also a member of Peaks Potential Karma Krew, and he has volunteered with Children in need of treatment Program—Region Dental Program and the City Department (C.I.N.O.T.)

Rinay is the co-founder of Elite Training Pros, a company designed to educate and help real estate investors.

You can reach Rinay Chand at:

rinay@elitetrainingpros.com

www.elitetrainingpros.com

REAL ESTATE - YOUR VEHICLE TO FINANCIAL FREEDOM

By Cynthia Habib

When you pull up directions on your GPS, you are typically given two ways to get to your destination—the fastest route and the route that may be shorter, but also has possible tolls, construction, traffic and it may even go right through the heart of a busy city. Both routes will undoubtedly get you to your destination—eventually.

So, what route do you typically choose?

I know I tend to go for the fastest, unencumbered route even though it may be longer (more kilometres). I prefer to get to my destination faster avoiding any annoying and time-consuming waits in traffic or trying to work my way through a large city at rush hour. Yes, the actual kilometres of my route may be more, but the time (and stress) I save is well worth it to me.

Well, the same theory applies to getting into the real estate investing business. *Real estate is your vehicle and the route you take is the manner in which you approach real estate investing.* That being said, there are essentially two ways you can go about this.

1. You can choose the shortest route, which in this case would be skipping all the preparation work, avoiding taking the time to speak to other professional investors with more experience and simply choosing an investment property because it happens to be available, now.

2. Like the alternative driving route above, you can also take the fastest route by doing your "due diligence," finding yourself a good mentor and actually taking the necessary time to learn about any possible investment properties and how they will affect your overall success as an investor.

While it is often tempting to just take the shortest route, it may end up being longer and more expensive in the end because, like anything else in life, when you don't bother to take the time to learn about the process, surprises (and usually not good ones) always pop up. And these unexpected turns in the route can be very time consuming and costly.

On the other hand, if you opt for the fastest route, by doing your homework and learning what you need to know before jumping into the market, you will ultimately be more successful from a time management and financial standpoint.

The Real Estate Fast Track to Financial Freedom

There is no doubt that real estate is one of the world's best and most profitable investments. Countless savvy investors have made fortunes using real estate as their vehicle to success.

If investing in real estate is how you choose to make your success, there are a few things you should determine about yourself before getting into the business.

1. **Can you apply** what you know to your business in a way that will propel you forward?

2. **Can you accept** that you may not know everything and as such, need to complement your skill set and resources by seeking out people who do?

3. **Do you learn** from your mistakes and adjust your course to get to your destination?

Although these three questions may seem logical, you would be surprised at how many people simply decide they can invest in the market essentially blind. These people usually end up failing and instead of working to make their dreams happen, they only sabotage their efforts by not doing what needs to be done to make them successful. These are the people who simply choose the shortest route, hop in their vehicle, put the pedal to floor and then are surprised when they hit their first roadblock, which usually comes quickly.

So, now that you have determined you are ready to invest, you must decide what type of investing profile is right for you. There are essentially two types of investor profiles: The Active and the Passive investor. The Active investor profile simply means that investing in real estate is your main professional occupation, often generating a substantial income.

While Active investing is your hands-on business, Passive investing is its exact opposite, meaning you are an investor who's regular and frequent involvement in this business is not required, yet you still benefit as an investor.

Both investment profiles can provide you with a good source of income. Since most people can't afford to just jump into the market right away, without backup income, a rock-solid plan, the right knowledge and a good network of other professionals in the field, for the purpose of this chapter, I am going to concentrate on few passive investing strategies.

<u>Why Passive Real-Estate Investing</u>?

- Positive monthly cash-flow. Passive investing provides you with a great way to make $2000, $3000 or $5000 or more in extra income without too much extra work.

- You get to experience the benefits of owning rental properties that are managed by professional companies and avoid the hassles of the infamous midnight emergency calls and tenant issues.

- Leverage. You can use the equity in your home or any properties you purchase to acquire more properties.

- The cost of housing is down in the US, making "Capital Appreciation" very appealing. As such, purchasing a turnkey property is much easier with properties ranging from $40,000 to $80,000 producing generous returns on your investment

- Rental rates are holding steady and increasing every year in both Canada and the US. Lodging is a necessity, not a luxury. Everyone needs somewhere to live and that is not going to change.

Now that you know some of the many advantages from passive investing, let's look at a few passive investing techniques, so that you may choose what best suits your needs and situation.

The 3 Best Passive Investing Techniques you can use - Now

1. **Joint Ventures (JV)**

What it is a Joint-Venture?

A joint venture is when you enter into a business agreement with a second party to achieve one goal—buy a property and convert it into a positive cash-flow rental unit.

How do you make Passive Investing work with a JV?

There are many variables when considering a JV agreement, but certain things should be considered. For instance:

- As a passive investor, you choose to become a silent cash partner, without the extra work.

- Your partner, the active investor, brings their expertise providing you with a hassle-free investment property you otherwise would not have access to.

- The split is usually 50/50; however, this can be negotiated.

- You provide the down payment with a mortgage or fund the property entirely.

- Your active JV partner, possesses "The Perfect Mutually Beneficial Deal," and specialized knowledge that gives you access to:

  ✓ Rare cash-flowing properties passively

  ✓ Contractors for renovations and repairs

  ✓ Property managers

  ✓ Title holding companies and attorneys

  ✓ Insurance companies and financing

As a passive investor, your biggest challenge will be to find a JV partner you can trust and work with. An open mind and solid due diligence based on historical facts should always be done prior to jumping onboard any contractual agreement.

What are the Best Places to Find a Good JV Partner?

- Your own real estate mentor/coach
- Private investment clubs or real estate clubs
- Real estate conferences and trainings
- Reputable companies
- Referrals

Example of a Good JV Agreement:

In late spring of 2014, I decided to pursue more passive JV opportunities in Kansas, MS and in various cities across Florida.

Just as an example, I'll take you through one JV deal that I did in Kansas City. In this case I was the passive investor and my mentor was the active investor.

Here's how the JV deal went:

- The property was fully renovated and already generating remarkable amounts of monthly positive cash-flow.
- The average expected ROI, just on a rental basis, without figuring in any appreciation, was very generous.
- Because we developed a great relationship with our mentor and some key people, we got access to exclusive financing.
- As a professional active investor, our mentor got us a great cash-flowing detached house in a good location. They ensured the fix ups, connected us with a professional management company and even negotiated with the seller to pay the closing costs.

- The property management company was responsible for:
  - ✓ Rent collection and tenant issues
  - ✓ Property upkeep and maintenance
  - ✓ Providing owners with a monthly status of property
  - ✓ Distribution of expected positive monthly cash-flow
- My mentor also helped with the paperwork, including the actual real estate agreement, the JV agreement and mortgage paperwork.
- In the future when the property gets sold, I will get all of my money back first and the rest of the net profit will be divided according to the JV agreement.

As you can see from this example, it was relatively easy for me to invest in a lucrative cash-flowing property with very little work on my part. My mentor not only did the majority of the work and created a win-win scenario, but he also showed us a path to passive monthly cash-flow.

2. Assignments

What it is an Assignment?

An assignment is different from a typical real estate purchase agreement in one way. Your name will not appear as the buyer on the purchase agreement. Instead, it will say *Assigns*. This term legally indicates that you, as the buyer, will be transferring the full rights of the purchase contract to an end buyer.

How do Assignments Provide a Means of Passive Investing?

When purchasing real estate to flip, an investor will buy and take full control of the property by putting an offer on a property along with a deposit. It usually takes between 30-60 days to close on the property.

It is during these 30-60 days, prior to actually closing; that the investor assigns or sells the interest in the property to someone who is looking to get access to a good cash-flowing property. In essence, assignment is like flipping property where the locater of the property doesn't actually close on it but makes a profit on the sale.

Here's an example:

Let's say I'm the active investor and you're the passive investor who doesn't have the connections, expertise or the time to locate amazing cash-flowing opportunities. In this scenario, I find a property for $60,000. After doing my due diligence to make sure it's a sound investment, I put an offer in to buy the property along with a deposit. I now have 30 days to close on the property.

As the passive investor, you then approach me saying you would love to grab this rare opportunity because the property is expected to produce nice monthly cash flow and/or you are buying it below market value.

In this case, I may sell the property for a $10,000 fee or profit, which means your total investment is $70,000 plus any closing costs.

I am doing all the hard work, including negotiating a good deal, doing my due diligence, doing my pro forma, putting many offers in to close on one good deal and helping you connect with the a suitable management company.

For you, it's a completely passive investment because all the work is done for you and you essentially get the deal served to you on a silver platter, ready to collect money every month.

How do You Complete a Real Estate Assignment?

As a passive investor, you can use your real estate network to stay in contact with active real estate investors, mentors or wholesalers who can give you access to opportunities that are generally not available to the public. Your ability to find and build a relationship with these insiders can be the difference between whether you'll become financially free or not.

Here's how you can find trustworthy, active investors and/or mentors to help you:

- Attend your local real estate clubs

- Google using keywords such as, "Real estate coach, real estate mentors or property wholesalers." Linked In and Yahoo are also good sources.

- Get referrals from your friends, lawyers, accountants or fellow investors.

- Do your due diligence on any partners you're thinking of investing with.

3. Hard Money Lending

What it is Hard Money Lending?

This concept is based on lending your money out to a borrower for a fee. The fee is typically dependent on the risk associated with the borrower and what they need the money for. So, you are essentially investing your money to make more money.

Competition among hard money lenders is high. To succeed, you need to be flexible to the borrower's needs and specialize in a known territory to minimize your risk.

How to Start Hard Money Lending

There are several general guidelines to help you get started in this type of investment.

1. Select a known market and territory to reduce your risk until your experience allows you to expand.

2. Determine the general loan percentage. It can vary on a case by case scenario depending on the borrower's situation.

   Consider: Many lenders in North America lend at around 65 percent of after repair value

3. Establish guidelines for what percentage of interest you will place on the hard money loan.

    Consider: Many lenders in North America vary from 7.5 to 29 percent

4. Establish whether you will be using an origination fee and what that spread will be.

    Consider: Many lenders in North America use a spread of 2-5 percent

5. Establish criteria for the duration of the loan.

    Consider: 3 months to a year depending on the size of the task

6. Don't just lend anyone money. Specialize in lending money to individuals that have purchased property and who need money to convert the property into a profitable flip.

7. Determine your sources of lending money (your money, your line of credit, money from private investors and money from financial institutions)

8. When using your own money, determine what kind of fees you want to charge along with the interest rate.

9. Temper the risk to your comfort zone. The more flexible you are as a lender, the more borrowers you will have access to, however, the greater the risks involved.

Example of a Hard Money Lending Deal

You have located an investor that needs a hard money loan to do repairs on a property, flip it and sell it. It's crucial to qualify the borrower prior to providing the loan. The rule of thumb is the best loans are the ones given in which the borrower is increasing the value of the property—which means higher profits for the borrower and better odds of success for both parties.

Ask yourself if this is the type of loan you want to give out—Yes or No? While a personal credit check is not required, you do need to be informed if the borrower has ever filed for bankruptcy or has a court demand/judgement against them as this will influence your decision to proceed or not. If you choose to proceed, you will definitely need to factor this risk into your rates.

Assuming you decide to proceed, there are several things you must first determine from your potential borrower that will help you decide what course of action to take next:

1. Is this buyer able to make the down payment (or buy the complete property) and cover the closing costs?

   Answer: The borrower bought it from a wholesaler. Total cost was $100,000.

2. Is the buyer able to cover the rehab costs, if applicable?

   Answer: Yes. He only needed to remove asbestos from the insulation. The work was completed and he provided paperwork as proof.

3. Is the property located in a favourable market where you will be able to get the best selling price?

   Answer: Yes. Comparables show houses sold for $200,000 in the area in the last 30-60 days.

4. Is the loan the borrower is requesting too high, rendering the property unprofitable or too low in profit to be of value?

   Answer: No. The profit margin has potential.

5. Does the property have at least 40 percent or more equity in it? (In case of loan default.)

   Answer: It has 100 percent equity.

6. How much will the repairs cost?

   Answer: $25,000.

7. Can the borrower fully describe the plan for implementing repairs?

    Answer: The borrower has a detailed plan with contractor estimates for each repair documented and it is available for review. Full disclosure.

8. What is the estimated after-repair value of the property?

    Answer: Based on the market, it's $210, 000.

9. What is the duration of the loan?

    Answer: 60 days to complete the work, plus 60 days to close on selling = 4 months.

10. Can you ensure that you will get 100 percent disclosure on all details of the project and the borrower?

    Answer: You realize this is the second house this investor has flipped. He is new and as such, he could have made some unforeseen errors in his plan.

Assuming that you have enough details to prove this investment will be profitable for both parties, explain the terms of the hard money loan to the borrower. Follow your own policy. Do not deviate. And then present the loan agreement, which should state:

- Hard money not to exceed 65 percent of after-repair value.

- The repair plan is detailed and backed up with professional estimates.

- Your origination fee is set at 4 percent ($1,000 payable upfront.) The cost of this loan is $26,000.

- Duration of the loan = 4 months.

- Interest is set at 20 percent (high interest rate to offset short duration.) Interest = $5,200.00.

- Total cost of the plan: $31,200.

- You require a balloon payment made at the end of the 4 months.

- Your profit: $6,200.

As you can see, there are many ways for you to enter the real estate market. The time has never been better to invest as the return on investment for real estate is actually better today than it has ever been—especially if you're open to investing in the US where there are currently countless new opportunities. All you need to do is look through the eyes of a successful seasoned investor that has already travelled the road you want to take and you'll find yourself on your way to reaching your desired destination.

About Cynthia Habib

Cynthia Habib is an accomplished Real Estate Investor, Author, Mentor, Speaker, and former Property Manager Expert. Born and raised in Montreal Canada, she first entered the real estate investing market in 1998 with the purchase of her first revenue producing property— a duplex. A few years into the investment, her position in quality assurance was downsized while she was on maternity leave. That was the incentive she needed to pursue her lifelong ambition to start her own business and redirect her professional orientation.

With the burning desire to be present in her family's lives and not be concerned with the never-ending fluctuations of traditional employment in today's market, the choice was simple. Real Estate became her chosen vehicle.

Having experienced multi-housing property management while helping others with the management of their buildings, the time had come to pool together with other aspiring investors. Using the equity of her original duplex and proven real estate techniques acquired through mentoring, she purchased two residential multi-family housing buildings for a total of 78 rental apartments. For over a decade the management of those buildings became her new career, while her associates enjoyed their journey as passive investors.

Today, Cynthia has a system in place that allows her to enjoy passive income by investing in the US, where she has purchased 12 properties and several lots in Florida, Kansas and Ohio. Now, Cynthia has chosen to focus on helping others achieve their goals in Real Estate by providing them with insider knowledge and deals through Mentoring, Public Speaking, Joint-Venturing and allowing others to take advantage of unbelievable cash-flowing opportunities that she has access to.

A Special Gift for your journey to Financial Freedom

Cynthia has developed a practical guide called *"Money Making Techniques using Real Estate"* to help investors across North America determine what kind of Real Estate vehicle is a good fit to reach their financial objectives. To download your complimentary copy go to *www. MMT-RE.CynthiaHabib.com*

To connect with Cynthia Habib you can send a message using LinkedIn.

ARE YOU IN CONTROL? HOW YOUR THOUGHTS AND FEELINGS DETERMINE YOUR SUCCESS

By Lynn Signoretti

"Mrs. Signoretti, you've just had a heart attack."

Have you ever wondered "Why me? Why now?" I don't think we would be human if we didn't have these questions at least once in our life. Usually, it's when something significant happens to turn our lives in a completely different direction. Or, at the very least, derail us from our current path. In my case, it was a heart attack.

When Tragedy Strikes

Everything seemed to be going great. My life was on the right track (at least as far as I was concerned). Things couldn't be better. So why was this happening to me? Why now?

I think we try to live our lives the best way we can. We deal with the daily stresses of work, family life, conflict with others and our personal and business relationships. This is all to achieve one goal—to make ends meet so we can be happy and live a fulfilled life. Then, without notice, something drastically changes everything we thought we had "under control."

So, what does this have to do with real estate investing and success? Everything. Why? Because every single thought and every single emotion or feeling you have, determines how your life will unfold. I can teach you everything I know about the technical end of real estate investing, but if you aren't aware of what future your mind and actions are currently creating, none of my experience and expertise will help you become successful. No one's will for that matter. Because simply put, *"life is an inside job."*

When the Universe Came Knocking on My Door

I have been in the fitness field for most of my life. At the time of my heart attack, I had spent 32 years dedicating my life to teaching others how to be healthy through exercise and nutrition. I also practiced what I preached and worked out every day and ate a healthy diet. In fact, in my eyes, I was the perfect example of how to live a healthy life. Have you ever heard the saying, "If you want to make God laugh, tell him your plans?"

Well, in the fall of 2012, while teaching a fitness class, I suddenly fell to the floor. There was no warning or explanation for the fall. I had taught this same class countless times without injury. But the force from the fall was so hard that I actually broke my lower left leg.

I was stunned. The injury obviously incapacitated me for some time, so, of course, I also had plenty of time to think about what had happened. None of it made any sense to me. I saw no rhyme or reason for this injury that completely derailed my life. My job was to be active and fit, a role model for my students, yet I was laid up for months.

I continued to go around and around in my mind, focusing on "why now?" yet never actually finding a good reason. I eventually recuperated from the injury and was ready to jump back into my regular routine. Little did I know that the broken leg was actually protecting me from something much bigger that was about to happen.

On Wednesday, June 12, 2013, I received news that my baby sister had just passed away. I was devastated. It was like any other day. I was at work when my husband showed up out of the blue. I could tell by the look on his face that something horrible had happened. When the words left his mouth, it was like he was speaking in slow motion. I could almost see the words slipping off his lips. I remember thinking, "What is going on? My stomach dropped as I pleaded with him to tell me it wasn't true. It was like the world around me had suddenly disappeared. It simply didn't seem real anymore. All I could think is, "I must be dreaming."

What Happens When You Don't Listen

Over the next few days, my emotions ran the gamut between sadness, anger and frustration. As I stood in the funeral precession line, greeting all the people who came to give their respects and blessings, I remember feeling strong and empowered. Seeing the rest of my family grieve I felt a strong need to help them, especially my parents. I somehow felt it was my duty to help them get through this tough time.

Around 7 pm on that Friday, I started to feel a throbbing pain in my back. It eventually moved down my left arm. I must have looked unwell because my husband turned to me and asked if I was okay. I told him I didn't feel well and that I didn't know what was wrong.

The next thing I remember is being taken away by the ambulance and rushed to the hospital.

As I lay on the small gurney, doctors and nurses rushing around me in the busy emergency department, my husband, daughter and I waited for answers. The scariest part was that we didn't know what was happening. One minute I was trying to help my parents deal with the loss of my sister, and the next, I was in the hospital myself. It was a very bizarre feeling. Then, a very brisk doctor approached.

"Mrs. Signoretti, you've just had a heart attack," he said, matter of factly.

"Did I hear you right?" is all I could muster. "That can't be. Are you sure?" My mind simply couldn't accept any more bad news.

"Oh, yes," he said. "We are quite sure, and we will be keeping you for a while and prepping you for more tests to determine the cause."

Shock would be an understatement for what I was feeling. I just looked at my husband and daughter, disbelief written all over my face. "How can this possibly be happening? I'm healthy . . . I'm a fitness trainer! I help people with their health so they can avoid things like this. How can this be?"

The questions came at me like rapid fire ammunition as my mind tried to make sense of everything. The only thing I knew for sure was that I was just told I had a heart attack. Even with that, I had a hard time accepting it. The doctor had to be wrong—denial was setting in for the second time that week.

I wanted and needed answers. "Why me? Why now?" But, as it turned out, I was not going to get those answers—at least right then. After all the tests were completed, I was simply told it must be genetics. Essentially, the tests were inconclusive. They didn't know the actual cause of my heart attack.

Looking For Answers

While I had no concrete answer for my sudden heart attack, between my sister's death and my own near-death experience, I came to some realizations that ultimately changed my life forever. It was like someone had simply turned on a light switch and I could now see everything clearly.

I saw how the majority of us go through life hanging onto our past traumas, hurts, beliefs, negative emotions and feelings, which ultimately keep us from living life fully. We go through the motions of our daily life—getting up, going to work, working at a job (most of us probably don't even like.) We come home, take care of our family, pay the bills, go to bed, and wake up the next day only to do it all over again. All the while, we push forward like programmed robots, in hopes we will someday, somehow, make ends meet so we can retire—so our lives *can really begin*. Then, and only then, we will be happy and fulfilled.

But for the majority of us, the reality is that day will never come. As I found out first hand, you either become ill from a disease, which then requires medication for the rest of your life, and you are left to fend for yourself because no one knows what to do for you, or you die. Not a bright scenario anyway you look at it.

I knew then that I had lost all hope. I felt vulnerable and wondered how I was supposed to live the rest of my life this way. The situation triggered feelings of despair, anger, frustration, hopelessness and fear of what the rest of my life would look like. All my plans for a happy retirement and a fulfilling life were gone.

As I looked back at my life as I lay in that hospital bed for over a week, pictures and pieces of it flashed before me. I started to question everything—"Why am I here?" "What is my purpose in life?" "Why did this happen to me?" All these questions kept haunting me. I thought I had it all figured out.

But then, something changed. Just one year later, as I now look back at what happened, I can clearly see it was a blessing—a true soul experience. A gift from God. I learned invaluable lessons that would change my life forever so I am able to continue on my life path to fulfill my dreams and my true purpose, which I believe is to live life to its fullest.

And these are the lessons I want to share with you.

Live Like There Is No Tomorrow

Be happy—NOW. Realize that at this very moment, even as you read this, you must start living your life right away, right now, not a minute later. Probably the biggest lesson I learned from my experience is that I need to live in the moment, each and every day. Life is too short and precious to squander on things that really don't matter.

I know now I was just going through the motions of living, like far too many people do. It could have been all taken away from me in the blink of an eye. It made me realize God, or a higher power, was nudging me to wake up and stop sleeping my life away. I was being shown I needed to take notice of all the little things around me that we normally take for granted. There is nothing in this lifetime we should take for granted. It's all precious and was put in our path to help us grow and fulfill our destiny. SO LIVE YOUR LIFE. It's all about living the highest quality of life possible while we are here on Earth. Be thankful and grateful for what you have right now. And when things get tough, just know and trust in your heart and soul that you are exactly where you are supposed to be, and it's all working out for your highest good.

Life should be opened up and cherished like a gift on Christmas morning. If you live today like it is your last day on this planet you will never regret it. The only thing you will ever regret is a missed opportunity. So live life like there is no tomorrow, because you never know when there won't be one. Ask yourself this question: If I only had one more day to live what would I do? Then go out and do it. Don't put it off. You really can't afford not to.

Exercise:

Live absolutely in the now. Always follow your heart, your gut, your intuition. It will never steer you wrong. Ask yourself these questions when opportunity arises:

Is what I am about to do truly what my heart and spirit want me to do?

Does it feel warm and fuzzy inside?

Does it make me feel excited and happy?

If the answer is yes, then take the risk and go ahead and do it. Since my heart attack I always follow my heart, my intuition, in every decision and opportunity I encounter. I was constantly worried and afraid of taking risks in case I failed. But what I realize now is that by not taking risks and following my intuition, I've already failed—I've failed myself. So I began taking risks and following my heart. I ventured into real estate in order to make passive income so I can enjoy life now, not tomorrow. And that is exactly what I am doing.

Love Like You Will Never Get Hurt

The second lesson is to truly love—you. As I sat in the hospital bed, I realized that love for yourself has everything to do with being happy and fulfilling your dreams. As I began to radiate love, miracles began to happen. The life I was born to live started to appear, as if by magic. Excitement re-entered my heart and soul to ignite and rev me up to new and challenging adventures. You truly do begin to live in this moment.

You must vow to help yourself and love who you are through and through. Trust your body, as the temple it is, and it will give you signs to nudge you in the right direction—on the path toward your purpose. We all go through challenges in life, but our biggest challenge is actually overcoming "ourselves."

We will always have emotions that lower our self-esteem and make us feel unworthy. We are conditioned through our past experiences to tell ourselves we can't do it, we're not smart enough or pretty enough. Some of us have been programmed to believe this from a very early age. As a result, we don't love ourselves. We don't respect who we are and we try to find love from others to fill that void. But the reality is that what we really need is to look within ourselves—first. To have love for ourselves, first and foremost.

So many people consciously and even unconsciously, put others ahead of themselves in too many areas of their lives. We let people walk on us. We do things we don't really want to do just to make sure we are "loved." But as you probably know, this only creates resentment, often to the point of self-loathing. If we can just look within and be kind to ourselves, truly love the person we are, inside and out, all of our dreams will come true. When you love, you attract more of the same into every area of your life—including finances.

Exercise:

Every day, as soon as you wake up, look into the mirror and tell yourself that you love you. Absolutely mean it to the core of your being. How often do we actually say these words to ourselves? Probably rarely or never. We are very good at telling others we love them. We are also very good at criticizing ourselves, even when we get a compliment. We justify putting ourselves down.

So get up every day, look into the mirror and say "I love and accept myself just the way I am. I am loved, and I am worthy." At first, it will be tough and maybe even seem a little strange, but with time you will truly see how perfect you are just the way you are. As you continue with this exercise, you will begin to look in the mirror and just smile. Love will begin to radiate from you to everyone around you and you will begin to witness miracles happening in your life. Love for life, love for everyone else and love for knowing you are here for a reason. Love is the key to peace, happiness and success. When there is love, there is no fear.

What You Think About, You Bring About

The third lesson is the most important. It's actually a mindset that relates back to the first and second lessons. The way we think, what we believe, our attitude and emotions, in turn play a significant role in our overall health. *Thoughts are things.* Once you accept this concept, you will notice how powerfully it impacts your life. We know that placebos work. Study after study uses them, and without a doubt, people experience the same results as the control subject. When you believe something is real, you can make it real—good or bad.

Every thought demands a response from your body. When these thoughts are negative (even if directed at someone else), these emotions then destroy your health, your mind and your life. Negative thoughts will creep into your life at different times for different reasons. Many people explode in anger, which then results in health issues. Others bury their feelings or push them aside and continue their life thinking they are "fine" because they don't feel anything. But just like the person who explodes, the person who hides their anger, is simply letting it fester into diseases like cancer, a heart attack, gallbladder issues, you name it.

The bottom line is that if your thoughts and feelings are negative, your body will respond in kind and release chemicals that change your body on a cellular level. So if you continue to have negative thoughts and feelings, like fear, anxiety, worry or stress every day, your body will continue to release these chemicals that ultimately end up destroying your health.

Adrenaline is one of these chemicals. It's the first chemical the body releases in defense physiology to counter your negative thoughts like fear. Adrenaline elevates your heart rate and tightens and tenses your muscles. Over time, your body begins to break down and disease and illness take over. Think about a finely tuned racecar. If you run it hard every day, not caring about how you are pushing the engine, it will eventually break down. Your body is probably the most finely tuned engine in the world. Imagine what is happening to it.

Exercise:

Think positive thoughts. By using positive affirmations on a daily basis you will eventually change your mindset. When a negative thought comes up, and it will, recognize it, say the word "cancel" and immediately replace the thought with a positive one. For example if you think "I feel sick today," immediately replace it with "I am in perfect health. I am healthy, I am energized." These positive affirmations will begin to help your body function the way God intended it to.

Easier said than done, you say. Yes, but by taking these steps, little by little every day and making this change, you can turn this around to have the health and life you want. Remember THOUGHTS ARE THINGS. There are positive things and situations all around you. You just have to recognize them. God gave you free will so you can change the way you think in an instant.

Health-Saving Realizations

Before my accident and my sister's passing, and of course, my heart attack, I had no idea what all my past hurts and traumas were doing to my health. Apparently, I didn't learn the lesson when I broke my leg. I went right back to my old thinking. Then my sister passed. And I stuffed all of my emotions again when I tried to ignore my feelings and help my family deal with theirs. So, life dealt me another lesson—my heart attack. But this time I listened.

It's so important to release any negative emotions. Find a safe way to deal with them. Be grateful for what you have and more good will come into your life. If you think positive thoughts and feel positive emotions, each and every day, you will begin to live your life as though today is your last.

God gave me another nudge—a huge one at that—to help me recognize what I was doing to myself. I was being shown that I needed to change the way I lived my life and my thinking. How was I going to help others heal and be happy if I could not heal myself?

Everyone has control over their thoughts, whether you believe that or not. No one can make you think something you don't want to think or believe. You are the creator of your life. If your life isn't the life you want, then own what is happening to you and do something about it. Life is way too short not to recognize the blessings we are given to push us in the right direction. So forgive yourself for not recognizing these signs earlier and learn the lessons NOW. Every obstacle that comes, or has ever come your way, is there to better you in some way. Take it as a lesson to be learned and not something negative you store in your body until it reveals itself as disease.

Forgive, let go, learn the lessons, love yourself and live your life for the present moment because your life really does depend on it.

About Lynn Signoretti

Lynn Signoretti was a personal trainer for 32 years. She currently resides in Sudbury, Ontario where she is a B.E.S.T. (Bio Energetic Synchronization Technique) Practitioner, using a mind-body healing technique that removes any interferences that may cause illness or disease. She is also a part-time professor at College Boreal and an active member of PIC (Private Investment Club.) Lynn is involved in single and joint ventures in residential real estate and currently owns investments in both Canada and the US.

Her goal is to help people become aware of their current thinking and how this is affecting their health. She believes that until we are able to accomplish this, we cannot be truly happy or successful.

Lynn is offering readers her eBook, free, for a limited time. You can get your copy at www.lynnsignoretti.com. You can reach her at lynn@lynnsignoretti.com.

Enlightened Real Estate Investing for Success

By Ramesh (RT) Sangani

More and more today, people are realizing that success is simply not about how much money you make. Success involves monetary wealth, of course, but in order to be truly successful as a person, entrepreneur (or employee or boss) and family man or woman, you need to be abundant on all levels of life—personal, physical and spiritual.

Many people are able to achieve abundance on one or even two of these plains, but very few, unfortunately, are able to say they are successful in every area of their lives. This is not from a lack of trying. I know many people who are sincere, hard-working people that try and desperately want to be abundant and happy with their life in general. But it's not always about how hard you try. It's about your mindset, and until you are able to grasp this concept, no amount of trying will ever result in achieving what you really want and desire in your life.

What is Enlightened Real Estate Investing?

Enlightened Real Estate Investing, or ERI, as I like to call it, is simply a specific mindset you must develop in order to achieve:

Material wealth

Peak health

Spiritual Abundance

And how do you go about achieving each of these? The answer is really quite simple—through the help and guidance of those people who can mentor you and support you as you make your journey toward a more successful and happier mindset.

Why Mentorship?

You would not go golfing for the first time and expect to hit a hole in one or come under par on an 18-hole course. Nor would you expect to jump into the captain's chair of a 747 and simply fly the enormous plane across the Atlantic. So why would you expect to be able to successfully invest in real estate just because you want to?

Successful people did not get that way by going it completely alone. Sure, some have tried and have made numerous mistakes that were both time consuming and expensive before they achieved anything worth talking about. But why reinvent the wheel? Why not use the experiences (both good and bad) of successful people who have already travelled the road you wish to take? Why not use their valuable knowledge to bypass much of the anguish and problems they have already encountered to catapult you into a successful career?

I know I would not be in the position I am without mentors in every area of my life.

Mentors can help you in many ways:

Modeling a successful entrepreneur can save you countless hours and money. You can learn from the mistakes and successes of a mentor. What worked for them worked for a reason—because there are certain things that are universal about real estate investing that every successful investor must know. Mentoring helps investors understand the market and the numerous strategies that can be used to maximize your profits. You can save yourself years of trial and error, not to mention money lost on bad deals.

Mentoring can give you an edge over your competition. If you are just starting out, you can achieve much more than someone who tries to go it alone. Investing in real estate is not easy because there are many intricacies that can either make or break your investment.

Mentoring does not have to be expensive. Finding an experienced mentor does not necessarily have to cost you an arm and a leg. Some of my most trusted and experienced mentors have been people who have simply shown up in my life for different reasons. What you are really seeking from your mentor is knowledge, and you can gain much of this knowledge through reading books about successful people and attending seminars, etc. Ultimately, though, you are going to want to talk to someone who can also answer your questions and steer you in the right direction.

You will have immediate access to a wealth of knowledge about the industry. Mentors can help you figure out what you need to understand about the market and the area you wish to enter and even help pinpoint your area of expertise. In order to be successful, you need to focus on one area and make a name for yourself before you expand into other areas.

A mentor can help you jump into the market with complete confidence. A mentor can help you hone your skills and prepare you for the market. Ultimately, this will give you greater control over your portfolio's growth. A mentor can help you grow into a strong investor.

A mentor can keep you on track in many areas of your personal life as well as your business. Apart from providing you with a wealth of knowledge, a good mentor can help you learn how to manage your time successfully in order to maximize your profits. This is imperative if you want to achieve the most out of the industry, especially if you are new to real estate investing. Mentors can help you develop a strong business plan and extrapolate the details of the plan to create a successful and working business model.

Mentors provide a variety of ways to learn. Not everyone learns in the same way. Some people learn best with simple positive encouragement and guidance. Others need to be taken more by the hand and kept on track with a more hands-on approach. The beauty of mentorship is that not everyone has the same personality, and neither do mentors., so you can find a mentor who fits your learning style perfectly. There is a perfect mentor for everyone.

How Mentors changed my life

I have been truly blessed to have people who have guided me in every area of my life. While I was not actively seeking mentorship, I believe these people were put in my life for a reason, and that reason was to help me achieve personal wealth and health and a strong spiritual understanding of what makes a person successful.

I remember how excited I was when I first graduated university. The world was mine for the taking, and nothing was going to stop me. Like most graduates, though, I had a lot of experience with theory, but little to no practical experience. I was lucky that my knowledge of seven languages helped me land a job in the Hotel/Hospitality industry. I was ecstatic, but scared to finally take my first steps into the "real world." I thought I was well-equipped with my newfound knowledge and a vast array of friends and acquaintances with whom I could network, but the thought of jumping into a very reputable and large organization was still daunting.

Like most new employees in any field, there is always a "training period." Mine was to be six months. I was trained by a number of supervisors in the front office of the hotel, but I was eventually assigned to the sales and marketing office, where I reported to the Sales and Marketing Manager, Veer.

Over the course of next 24 months, Veer guided me. He helped and monitored my progress at every step. It was during this period that I was able to garner much of knowledge and confidence in the business world that I maintain and rely on today. He led, encouraged and helped me move toward my goals and dreams at the time. Veer had a very dynamic personality. He had an effective way of bringing out the best in me, which ultimately helped me to to progress in my career.

Although these were the early days of my career, he had a profound impact on my success today. At the time, I just thought he was a very nice "boss." I had no idea how much of an impact he was actually making! This is part of the lesson I am trying to impart on you. *Mentors can literally guide you from the beginning stages of your career to the apex of your success.* Had I known this then, I would probably have hired numerous mentors or at the very least, looked to others to lead me in all the areas of my life where I wanted to achieve success.

After the guidance Veer provided me in just a few short years, I was promoted to another area within the organization, but we kept in touch, and he was always there when I needed his advice or input. We both eventually left the company. Later, fate brought us back together in another venture where he continued to be an integral part of my business life over the next several years.

We still keep in touch today, and I continue to cherish his friendship, caring and wisdom. I now know that he is truly one of my very first mentors, and I feel blessed. Without his guidance, I would never be where I am today.

What Did I Learn from my Mentor?

Veer provided me with so many things, but most of all he taught me:

How to use my theoretical skills in a practical manner for ultimate success.

How to have confidence in myself and my work.

The necessary skills to survive in a large organization.

How to balance my work and home life so I can be more successful in both.

How to manage my time in order to utilize every minute and hour for success.

Without Veer's knowledge and his willingness to mentor me (without me even realizing the value of his skills and experience), I can truly say I would not have had the skills and know-how to cross over into the various careers I have taken on, which eventually led me to real estate investing.

Mentor # 2

I always think it's funny how, when you look back on your life, everything you have done that seemed irrelevant to your success at the time is actually connected. It's like we are picking up pieces to the puzzle of our success as we journey through life, whatever path we choose to take. Every piece, no matter how small or seemingly inconsequential, really has to be in place in order to ultimately create the finished puzzle that we call our life—our success.

Following my career in the hospitality industry, I found myself in construction. Part of the reason I was able to make this jump was the confidence and skills Veer had imparted on me earlier in my life.

My new mentor would be Richard. He was a much older man than I was at the time, and as such, he had vast experience and knowledge I could never have learned without him—at least not in the short time we were connected or without making many costly and time-consuming mistakes. He guided me to expand my horizons and exposed me to some incredible experiences in the international arena.

Often, with mentors, because of the time you spend with them and because they truly are a unique and strong presence in your life, the relationship can turn into one of mutual respect and friendship. This was the case with my earlier mentor, Veer, and it would also be the case with Richard. This friendship eventually transformed into a business partnership. Our journey together lasted over 7 years. And I believe this was another gift that fell into my lap in this incredible journey we call life.

What I learned from Richard

Acquiring Distributorships from major international companies in manufacturing construction, materials and equipment

Negotiating and signing contracts with international construction companies

Liaising, influencing and working with multinational architects and consultants

Managing multiple installation teams and work sites

Overall business acumen and expertise

Mentor # 3

Just over three years ago, I was introduced to the concept of *"Merging with the Infinite."* I have always been a very spiritual person. Like most people, however, I often wondered what life is really about. I struggled to understand the meaning of life, however clichéd that may be. I think we all go through this at one point or another, especially when things seem difficult or without meaning. It's how we learn and adjust to the hills and valleys of life.

Merging with the Infinite is a concept that essentially states that everything is made up of energy. From the water we drink and the food we eat to the desk we sit at as we work each day, it's all energy, constantly moving at specific vibrations. We too are made up of energy, and unlike the desk or other seemingly inanimate objects, to some degree we have control over the energy vibration we emit. It's this energy vibration that either attracts or repels the experiences we have in life. You likely learned in high school science class how magnets work. Well, our bodies are similar in that they produce a specific energy based on how we feel or what we do. For instance, if you are in a bad mood, you will attract similar negative energy.

Have you ever had a day when nothing seems to go right? You start out by losing your car keys, for example, which puts you into a bad mood because you will be late for work. From there, you then find yourself pulled over for speeding because you rushed to get to work on time, and then, when you finally get to work, there are no parking places, or someone is on your parking spot. Then maybe you have to listen to complaining co-workers all day or customers who are not happy with your service. With each negative experience, your mood escalates until finally, you feel defeated, frustrated and even angry.

The same is true when you start out in a great mood. Maybe you wake up feeling especially good from a restful night's sleep. You are happy and content. You leave for work exactly on time and miss all the traffic. You find the perfect parking spot. Your co-workers are happy to see you, and your customers sing your praises. With each positive experience, your mood becomes happier; you are more excited about your job and life in general, and as such, you keep attracting wonderful experiences into your day.

My next mentor or "Guru," ShivAnandji, which means Infinite Happiness, introduced me to this concept. I realized I have a responsibility to project the best possible energy I can, as my energy or "mood" can not only impact my success or ultimate failure in life, but it can also affect the people around me. My energy (and yours), can either bring positive experiences to the mix or promote "bad energy," which can only lead to demise.

I further realized this concept applied to my businesses as well. If I want to create a successful business, no matter what industry I am in, I need to create harmony through my actions, which are based on respectfulness to the people I meet and encounter on a daily basis.

Through this mentor I was able to create spiritual abundance in my life that has ultimately promoted my material wealth. He awakened my true potential. I now know I have the power to unite with the *Infinite Energy Force* of the universe.

Because of this mentor, I am going through this incredible journey on a spiritual level as well (which is truly the only way we can succeed with any real joy or happiness). Again, for that, I'm thankful to my GURU, ShivAnandji, for helping me with his spiritual mentorship. He is my guide and my strength. I truly believe this was again a Godsend.

Lessons I was blessed with from Shivanandji

Understanding that I am the SOUL— and a part of the purest form of Energy

The effect of our self-created Karma—actions and intentions

Patience and belief in the Infinite

Every soul has its own agenda and path to follow.

Total and complete forgiveness, respect and unconditional love

Entering the Real Estate Arena

When I decided to focus on real estate investing, I immediately knew I needed to do an incredible amount of learning. I spent days and weeks acquiring the knowledge to help me make the right decisions moving forward. I attended courses, seminars, conventions and numerous real estate events.

And while doing this, one thing remained constant. My past experiences had taught me the need and the value of having a good mentor. Someone who could guide me in the right direction. Someone who could help me decrease the time it took me to become knowledgeable and experienced in the field. Finally, someone who could give me the confidence and empower me to pull the trigger when needed.

With this in mind, I set out to find another good mentor, and I found the perfect person! Over the next few years, I was able to build a nice real estate portfolio both in Canada and the US, which is now providing me with great passive income.

Currently, I have three mentors I work with. One is based in BC, Canada. Another is in Ontario, and the third is in Dallas, Texas. While these mentors did not fall into my lap as my previous ones had, they are just as important as my previous mentors who, collectively, brought me to the stage in my life where I was confident enough to enter the real estate investing arena. In a short time, I have built a portfolio of US real estate investments, many of which realize a yearly return of 16 to 18 percent! I am financially free, and even more important, I am healthy, spiritually wise and happy. Really what more do we want in life?

A Final Lesson

Mentors can help in every area of your life, whether that be emotional, spiritual, physical, or in business. They are the coaches who work with you to achieve whatever you want in life. Sometimes, they come into your life unannounced, silent warriors who tread the path before you to provide invaluable knowledge and expertise. At other times, you have to look for them, but once you find your mentors, you must cherish them and be grateful to them for being part of your life; these are the people who will be the co-pilots in your journey to success. And let's face it, you are NOT flying that 747 without a co-pilot, no matter how much you think you know!

About Ramesh "RT" Sangani

Ramesh "RT" Sangani is the President, CEO and Co-founder of Sai Investments & Consulting, Inc. (www.sai-investments.com), located in the Toronto, Ontario area. His company locates, analyzes and structures complete "turn-key real estate investments" in Canada and the US. These investments are expressly designed to maximize profitability and minimize risk on the part of investors.

RT was born in India and spent most of his childhood in Ethiopia. Over the past four decades, he's created, grown and worked with businesses across the globe, including land development projects in India, construction projects in the Middle East, export businesses in the US as well as travel agencies, financial brokerages, and a major international hotel chain.

In 2011, he began building a US real estate investment portfolio, including many properties which realize a yearly return of 16 to 18 percent. By working with an expert network of Canadian and American partners, he packages "done-for-you" investments for properties located midwest and eastern USA. His company specializes in joint-venture partnerships, creative financing, Real Estate due diligence, raising capital and business consulting and effective strategies.

RT is passionate about property investments and wishes to help others build long-term wealth through the power of real estate. As such, he invites all who are interested in real estate investing to contact him at (416) 494-2179 or email him at rt@sai-investments.com.

The Secret to Creating Powerful Financial Independence

By Alex Fracassi

"The future depends on what you do today."
—*Mahatma Gandhi*

Creating a Perfect Mindset

Change. What does this word mean to you? Do you feel excited when you think about change? Do you feel anxious, even terrified? Change can bring up a whole slew of emotions in people. As humans, we don't typically like change. We resist it—even good change. Why? Because of a little something known as our *ego*.

If you think of your ego (that subconscious part of your mind that continually "talks" to you) as something that is alive, you can then see that any change usually means something has to give—and that typically means a change to our ego. As something alive, your ego wants to survive—as is. So when you even think about change, if your ego is not on board, it will bring up feelings of anxiety, frustration, anger, and in some people, actual terror.

It's hard to believe that something we are not even aware of, for the most part, can have so much control over us. If someone else in your life tried to control you to the extent that our egos do, there's no doubt you would see it differently. Likely you would not put up with it or would at least question that person.

So in order for change to occur, we must first deal with our egos. We must change our mindset. If you do not make this one change, no amount of will or intention will bring about true and lasting change in your life—in any area. And for this to happen, you need to have an open mind and realize that what you're doing today may not be working as well as you think it is.

Changing your mindset does not have to be overwhelming. In fact, it can be just a minor adjustment. In other cases, however, depending on your current thought patterns, it can entail significant change; you may even need to re-invent yourself altogether.

One of the hardest mindsets to change is often our thoughts about money. Even though money is really just a "thing" we use to purchase those items in life we want or need, we tend to relate to money with extreme feelings—such as love, hate, frustration, a sense of freedom. The truth is there really is no other object that people have such strong feelings about. Think about your own feelings toward money and wealth. What is the first thought or feeling that comes to mind when I mention the word MONEY? Do you have the same intense reaction to the words CAR, FOOD, GIRAFFE, or PLANT, for instance? Likely not.

I think what most people will notice is that they have no feelings around these other words other than possibly like or dislike … but certainly not the extreme emotions of LOVE or HATE, which really are very strong words. You may also find that words such as CAR elicit stronger feelings than GIRAFFE. Why? Again, because CAR is associated with money in the sense that you need money to get a car (for the most part), and the type of car will depend on how much money you have. The closer an object is linked to money, the more intense your feelings become.

It is also no secret that the less or more money you have, the more ingrained these feelings will be. So how does this relate to your current financial state? Simply put, you need only to look at your current financial state to see how you view money. Those people who have a lot of money certainly don't hate it—if they did, they would not have it, or if they did, it would not last. Your emotions and feelings attract or repel objects according to the feeling. Hate brings negative situations, and love brings positive situations.

So what does this mean for you and your current financial state? It means that if you are currently experiencing financial difficulties, then you need to change your mindset with respect to money. Start by changing the way you view it. Appreciate it, be grateful for what you do have (there are always people who are much worse off.) Once you change your feelings toward money, you will see your finances begin to change.

This in no way means, however, that all you have to do is "love" money. Not at all. It actually means you must also respect it, not throw it away or squander it on needless things when you are trying to build wealth.

I have just the tips for you and your family that will help you to grow your money so you can experience the financial freedom you deserve.

> "If you can change your mind, you can change your life."
> – *William James*

My Household Inc.

One of the best ways to create and grow wealth is to become a micro-manager of your finances. By this I mean *know where your money is going*. If you have no idea what is coming in and what is going out, how can you possibly manage your finances accordingly? When you take emotion out of the mix, it becomes much easier to see money as simply something to manage.

So if you treat your household as you would a company, you will be infinitely more aware of your bottom dollar and as well, relieve much of the stress you needlessly put on yourself when you have no idea where your money has gone.

Here are a few steps and tips to help you:

1. Develop a Good Budget and Savings Plan

A *Budget and Savings Plan* is made up of two components: the *Net Worth Statement* and the *Cash-Flow Statement*. These two statements are like the foundation of a building. Without them, the building would collapse. They help establish financial discipline, measure your financial progress on a regular basis, and prepare a strategy to achieve your future financial goals. As an "incorporation," you would divide your "fiscal year" into four quarters. So let's start.

It's important to know where you are right now financially, where you want to be in the future and the financial resources you have to reach your destination. In order to do this you will have to use a concept known as *Net Worth Planning*. There are several steps you can follow to achieve this:

The first step of *Net Worth Planning* is to construct a *Net Worth Statement*. This statement is the equivalent of a company's balance sheet. It represents a snapshot of your financial assets that will eventually grow over time and can be used to fund future spending needs, such as retirement, your child's education or for emergencies. The calculation of your net worth at any one given time is not as important as *calculating your net worth periodically,* so you can see whether it's growing toward a specific goal or if it's falling short of your goal. Like a corporation, you should create a *Net Worth Statement* every quarter, so every three months you can see your progress. It doesn't matter when you start; the trick is to just start and get into the habit of calculating your own net worth! Then, when the following new calendar year comes around, start with January and calculate your net worth every quarter. You can then look back and see how you did every calendar year!

You may also want to do this on a monthly basis at first so you get accustomed to it as it allows you to track and see your progress from month to month.

I have both the *Net Worth* and *Cash-Flow Statements* already prepared for you on my website (www.AlexFracassi.com). Feel free to download and use these to get started right now.

As you are filling out this statement, you will notice there are two main sections. The first one is *Assets*, which are items such as the current value of your house or condo, stocks, bonds and other securities you may own. The second section is *Liabilities*, which are items like a mortgage, credit card balances and other outstanding debt. Once you subtract all your *Liabilities* from your *Assets*, you arrive at your *Net Worth*.

The second concept we'll look at is *Cash Management Planning*. The first step of *Cash Management Planning* is to put together a *Cash-Flow Statement*. A *Cash-Flow Statement* is the equivalent of a company's income statement. This paints a picture of your cash-flow over a period of time. **The only way net worth can grow is by having positive net**

cash-flow, which will then become your savings.

If your cash-flow is not where you want it to be, you can apply the following techniques: 1) control your current household spending; 2) restructure any debt; and 3) reposition any assets (speak to your accountant about the best options for your particular scenario.) This will help you increase your net worth over time.

The *Cash-Flow Statement* can also be used to identify areas of excessive spending so you can manage your spending patterns to lower your cash outflow to a level you're more comfortable with.

By using these two statements together, you will develop a systematic *Savings Planning Strategy,* which is the driving force to long-term financial success. Simply put, these two statements will help you to **SAVE MONEY,** which is the key to successful finances.

2. Savings Planning

Once you start having money to put aside as savings, there are things you can do to maximize these savings.

Some general savings strategies include:

a) Treating Your Savings as a Fixed Expense

You can create a "savings expense" every month, which means putting money into a high-interest savings account or a mutual fund that forces you to save. You should also shift any excess money in your bank accounts and transfer them over to at least a high-interest savings account so you earn a better return on your money.

b) Reduce Expenses

By looking at your *cash-flow statement*, can you see what expenses are not necessary? What I have found is that people tend to overspend in certain areas, and if they pay attention to these areas, over time they will save a lot of money. The first area where I usually find people overspending is in what I call the *"Latte Conundrum."* If you're spending a lot of money on, you guessed it, Starbucks, this is an easy expense to reduce. The solution is simple: Buy your Starbucks coffee beans in bulk at places such as Costco and learn how to brew a killer cup of coffee yourself!

Other easy reductions are looking at your cable bill. Do you RE-ALLY need the best package? Ask yourself "How much TV do I really watch per week, and does it justify my cable bill?"

Speaking of electronics, do you have a cell phone? How about a laptop or a tablet, or both? How often do you upgrade your devices? Ask yourself if you really need the latest and greatest devices, or if your three-year-old tablet still does the job. I think in most cases the answer is "yes, my old device is perfectly fine." So be prudent in this area and update your devices only when they can no longer perform the tasks you need them to.

You can also look at your bank accounts. How much are you paying in bank fees? Have a chat with your banker and ask how you can minimize these fees by reducing the number of bank accounts and simplifying your monthly transactions.

A big common expense is buying a vehicle. Sure, the new car smell is great, but as soon as you drive that beauty off the car lot, it starts to depreciate—immediately! Have a look at the price of your next vehicle if you were to buy it brand new, and then compare it with a used one that is 2-4 years old. You will find the same car, just 2-4 years older, is 25-40 percent less! So let someone else buy it brand new. Let them carry the depreciation. You'll get a very good vehicle at a significantly reduced price. And if you're concerned about a warranty, buy your used vehicle at a dealer and ask about purchasing an extended warranty or purchasing from their *certified pre-owned program.*

The last common sense savings tip is *shopping.* Try shopping at outlet malls and discount stores vs. shopping malls. You will find almost everything you're looking for in the outlet world and drastically reduce your shopping bill.

3. Increase Your Income

Now this is what I call creative income planning. Let's take a look at your real estate situation first. An example is the house you live in. If you are not using your basement or every room in your household already, you can rent it out and collect monthly income. You can section off your basement and build a separate entrance for your tenant. If you want to rent out individual rooms, this is called "shared accommodations." You should learn more about this, however, before you decide to go this route. If you have an empty or half-empty garage, you may also want to rent this space out as storage space.

4. Enhanced Investment Return

Most people have a traditional investment portfolio that consists of stocks, bonds and mutual funds. This is usually where people start to invest because it's rather easy, and you don't need a lot of money to get started. In addition to these financial instruments, though, you should open your mind to other investment opportunities—like real estate.

Real estate is a very important component to any investment portfolio. It offers other opportunities that are not available if you just stick with financial instruments. Real estate offers opportunities such as owning hard assets like single family homes, apartment buildings, commercial property, land and tax liens, just to name a few.

Over time, as you build your investment portfolio, you should assess how much risk you are willing to take on and move any existing funds to the highest risk category you are comfortable with, as *greater risk usually brings greater returns.*

> "Someone's in the shade today because someone planted
> a tree a long time ago."
> —*Warren Buffett*

5. Credit and Debt

Another important component to your household finances is how you and your family handle credit and debt planning.

When you think of credit cards, having overdraft protection on your account or having a line of credit, often you think of the negative implications associated with each of these. For instance, having too many credit cards or not using them correctly can cause huge problems down the road for your credit score. I caution people about having too much credit and consumer debt, but before we get to the negatives, let me tell you about the positives and how to use credit **correctly**.

The rule of thumb in financial planning is that you should ever have only two credit cards issued by two different financial institutions. The reason for this is that if one company's system goes down and you're in the middle of making a purchase, you can always use the other institution's credit card so you won't get stuck.

Shifting all of your monthly expenses, such as cell phones, hydro (electricity) and literally all of the rest of your bills and purchases onto a credit card is actually a **GREAT** idea. Why? Because it provides you with a monthly statement that is already prepared for you—for FREE. And it shows an itemized list of your monthly expenses and purchases! This allows you to quickly see all of your yearly expenditures in 12 simple statements.

A credit card that has some kind of rewards program is a good idea because not only are you organizing your expenses, over time, you're building up points toward a purchase you would make anyways. The difference now is that you're going to get it either at a discount or for FREE. Some example reward cards include travel rewards, cash-back rewards and vehicle rewards. Even though some of these cards may have an annual fee, your purchases may far outweigh the cost of the card. Beware, however, that you don't get hooked on making purchases just to rack up points. That defeats the whole purpose of getting a rewards credit card.

Now here is where a change in mindset comes in again. When you use credit cards or a line of credit, you are borrowing the financial institution's money to fund your purchases, but they charge you a hefty interest rate to borrow!

With credit cards, you're paying interest only after 30 calendar days. For lines of credit, you're paying interest immediately upon borrowing. So whatever you buy with your credit cards, ask yourself, "Can I pay this back by the due date so I don't get charged interest?" If the answer is no, then leave it alone!

As for lines of credit, it's wise to obtain one line of credit and use it ONLY for emergencies. Have your line of credit all set to go today before an emergency happens.

Any other credit cards or credit products are not necessary for your overall financial plan. Some people may take on extra lines of credit or obtain additional credit cards at lower rates to use toward an investment opportunity; however, for the purpose of personal financial planning, the rule of thumb is only two credit cards and one line of credit. So, for this reason, when offered more credit, just say no!

> "By failing to prepare, you are preparing to fail."
> —*Benjamin Franklin*

6. Take Action Now!

After reading this chapter, put this book down, go to my website, create your *Budget and Savings Plan*, and review it! It doesn't matter what your financial situation is:

Put this into your schedule and create your statements at least every quarter. Remember, you are now the CFO of your household, and you must run it with financial discipline.

I hope this will set you on a new financial path to financial responsibility and lead you, your family and future generations to financial prosperity. To your financial success!

About Alex Fracassi

Alex Fracassi has a BA in Economics and is a licensed Professional Financial Planner (PFP) in Toronto, Canada. He has been working as a licensed securities trader for one of North America's largest financial institutions for over 14 years. He is also active in the stock market and regularly trades stocks for his own personal account. In 2012, with his strong financial background, he dove into the real estate market as an investor and has been purchasing investment properties ever since.

In his spare time, you can find Alex working out at the gym, playing a game of beach volleyball, reading self-development books, and you just might find him relaxing on a tropical beach somewhere. Alex enjoys educating people on personal finance, investing and financial planning. If you would like to connect with Alex, he invites you to join his network at: www.LinkedIn.com/in/alexfracassi or visit his website at www.AlexFracassi.com to get started on your budgeting and savings plan today!

How to Make Money in Real Estate without Losing Your Shirt

By Tony Miano

Sound too good to be true? Well, it's not . . . if you follow a few simple guidelines.

Real estate investing is as old as there is land to invest in. Property ownership has always been held in high esteem in almost every culture. Those who had property, even if just their own home, have always had something to fall back on in hard times. Banks like property owners for the simple reason if they ever default on any loans the bank has a tangible asset to go after.

Today, however, real estate investing is easier . I have seen properties sell with no money down. And more common now, there is also the option to rent to own for people who can't get a traditional mortgage. But it's not all rainbows and puppy dogs, as they say. If you don't know what you are doing, you can also lose your shirt. The people who make millions in real estate are the ones who are educated in the industry or those who have a good mentor. Today, I am going to be that coach for you.

The very first thing you need to look at before even thinking about investing in real estate is your current mindset. And by mindset, I mean the predominant way in which you view life—money, happiness, health and general wellbeing.

Change your Mindset, Change your Life!

As I immerse myself in writing this chapter I realize that I would never have believed I would be where I am today.

For many years I had wanted to be financially free and live my life on my own terms. I had absolutely no idea, however, of how I was going to accomplish this. Back in the 80s, before the Internet revolution, I started to answer magazine ads on how to "get rich." I knew you couldn't simply *become wealthy* working for someone else)

Back then, the "get rich quick" hype was all about mail order, stuffing envelopes, franchises and a dozen similar programs that required little to no money for doing almost nothing.

Needless to say, my dreams of financial freedom never materialized. Then, one day, I came across a book on *Real Estate Investing*. I was absolutely amazed to learn that you can actually buy property with little or no money down using the magic of "leverage," which is unique to real estate. So I learned what I could and gently stepped into the investing business while still working full time in my hairstyling salon.

This kept me busy and I was financially comfortable. I soon began to realize, however, that I was no longer focusing on "why" I had gotten into the investing business in the first place. Yes, I was making a decent income, but for me, wealth is more than just money. It's more than owning a luxury home, fancy cars etc. For me, true wealth means finding my *purpose* in life and living my passion. That's what I call *freedom*.

You have probably heard that your mind is a very powerful tool. We also know there are many areas of the brain that are still a mystery. Regardless of the vast amount of information we gather every day, we only process about 1 percent of what is actually available to us. The rest is a mystery. And part of that mystery is our *subconscious* mind.

The Importance of Mindset

If I have learned nothing else in my journey thus far, it's that in the pursuit of wealth, there is no action that is more important than developing the right mindset. Wealth is the result of one thing— your current mindset. The creation of wealth is not at all random. It is a psychological way of being that involves your mindset, attitude and beliefs. Essentially wealthy people think differently than those who are struggling in life. The wealthy BELIEVE in their ability to create wealth, while those who are struggling, have doubts in their ability to achieve what they want in life.

"I always knew I would be rich. Even when I didn't have much
money, I acted rich anyway."
—*Ray Kroc, owner of McDonald's*

Once you learn how the mind works and begin to harness its
unlimited power by choosing to believe that all things are possible, you
will begin to see that all things truly are possible.

Conscious and Unconscious Thinking

Our beliefs are habitual thought patterns that once formed, no longer require us to continually think about them. They *happen* regardless
of whether they are based on the truth or not.

These beliefs and thought patterns are actually deleted, distorted
and generalized according to our current beliefs and the things that are
important to us at the time—our MINDSET.

Your mind consists of two elements: the *conscious mind* and the *subconscious mind*. The *conscious mind* thinks logically and analytically. It
makes choices based on fact and directs your body to make deliberate
movements. It sets goals and directions and it monitors the progress of
those goals. The *subconscious mind*, on the other hand, is responsible
for vital activities. It governs your bodily functions such as breathing
and your heartbeat and other organ functions that happen automatically. The *subconscious mind* also stores your memories and retains
your habits, routines, attitudes and beliefs. And your beliefs are nothing more than thoughts ingrained in your *subconscious mind* that have
become automatic, like how you breathe without noticing.

What is truly amazing about the *subconscious mind* is that it *cannot differentiate between real or imagined beliefs*. So, if you have the
ingrained belief that you are not capable of becoming rich for example,
no amount of conscious desire will get you there.

What does this mean? It means that your *conscious mind* alone cannot bring you wealth; it merely sets the direction for the creation of
wealth. You need to reprogram your *subconscious mind* to *want to* create wealth. If you can do this, obtaining wealth will becomes as automatic as the beating of your heart.

How to Train your Subconscious Mind to Create Wealth

In order to reprogram your subconscious mind, you will need to go through two steps:

1.   Choose the beliefs you want to hold about money.

2.   Impress these beliefs upon your subconscious mind.

Once these beliefs are ingrained in your *subconscious mind*, there will be nothing to stop you from attaining wealth.

And how do you achieve this? *You need a vision.* Without a vision you will never attain anything. People who do not have a clear vision of where they want to go in life will never get there. If you have no idea in what direction you want to drive your car on a trip to Florida, for example, how do you expect to ever arrive at your destination? The only way you will ever reach your end goal—your destination—is to have a clear vision of a) where you want to go and b) how you will get there. Studies have shown time and time again, that visualization has significant effects on real-world performance. Ask any world-class athlete how they got to where they are today. Their answer will undoubtedly include visualization.

So now that you know you must visualize your wealth, the next step is to *take action.*

> "The ancestry of every action is a thought."
> —*Ralph Waldo Emerson*

Over the years, I have learned that if you have a thought, no matter how small or insignificant, you must act on it, as it can ultimately lead to greater things. And whatever you do, don't ever let anything discourage you from taking immediate action. So, right now, begin to cultivate a mindset of wealth consciousness. I guarantee that when you do, the right opportunities will show themselves to you.

So now that we have your mindset under control, we need to look at the technical aspect of real estate investing—the Dos and Don'ts.

Here are some things successful real estate investors avoid and things you definitely need to know before taking that leap into the real estate investing arena.

The Biggest Mistakes New Real Estate Investors Make

1. Improper Financing

The first big mistake new investors make is that they don't fully understand how financing woks and what that means to their current situation. There are a variety of financing options available to real estate investors today. Many of these mortgages allow buyers to purchase homes they might not otherwise have been able to afford using a conventional 25-year mortgage. Before you lock yourself into a variable mortgage that seems great because interest rates are currently low, you need to understand how that particular mortgage works and if you have the financial flexibility to make the payments should the interest rates go up. You must also make sure you have a back-up plan and are able to convert to a more conventional fixed-rate mortgage should you need to.

2. Not Doing your Homework

If you have kids, "have you done your homework?" probably rolls off your tongue with ease by now. But what about you? Have you done your real estate investing homework?   I'm talking about doing your "due diligence" prior to investing in real estate. There are countless variables to consider before purchasing your investment property. Things like area: Is the neighbourhood conducive to your needs? Is it safe? Is it an area that has historically good resale value?

3. Going it Alone

It's not uncommon when you decide to invest in your   first investment property to overestimate your ability to do everything. While you may be capable of doing many things, this requires a lot of attention to detail, legal issues, accounting issues, market knowledge and general investing know-how. If you want to succeed as a real estate investor, you must find a good team to help you. You will need:

- a knowledgeable real estate agent

- a good contractor and an home inspector

- a good real estate attorney a good insurance agent and tax accountant

- a creative lender

4. Paying Over Market Value

If you have done your homework, this should not be an issue. Too many people end up paying too much for a property.

It is understandable why many new investors simply jump on a property they like. After weeks of looking at properties and never finding exactly what they are looking for, when that good property does finally appear, they want to snap it up before somewhere else does—and they are willing to pay top dollar for it! This is emotional buying. You need to buy based on the expected return on investment.

5. Overestimating your Budget and Underestimating Your Expenses

If you have always rented a home, you know that any repairs and taxes are typically covered by the landlord. But when you purchase an investment property, you are now responsible for the taxes and the repairs.

You have likely heard of the term *house poor*. This is when you have sunk all your money into a home. This is obviously not a position you want to find yourself in. To avoid this, make a budget from the get-go—before you purchase the home. Do a little research into things like the property taxes, water and sewer costs, other utilities, maintenance on the property, what has been replaced, what hasn't and your mortgage rate, etc. This will be an eye opener, but hopefully it will save you from locking yourself into something you cannot afford.

What It Really Comes Down To

When buying an investment property, you need to do your research. There are all kinds of hidden costs in owning a property, and if you are not fully aware of everything these entail, you are only setting yourself up for disaster. The bottom line is that real estate investing can make you millions, but you have to know what you're doing. That being said, here is the top 10 things real estate investors do to become successful.

Top 10 Things Every Successful Real Estate Investor Knows

1. Do You Have a Plan?

Planning is the most important thing you can do to ensure you are successful at anything. Whether it's parenting, moving or investing, without a concrete plan, you are likely to fail—or at the very least, postpone any success. I always make the analogy of taking a trip around the world. Do you think you can just decide you want to travel across the planet without making the appropriate plans first? Of course not. There are passports to consider, the best time of the year to travel, which countries are actually safe to travel to, hotel reservations, flight schedules and the list goes on and on. So what makes you think you can just dive into purchasing properties without having a solid plan in place?

2. Are You Even Ready to Invest?

This is a question that every successful real estate investors should ask themselves. You need to know whether you can afford to jump into the market, no matter how good it may seem. There are other factors to consider as well such as do you have the time to commit to investing successfully? Investing can take a significant amount of your time. If you plan to buy rental properties, it can become a full-time job if you don't have help. Do you know enough about the market, the industry etc.? Investing in real estate is not for everyone. So, take a long, hard look at your life, and determine if investing is right for you—now.

3. What Type of Investor Do you Want to Be?

You need to decide what type of investor you want to be. For instance, do you want to be an active or passive investor—this will depend largely on your financial situation and your time commitment. You must also decide what type of property you want to invest in. Do you want to 'flip' houses? Do you want to buy single family rental homes? Do you want to buy commercial properties? Do you want to buy apartment buildings or a condo? Whatever you decide, you need to go back to the above questions and make sure the type of real estate investing fits into your lifestyle and financial situation.

4. Money—Do you Have Financing in Place?

As we discussed , if you don't have the proper financing in place, you will likely fail. You must also find the right type of financing for your particular situation and the property you are looking to buy. There are many options available from a joint venture deal or no money down to a full outright purchase for cash. So, determine what you need to do and make sure you have everything in place before you look any further into real estate investing.

5. Do You Have the Proper Team in Place?

I won't go into details about this, but I must emphasize how important it is to make sure you have a good team in place to help you make your investing business successful. Remember, as John Donne said best: "No man is an island entire of himself!"

6. Location, Location, Location

Successful real estate investors know exactly what area they are buying into. Before you even think about purchasing a property, you must understand where you are buying and how it will affect your ability to rent and or resell it. For example, if you are looking to rent to seniors with an established and consistent income, you are not going to want to buy a home close to a university where the majority of the population is rowdy students. Talk to people in the neighbourhood in which you are looking to purchase. Drive by at different times of the day. In the above example, the area could seem very quiet and peaceful during the day because all the students are at school. But come nighttime, when the parties are in full swing, it can look much different!

7. What is the Likelihood of Finding Tenants?

In other words, is the property located in an area that has low vacancy rates? Is it an area that is season specific? Some areas are reliant on the weather. Ocean front properties are a good example. Many of these properties may be able to make you astronomical amounts in rent during the busy summer season, but they may not be good long-term rentals. So again, do your homework. Successful investors know exactly what they are buying and where and what they can expect. There are many good sources for find out vacancy rates. A quick Google search or a talk with a real estate agent or local business owner can give you a good idea of what you are getting into.

8. Have You Done the Math?

This is something I covered in the top mistakes new investors make, so as a successful investor, you will make sure you know exactly what your expenses will be for any given property. And don't underestimate the numbers because you are only setting yourself up for failure. Taxes and repairs can be costly, but if you know ahead of time that you are able to manage these expenses, even if you don't have a tenant, then you will not be surprised when the bills come due.

9. To Manage or Not to Manage—That is the Question?

Successful real estate investors know their limits. They know if they have the know-how and time commitment to manage any properties they take on. This is definitely not the time to let your ego take over. Admit whether you can successfully manage being a hands-on landlord or if you are better off letting a professional management company take it on. Yes, it will cost you to hire an manager, but is that worth not having any potential headaches down the road? Only you can decide this.

10. Can You Get out Gracefully and even better, Profitably?

Do you have an exit plan? What if the market falls and you can no longer afford to hold onto a property? What if you need to liquidate your assets? Can you to sell your properties on time and not lose your shirt? This is part of doing your homework. If you know ahead of time what you will do in such cases, you will not panic and you will have a better chance of remaining profitable.

The Bottom Line

Real estate investing may not be for everyone. But for those who choose to get into the business, with the proper knowledge, guidance and financial backing, you can make a lot of money—even millions! The key to successful investing is to first believe you can be successful. Once you know this, look for a good team of professionals to help you achieve your dreams.

About Tony Miano

Tony Miano is a native of Sicily, Italy who now resides in one of the Seven Wonders of the World—beautiful Niagara Falls Canada. He and his wife, Mary Ann, have three adult children who are a big part of their lives. Tony has been an entrepreneur his entire life, owing and operating various businesses across the country.

Today, Tony is retired from all of his businesses except Real Estate Investing. Over the years, he has perfected a very unique strategy for generating continuous streams of income that he now shares with interested investors. His expertise lies in single family homes as well as multiunit buildings in both in Canada and the U.S. He currently owns and manages several rental properties and as well, he continues to flip properties "remotely," using his tried and true system.

Tony has written a digital book called "THE "LAZY MAN'S WAY TO REAL ESTATE RICHES" which he would like to share with you. To get a complimentary copy, go to:

WWW.MIANOINVESTMENTS.COM/TLM

Or, if you would like to contact Tony, you can reach him at:

MIANOINVESTMENTS@GMAIL.COM

How I Turned Adversity into Cash

By Eric J. Carpenter

"Adversity causes some men to break; others to break records."
—*William Arthur Ward*

I bought my first duplex when I was 18. By the time I turned 20, I had 5 houses and 4 corporations. There was nothing that could hold me back—except me.

Instability and Chaos

If statistics have anything to do with it, some would say that I would never amount to anything, at least in a good way. My childhood was less than stellar. By the time I was 13, we had moved to 36 different houses, and I had attended 12 different schools. In Grade 4 alone, when most kids don't have a worry in the world, I was moved to 4 different schools. No, my parents were not in the military. My father was not being sent to different bases, nor was he or my mother a foreign diplomat that required them to move from country to country. Those 36 moves—they were because we were constantly being evicted from our "home."

For me, instability was normal, at least in my world. Alcohol, drugs and chaos: They were all just part of how you grow up. One of my strongest memories is when I turned 11—it was my birthday. I had come home from school, only to find my key wouldn't open the door because our locks had been changed—again. I waited outside the door until 11 p.m. for someone to come home.

Adversity Creates Power—If you let it

"I do not think that there is any other quality so essential to success of any kind as the quality of perseverance. It overcomes almost everything, even nature."
—*John D. Rockefeller*

That night was a turning point for me. It was like something in my mind snapped, and I realized I never wanted to be in another situation like that again. It's hard at that age to separate the natural love you feel for your parents and their actions, but I knew what was going on was not "normal." I knew I had to make my own way in the world if I was to ever pull myself out of this life. And I did.

I started reading every book I could on making money, on real estate investments, and on successful entrepreneurs like John D. Rockefeller. I soaked it all in and began changing my mindset.

My family had a constant string of drug-dealing boyfriends coming in and out of our lives. This used to upset me, but after reading about successful people and how they turned "disaster into opportunities," I jumped into my first "business" at the age of 11. I had always worked or saved any money I got from birthdays, etc., so when I saw these boyfriends using the Money Marts for short-term loans until their paycheques arrived, I figured I had just found a perfect opportunity. I began lending them money at a lower interest rate than the cheque cashing companies, and I was able to turn $1000 into $6000 in a short time.

The Lesson

Look at any negative situation in your life and spin it. Find the positive in it and how you can leverage that into an opportunity. If need be, take a piece of paper and write out every possible positive scenario you can find in the situation (this will take some imagination) and then think about how you can turn that into something you can either learn from (because lessons are always a gift) or turn it into something you can profit from.

Making Lemonade

> "A dream doesn't become reality through magic;
> it takes sweat, determination and hard work."
> —*Colin Powell*

I had been visiting my Father about once a week at this time. He was a stable man with a girlfriend and family, living in a middle upper class neighbourhood. To me, it seemed like paradise after the rundown shacks I had been living in. The thing that I craved most was the stability they had. As a top car salesman for over 10 years, he had a fairly good income, and he was always driving great cars. I wanted some of that in my life.

At 14, then, I moved in with my Father and was immediately put into school. Coming from a background where I had simply given up on school (moving so many times, I figured there was no point), I found this change difficult. I had also come from a very rough upbringing—the houses we were able to afford were rarely in a good neighbourhood, so gangs, fighting, and drugs were normal for me. As such, any time conflict arose in the new school, I turned it into a physical confrontation. This obviously didn't fly with the school board, and eventually I was expelled from more schools than I care to remember. After my last expulsion, my Father told me I was not going to sit at home and do nothing, so he borrowed a power washer from my uncle and had me power-wash our neighbour's back yard deck.

My first job turned into 20 hours of work, and I made $220. The customer was so impressed he hired me to sand and stain. My first job paid me $500. By 16, I had turned this into a real business that was bringing in some decent money. Since I was just getting my G1 driver's licence, I still couldn't drive, so I hired someone just to drive me to every job.

Lesson

There are money-making opportunities everywhere. In this case, my opportunity was the wooden deck right under my nose. We just have to see their potential and use it to our advantage.

Look at all the areas in your life and see where others are making money from your efforts.

Look at what the people in your neighbourhood need. What are types of things are they willing to pay someone to do for them?

Even a part-time business can turn into something huge. Apple started out of Steve Jobs' garage! Now this deck business has grown to cleaning the Air Canada Centre and many more large commercial and historical buildings.

Making Goals

"What you get by achieving your goals is not as important as
what you become by achieving your goals."
—Henry David Thoreau

At 16, I was sent to a reform school. No other school would take me. With my recent success with my restoration business, I knew I wanted to make more of myself so I could become as successful as the entrepreneurs I had read about, so this time, I made school a priority. I got 11 credits in 4 months, which showed I was ready to return to "regular" school. When I did, I simply kept my mouth shut, my head down and concentrated on the end goal—graduation. My mother always told me my grandfather had put a university fund away for me, and a higher education was my new objective.

I pushed myself hard. I did all my homework, I listened in class, and I ended up with an 87 percent average. When I mentioned the university fund at the end of Grade 11, though, I was told it never existed.

I saw myself at a crossroads. Would I take this as defeat and revert to my old ways (neglecting my homework) or would I persevere and carve out my own future? I chose the latter. I went full-speed ahead with my restoration business and continued to finish school.

I also set some pretty lofty financial goals for myself at this time: I had actually planned my entire life up to age 80, plotting exact dates for things like purchasing a rental property, how many new investment properties I would have by certain dates, etc.

I quickly realized that in order to achieve these goals I would have to want them as much as I want to breathe. I knew there would be sacrifices, but I learned early on that you have to figure out what it is you are willing to give up to achieve your goals, and that is what I did. I took on two more jobs on top of my growing business and continued to finish school.

In Grade 12, I would get up at 4:30 a.m. to head to the gym. I would come home, do my homework, and then head off to school. After school, from Monday to Wednesday, I worked as a cook at a local restaurant.

On Thursday to Saturday, I not only worked at the restaurant, but I would then head to a nightclub where I worked until 4 a.m. I saved every penny I could and graduated with my high school diploma at 17.

I was on track for my long-term goals.

Lesson

Goals are great. Most people have them in one form or another. The difference between people who just set goals and expect them to happen *somehow* and successful people, however, is that people who actually meet their goals have done so because they have lived and breathed that goal. They have done whatever is needed to meet that goal. Here is what to do:

> "Vision without execution is just hallucination."
> *--Henry Ford*

Pick a goal.

Now think about this goal and make a conscious decision to see it as not only a goal, but as a MUST.

Write out everything that will need to happen in order for that goal to transpire. Will you need to stop drinking four coffees a day from your local café? Will you need to get a second, third job? Will you need to sell something you don't necessarily need?

If you want to set long-term goals, you will also need to separate each goal, i.e., career, relationships, education and retirement.

Write out what needs to happen under each category in order for these long-term goals to happen. When dealing with long-term goals, you will find that you will need to set smaller goals within that long-term goal in order to make it happen.

You will also want to concentrate on only one or two goals at a time. If you overwhelm yourself, you are just setting yourself up for failure.

Make your goals achievable—at least in your mind. Don't listen to what other people say when it comes to what you can and cannot achieve. Only you can decide this. I would not be where I am if I listened to anyone that hasn't already walked the path I desired.

So, decide *right now* that you are willing to make sacrifices to see your goals as reality. Visualize yourself already achieving these goals every day. Bring these goals to the forefront of your daily life. Don't let them fade to the back of your mind like many people do after they set their goals. Put them in your face every day and make them happen.

Set Your Goals into Motion

"Discipline is the bridge between goals and accomplishment."
–*Jim Rohn*

With my goals clearly set and some already achieved (graduating high school and putting money away for a down payment), I set out to achieve the next one on my list—purchase my first income property by the age of 18.

When I had found the perfect investment property, I approached numerous banks for a mortgage. I remember my first meeting with the RBC. The Bank's mortgage specialist simply looked at me, an 18-year old kid, recently graduated high school, self-employed, no plans for college or university, looking to get a mortgage for an investment property. She actually asked me if this was some kind of prank. I assured her it wasn't. I was eventually told to leave. My credit score was new. I really only had 5 months of credit history, and my income was only around $20,000 for that year on paper. I was told to come back when I was 21 and had some credit history behind me.

Then I hit Google, determined to find a mortgage professional who understood my goals. I found a very credible Mortgage Broker by the name of Bruce Hale at Coldwell Banker. I was again told they couldn't help, but Bruce told me his son was working with untraditional mortgages. He put us in touch, and as soon as I showed him the potential deal, he quickly realized it was a great opportunity. I closed the deal in July 2006. With the help of Adam Hale, I had met my goal of purchasing my first income property by the age of 18.

Adam further told me that I could purchase up to 10 more properties, so I started looking for the next one right away. In February 2007, I bought my next income property. In March, I bought a triplex, as I had learned how high cash-flow properties can catapult your income quickly. I bought my 4th home a few months later, and then, a few months after that, I bought a 5th home. That is when things started to change—and not for the better.

Lesson

Never take NO for an answer. Too many times we see NO as an unsurpassable roadblock, but nothing can be further from the truth. "No" is simply the universe telling you "Not this way," or "Not with this person," or even "Not right now." It is simply asking you to find another way. Whether you do this or not is what is going to set you aside from the rest of the world. I won't even go into how many times Walt Disney, Henry Ford, R. H. Macy and countless other now successful entrepreneurs have been told "No" because you have probably heard this a thousand times.

So, next time someone says "No" to you:

Step back from the situation.

Resist the temptation to take it personally or as a failure.

Write out all the possible reasons for why this situation is happening, such as: There might be a better offer down the road, this may not be in your best interest, maybe that particular investment property you wanted to buy would have been more trouble than it's worth, or maybe you are supposed to look somewhere else.

Change your thinking. You may never actually know the real reason, but when you start changing your mindset by looking at the positive in the word "No," you will find new opportunities coming your way.

Know that *where one door closes, another opens.*

Fighting Your -fulfilling Prophecies

"Nearly all men can stand adversity,
but if you want to test a man's character, give him power."
—*Abraham Lincoln*

Probably one of the biggest things I had to overcome in my life to date is myself. I was so busy setting my goals and pushing to be the furthest thing from my past that I forgot to *deal with my past.*

From my experience, we are all a product of our environment from one degree to another. My environment was obviously not a good one. While I may have made conscious decisions to remove myself from it and set lofty goals to propel me away from this experience, I never actually dealt with all the inner turmoil my past had caused me. I thought that by becoming successful, I could essentially just walk away from it and never look back, but all the success in the world cannot deal with unhealed emotions and feelings.

And I found this out the hard way.

My father eventually quit his job and decided to join my restoration company full time. Ultimately, this did not work out, as I felt he was continually taking money out to pay his family's bills, while I was reinvesting my money into it. This, of course, resulted in resentment, and I ultimately left and moved to Hamilton, Ontario. Looking back, I can see this is one those many crossroads we will all face in life. The option I chose led me down a slippery slope that turned my life upside down.

I moved in with friends, or at least people I saw as friends at the time. They were dealing drugs and making significant amounts of money. By this time I also had a ton of toys like boats, fast cars and extra cash to blow–and I did. Being back in the type of environment where I had grown up (drugs, instability etc.), I started to digress. I eventually started lending money to these people with interest, thinking I was making a good investment as I was getting a good return on my money, not considering the ramifications of how I was making that money.

But one thing I can tell you for sure is that if you are going down the wrong path, the universe will definitely send you a message. My message came in the form of an arrest. Because of this, I lost almost everything I had. Everything I had worked for was essentially blown up by a few stupid lapses in judgement. I let the newfound power I was feeling take control of me, instead of me taking control of it and using it in a positive way to better myself.

I have since turned my life back around. I am still dealing with the repercussions, however, such as repairing my credit and repaying the money I owed over ($200,000) CDN. But I also now see where and why I veered off the path, and this is truly the most important thing. If you do not learn from your lessons, you cannot possibly grow or succeed, and honestly, you will only get the lesson again, except worse, until you finally see what it is you are supposed to see.

Lesson

Life has a funny way of catching up with you. We will be tested at every step. The key is to stay grounded. As Abe Lincoln said, the true character of a person will be shown when he is given power (which can come in the form of money). No matter how well you do in life, you need to keep yourself grounded to your values, principles and your sense of what is right and wrong. Without this, it can be a long fall to the bottom.

Here are the things I have learned that will get you to the top—and keep you there.

Figure out your *why*. Why do you want a particular goal? The *why* shouldn't be about money, either. Your *why* should be something closer to you heart such as a) you want to be able to send your kids to university; b) you want to be able to retire comfortably with your spouse; or c) you want to be able to give back to your parents. Once you find your *why*, you will find your *will* to achieve your goals.

Do not succumb to what I call the "Disease of mediocrity." You do not have to be like everyone else on this planet. It's okay to want more and to go after it. Set your goals, no matter how insurmountable other people may think they are. If you believe you can achieve them, then you can.

Find someone to help you on your journey. A good mentor and coach can help you keep on track. They will teach you what they already know and have learned through their ups and downs. If I had a coach earlier in life, as I do now, I would not have gone down the path I did. Behind every great athlete, you will find a great coach. Why would life and business be any different?

If you can remember just these three things and set and work toward your goals accordingly, you will find success will meet you half way.

About Eric J Carpenter

Eric J Carpenter is an entrepreneur in Mississauga, Ontario. He currently owns 3 companies outside of his real estate and property management companies. He was able to turn $17,000 into over $500,000 by the time he was 20 years old. His goal is to own 100+1 properties before the age of 30.

Eric J Carpenter can be reached at: 905-208-4208

For a FREE INSTANT COPY of my e-book that explains the step-by-step details of how I structured my deals and earned over half of a million dollars in less then a year and a half.

Go to www.ericjcarpenter.com/18to20

MAKING THE NUMBERS WORK
HOW A FINANCIAL ADVISOR CAN KEEP YOUR
BUSINESS ON TRACK FOR SUCCESS

By Larry Cooper

Do you have an Accountant or a Financial Advisor/Business Partner in your business?

Early in my career I was an accountant who knew Generally Accepted Accounting Principles (GAAP). I had a general knowledge of tax issues, I was quick to make financial calculations, and for the most part, I handled any financial-related matters. Most accountants continue to do this throughout their careers, simply because that's all they know, or their customers (senior management or business owners) don't know any better to ask or expect more.

The older accountant has just experienced the same transactions more frequently than his younger counterpart. Does this describe your current accountant? Or are you an *enlightened business owner* who recognizes that a good accountant sees all aspects of your business. He or she has a disciplined perspective to your specific business and has a very logical approach to the issues you face. More importantly, does your accountant speak to you in a language you understand—not some technical GAAP-type talk you don't understand? What you really want for your business is an accountant who can be more than a regular accountant, which honestly, is a dime a dozen these days. What you want is a Financial Business Advisor.

I know, because I am a *Financial Business Advisor*. I have been a Chief Financial Officer (CFO) in many industries (Pharmaceutical, BioTech, CPG, Food and Automotive) in all sectors of the economy (Manufacturing, Distribution, Service and Retail) with different organizational structures (public, private, owner managed, multi-national and not-for-profit). But what I think sets me apart from other accountants is that I simply don't think like, nor do I act like, a typical accountant. I am a financial business coach that can bring huge changes to your current management philosophy so you can finally achieve your long-term goals—without ruffling any feathers.

I am known in the business sector as the "Red to Black" CFO because of my experience working with profitable companies in the black and bringing losing companies in the red to the black.

I consider myself a student of learning, and I am always on the lookout to improve myself and the businesses in which I am involved. Here are some of the key things I have learned over the years that can either make or break a company—ultimately determining how successful it will be.

1. NOT PAYING ATTENTION TO YOUR CUSTOMER

As obvious as this should be, I see too many businesses get so caught up in what the owners want or just in their day-to-day activities that they ultimately lose sight of the real person who pays the bills—the customer. Whether you provide a service or a product, without customers, you have nothing. Here are some practical actions that keep the customer at the front of your mind.

Is your management presence easy for the customer to contact? Whether you have a retail business with a storefront, an office, or an online company, it must be easy for your customers to talk to someone in a position of authority. Can a customer get instant gratification?

Customer complaints are a gift. This means your customer cares and takes the time to tell you. Do you make it easy for your customers to approach you? Do you listen when they do? Do you give them something for taking the time to inform you? These are all the ingredients to make sure your customers come back again and again.

Advertising. Do you offer something different on a regular basis? That is, do you have changing specials? Do you communicate with your existing and potential customers through different forms of media?

Community Activities. Is your business seen as part of the community? Does it help with local charitable activities? Regardless of whether you are a national chain or just one store, you want your customers to feel empathy toward your business, whether you provide goods/services they like or not.

Do you care about your customer? Do you do things to make your customers see that you value them? Simple examples are: How long do they stand in line? Do they have to wait to get a question answered? Do they feel your staff shows empathy toward them? The key question as they walk out of your store is: DID THEY HAVE A GOOD EXPERIENCE?

Good Value. The fundamental rule of any business is to provide good value at a fair price and more importantly, to keep your customers coming back.

Always be on the lookout for any trends that show any of the above thoughts are not being met and then ask yourself, "WHAT ARE YOU DOING ABOUT IT?"

2. DO YOU HAVE WHAT YOUR CUSTOMER WANTS?

This is really two questions:

Do you have a reliable, consistent method to predict what your customer buys?

Do you have the product customers seek when they come to your store? In other words, do you have the inventory at the quality and price your customers want?

In order to fulfill these objectives, you need both a reliable method to forecast what you think you will sell and then a process to order it and stock and restock it. How many businesses have a great idea and then can't deliver?

Sales forecasting:

This is the system to predict which products will be bought and in what quantities. These estimates are known as forecasts and are used as the basis for ordering the inventory you will stock and in what quantity.

The system needs to incorporate these components:

A robust computerized system that tracks each Stock Keeping Unit's (SKU) purchase and sales history by date so it can be displayed in monthly data charts.

Your system should have mathematical formulas that can predict future customer sales based on past purchases.

Your staff should be competent to use and understand these mathematical formulas to assess the likelihood of these predictions and what changes, if any, should be made before inventory is ordered/produced.

Your staff needs to be sophisticated enough to factor in the impact on customer purchases of marketing incentives.

Typically, this forecasting function is best centralized to gain economies of scale for the operation.

This forecasting function is typically done monthly for a 3-6 month period, shortly after the previous month's actual results are known.

Inventory Purchasing

The purchase of inventory is determined by the sales forecasts. Purchase/Procurement staff take the sales forecasts and negotiate with suppliers for the best price possible and for the quantities you need. Usually the price is negotiated at the beginning of the year (it can be calendar year or fiscal year), and then it will remain the same for all purchases during that year.

An effective purchaser will seek incentives for buying more than a preset amount or the prior year's sales. Co-operative advertising is one of the most cost-effective incentives to work out with suppliers.

Companies establish financial/operational guidelines of how much inventory they will stock of each SKU. In other words, based on the sales forecast, a purchaser will buy the amount of inventory that will position your company to have about 60 days of inventory in stock. The determination of whether the target should be 45 or 60 or 75 days is dependent on a number of factors:

Customer service culture. Do you always want to have stock so stock-outs are an unacceptable result for your customer (no empty shelves)? Many companies will establish a backorder policy and what quantity of backorder is tolerated.

What is the **lead time** to order your next round of inventory?

The accuracy of your sales forecast system, based on your past track record, will determine your confidence level of **how much safety stock** you need to create in your inventory.

Is there any **uniqueness to a product**? The more unique the product, the more reliant you will be on the supplier.

Reliability of your supplier is a critical aspect of how much inventory you stock.

Company's financial strength: The more capital available, the more money can be invested in inventory.

Products that are **special order** because they are customer-specific by definition are not stocked in inventory.

3. MENTORING IN YOUR COMPANY

Business goes in cycles, and one of the top business concepts is *mentoring*. Academics, business people and entrepreneurs always recommend a coach/mentor to help you realize your full potential.

Luckily, I had the good sense to ask lots of questions about my performance as I grew my business and career. I have also been both a mentor and mentee throughout my career.

I learned that a mentor/coach does not have to come from the same functional area. In fact, the likelihood is that if you are being mentored by someone in the same functional area, the expanse of different experiences and learning will likely be minimal. Someone in the same functional area, but who has more experience in the same area you are working in, will likely just help you be better in that area. What about developing into a more rounded and experienced business person? The best way to do this is to find someone who has a different personality and experiences than you, both in a practical sense of their work experience and more importantly, their functional skills, which will provide you with a different perspective.

I knew a young sales manager who showed potential, but his only experience was in sales. He knew he could become a good sales manager, but he also wanted to become a general manager. In order to do this, he also needed financial management skills. Accordingly, he asked if I would mentor him in finance. I was more than happy to do so. The mentoring involved teaching the necessary core knowledge a finance executive learns in school and on the path toward gaining accreditation, but what was also imperative was the need to look at the problems a financial advisor would encounter in doing business and how he or she would suggest solving these problems. This thinking was invaluable for this young sales manager as it exposed him to looking at problem solving in a different way.

As a mentor I have worked with many individuals who have gone on to perform better, and in fact, achieve positions that are senior to my role. As a boss/mentor/coach, you should be able to elicit not only better performance from your "mentees," but as well, provide the environment for them to do the work that gives them confidence in themselves for the future. This is a role that any good boss performs, both because it is his or her job and because it is the way in which you build a better company. The hardest part is to get those senior managers who are good at mentoring to fulfill this role throughout your organization, not just in their functional area.

As a CEO you have the leadership position to make this happen. Do you praise the strong manager/mentors in your company? Do they get recognition for it? Do you champion cross-functional teams and relationships that serve your company and promote improvements in all staff receiving this mentoring? Is formal training provided or encouraged for leaders/mentors in your company? These people are the pacesetters within your organization who will lead by example. Many employees today are simply not satisfied with just doing a task as part of their job. They want to know how to do the job, and how it fits into the greater company good. They are impatient for promotions and more challenging work. Part of this can be averted or channeled if you have an experienced person giving advice to your younger staff.

Mentoring is, of course, only one aspect of managing employees in order to reach their full potential. It is an underutilized tool because it is usually a voluntary activity that may only be applied to high potential employees within your company. But why limit it? Other than the time of senior managers, there is very little cost, if any, and more importantly, good mentors enjoy doing it—they usually just need to be asked.

Accordingly, enlightened thinking would make mentoring one of the top ways to develop solid managers. This should be a core responsibility of an HR department. They should facilitate and encourage the implementation of a mentor for all employees who reach a managerial position.

4. CASH FLOW

In its simplest form, cash-flow is divided into two components:

Collections—the money owed to you, which you collect

Disbursements—the money you owe others, which you pay out

In finance we have named these two components:

Accounts Receivable—the amounts you charge for your product or service and are owed by your customers

Accounts Payable—the amounts you owe to your suppliers for the products or services you used/acquired. It should be noted that if you have employees, they are in essence "suppliers of labour" for your business and should be considered part of accounts payable for wages.

As such, managing cash-flow means *collecting your accounts receivable* in sufficient *amounts so you can pay your accounts payable*, providing you are operationally profitable. If you are not operationally profitable or are incurring capital expenditures or you have existing debt repayments, you will need cash-inflow from your shareholders or you may need to arrange some type of new debt (long-term notes of some type or an operating bank line of credit—LOC.)

The fundamental principle of managing cash-flow effectively is to collect more than you pay out and not pay out in advance of your collections (assuming you have the finances available). This can be very challenging in struggling businesses, but I have some good tips to help in this regard.

Accounts Receivable

In many companies, the credit department (this is the name usually given to staff within the finance department whose responsibility is to collect accounts receivable), are seen by sales staff as wearing the black hat because they chase customers to pay their bills. Unfortunately, although technically correct, credit department staff are just ensuring the company is paid for the services/products it deliveries. No one within the company should have to apologize when calling/meeting customers to get them to pay for what has been delivered on the terms agreed upon prior to delivery.

Some customers, however, do not fulfill these terms, or in fact, may be having financial difficulty. Credit staff that are able to have empathy for customers while being able to secure payment without creating bad feelings are truly invaluable to a company. Good credit staff needs to have the same customer orientation to service as sales staff to be effective.

Even if some customers are not paying for what may seem like invalid reasons, they are still customers and thus need to be fully respected. The most effective credit staff are those who not only have this customer orientation, but who also work together with sales staff to secure the amounts owed. There are many instances where a customer has issues with your company. It doesn't just have to be sales staff that resolves these types of issues. Credit staff can fulfill this function and thereby enhance their relationship with the customer. Credit staff that operate with a customer-orientated mindset first become problem solvers within your company, not just bill collectors.

Accounts Payable

How strong are your controls on your disbursements? This is an area of your business that can be easy to monitor. It further provides owners or senior management with quick insight into how their money is being spent within the business. Purchasing systems are also important and must ensure money is spent wisely. You want a purchasing system that requires competitive quotes on any large purchases. The definition of *large* depends on the size of your business, but typically capital expenditures (CE's) are of a capital nature and are over $5,000. CE's all should have at least three quotes. This is especially appropriate because a CE is usually done infrequently, so you need to be checking on prices in the market at the time of your purchase.

Ongoing purchases within the business are best handled by a quoting process, and then the best quote should be valid for at least one year, with this process being repeated each year.

The process of accounts payable is to pay "authorized" purchases. These would be purchases as defined above that have gone through the quoting process or if they are too small, then the manager closest to the responsibility for the purchase should be signing the invoice, indicating their approval. This approval means this manager agrees the goods/services were received as invoiced and the price is correct.

The actual signing of the cheque (if not automated) is a critical process to complete the disbursement cycle. It adds a layer of internal control and provides senior management quick information on how/where money is being spent. I can't count the number of times when signing a cheque that I either found errors in the amount or gained insight into activities in the company I was unaware of or had cursory knowledge of. The process of signing the cheque served as an information system to me, as CFO, to make inquiries into the specific activity for which payment was being made. Thus it allowed me to be better informed in my job, and it provided valuable insights and suggestions.

In managing cash-flow, many businesses hold off paying bills until the supplier's credit department calls enough times that you can't hold off any longer. This is a win/lose mindset. You made an agreement with your supplier on specific terms, and you should honour these terms, particularly if you have the financial ability to pay. This not only builds a win/win relationship with the supplier, but if you are ever in the position that you can't pay, you now have the creditability to talk directly and honestly with that credit department to request extended payment arrangements.

This goes to the old axiom "Build relationships early so they are there when you need them." The concept of talking to credit staff in an honest manner also reminds me of the favourite habit in accounts payable to say, "The cheque is in the mail." This is, again, a very poor policy, as it destroys your company's "creditability." Any good credit department takes notes or tapes all conversations and thus they will have the conversation on file. When the cheque doesn't show up, it becomes another mark against your credibility. Don't risk ruining your reputation for the sake of delaying a payment for a few days. Always fulfill your promises, or simply don't make the promise. There is nothing that builds more credibility with credit staff than fulfilling your promises.

Daily cash-flow monitor reports

These reports are done daily from your banking information and disbursements. It is timely, as it should be on the desk of all executives by 10 a.m. each day. It provides a quick overview of both the revenue and disbursement side of the business. It gives feedback on key aspects of the business such as:

Sales—If you are not selling, then your collections will be lower.

Collections—Are you collecting what you sell?

Disbursements—Are you spending in line with your sales and your original business plan?

Net Cash—Are you spending only what you collect? Are you holding back if you create negative cash-flow?

These suggestions are just a few of the ideas you can find in my book *Red to Black*, which I am happy to share with you. Please go to www.RedToBlackCFO.com for my eBook with more tips and strategies for effective business accounting practices.

About Larry Cooper

As a seasoned business executive with a strategic planning, top-notch financial acumen, excellent business sense and entrepreneurial mindset (with a bias for action), Larry Cooper provides a unique brand of expertise to help companies improve their bottom line. Larry has been a CFO in many companies in many different industries, providing invaluable leadership and financial experience. He is currently offering his services on a consulting basis to companies in almost every industry. If you are looking for a financial business advisor who can offer you experience and advice on changing current management philosophy to one that challenges the status quo, creating interest among potential investors, negotiating revenue- or profit-enhancing projects and/or developing and implementing a "customer service first" vision for your finance department, Larry is willing to help you achieve your goals. You can reach him by calling 416-818-4217 or by email at: l.m.cooperc.a@sympatico. ca or his web site at www.RedToBlackCFO.com

"Rewired 4 Success"

By Heather Ramsey and Colin Campbell

What if you had earned 1 million dollars for every major challenging or traumatic experience you have ever had! What would your net worth be? All of us would at minimum be millionaires, and the majority of us multi-multi-millionaires. Why haven't you earned all those "challenging millions"? And a more interesting question; "What if you knew how to earn one million dollars for every major challenging experience you have ever had or ever will have?"

You can "Cash In" on these experiences, but few of us do. Worse yet, most of us are still "Paying Out" because of them–paying out in emotional energy, in missed revenue and relationships that we didn't even know we repelled, in discomfort that generates in our cells because our body is eavesdropping on all our unsupportive thoughts and emotions. That is how we are "Paying Out" all the time, drawing a negative return on our investments–because we're unconsciously running our mind, our body, our life on old unsupportive stories, emotions, beliefs–old "wiring."

To clarify, when we ask, "Did you ever 'Cash In' on that challenging experience?" we do not mean "revenge"—quite the opposite. We mean not just "See the Good" in people and situations, nor just "Mine for the Gold," though both are highly recommended; instead, we actually mean "Reinvest the Gold!"

But we're getting ahead of ourselves.

Let's first look at what is the cost of your old "wiring," the old "hardware" that has been designed to see problems, limitations, worries, threats, and the limited or out-dated "software" that it is restricted to run on. Then we will take a look at why the majority of humans are "wired" that way, and finally how you can "rewire" for higher success and happiness.

Let us see what it takes to move from "paying out" to "cashing in." From old to new wiring, from worst to best case scenario, from surviving to thriving with the cards you have been "dealt."

Have you ever had a traumatic experience–bad relationship, upsetting news, business break-up? Most of us have. But then what? Do you still talk about it, think about it, engage others in the story? Is it still affecting the rest of your life in some negative way? Is that experience still sitting on the debit side of your heart account, your mind account, your bank account, your health account?

"Cashing In" on life's challenges means moving those ""negative" experiences from the debit or negative side of your heart account, your mind account, your bank account, to the credit or positive side of your accounting ledger of life. It means more than just dissolving, solving or resolving, though all of those have merit. Just getting an experience to "neutral" or "getting over it" is more than most manage to do in a lifetime. If you manage to stop "paying-out," you have dealt with your "debt," and yet if this is "all" you do, you are leaving big wins on the table. The next big step is not just to get rid of your debt, but to transform it into an "asset."

Alchemically transforming a seeming negative to an unequivocal positive or asset in your life—that is what we mean, and not just a one-time positive "Cash-In" that you spend, but positive assets that get set up as passive investments generating continuous returns in your exponential growth–daily, monthly and annual returns.

How do you turn an experience with a "jerk" into actually putting returns in your financial, mental, emotional and spiritual bank accounts? We all have seeming debts that we have not yet cashed in on, just waiting for us to turn into perpetual happiness, success and money-making machines.

The Cost of "Paying Out"

Before we dive more into "How to Cash-In" or "Rewire," let's look at the cost of "paying-out" through the eyes of one particular human, say an entrepreneur, 100% dependent on his ability to sell his service, let's say someone whose service is real estate investing. Let's call this person

Jordan, and let's say that Jordan has invested in his own professional development. He's trained with one of the most successful investors; he's learned how to assess, put offers in on properties, close, renovate, and create a decent return on investment. Then with great enthusiasm for this opportunity, Jordan goes out to attract investors whose funds he would manage and generate an excellent return for.

Objectively the investment opportunity yields the top returns compared to most other options such as government bonds, mutual funds, etc. Objectively, it is less risky than many potentially high-yield opportunities such as new business IPOs (Initial Purchase Offers) because it is backed by the real assets of the property, and the real estate market has continued to appreciate, especially where Jordan is investing. Yet in reality, despite Jordan's countless efforts to network and present the objectively excellent opportunity, he cannot figure out why he has not yet attracted any investors–and why, in fact, even qualified prospects he had courted who expressed interest in real estate, in real estate investing specifically, even in his geographic areas, had yet taken the action to "seal the deal."

Jordan was overlooking–as most people do–the biggest variable that people don't factor in, study, or master–himself, and more specifically the human dynamics of success. When one set of human "wiring" meets another set of human wiring, there is a dynamic interaction. Why does such a high percentage of our interactions generate little to no returns? Typically 70 to 80 to 90% of prospecting does not generate any sales, income, returns, not one penny. Is it "just" Jordan's selling system that needs to change, is it "just" his action-taking follow through he needs to improve to increase his closing ratio?

Or …

Does Jordan have 1000+ thoughts an hour, and does his prospect have 1000+ thoughts an hour, any one of which can "take him out" or "take them out" of the game, in this case the game of real estate investing?

One single thought during an entire meeting from either party such as "I'm not sure he's successful enough," "What if the market drops," "I don't think they're going to invest," or "I don't want them as a client anyway" can "kill the deal." That's the power of our thoughts.

Jordan is left frustrated, defeated, broke, and bewildered ....

Why can we have a great opportunity, but few takers? What is this thing, this potential "show-stopper" to our success called "human thoughts and dynamics?" What is this thing that causes us to waste such a huge percentage of our time, our efforts, our life not producing any tangible results? Why do we seem to "Pay-Out" much more than we "Cash-In"–whether in tiny or epic experiences?

What Stops Us from "Cashing-In"

Here's a closer look at the wiring that is in the way, or stops us from "cashing in" on opportunities.

Let's cut right to the chase and look at the thoughts and emotions that an average human generates on an average day. First we will start with how many, and then we will go to what is in them. The average human has about 70,000 thoughts each per day, or about a thought per second! More interestingly, take a guess as to "For an average person on an average day, what percentage of that person's thoughts and emotions are negative versus positive?"

Go ahead write down a percentage without peeking ahead. ☺

On average, 70% of a human's thoughts and emotions are negative. That is on average, so the moment that we get mentally or emotionally "hijacked" or triggered, it can shoot up to 85% or 95% in a heart-beat. If you guestimated that high, you probably understand why. If you guessed lower, just imagine this. Let's say you have a "positive" thought of "I'm going to Hawaii," and then a plethora of "negative" or worry thoughts naturally follow, such as "Where am I going to stay, with who, how much ... what if ...." The percentage of negative to positive seems much more understandable.

Now, tune into your own "inner radio dial" and ask yourself "On an average day, what percentage of my thoughts and emotions are negative versus positive? (These could be even mild, low grade worry, stress, anxiety...) Go ahead, write down that percentage too.

Now let's imagine that you live to be 100 years old.

Take your average percentage of negativity from above and fill in your number to this sentence while reading it out loud; "If I live to 100 years old, I will have 'wasted' ___ years of my life in negative unsupportive thoughts and emotions."

We will not leave you here, and yet it is vitally important to your success and happiness to get really present to the content of this sentence because it is the lowest risk, highest-motivation wake-up call you may ever have. Just think of the much higher-risk wake-up calls many of us have had–accidents, health scares, bankruptcies, abuse, financial ruin … or the opposite, the lack of wake-up that leaves people at the end of their lives saying "I missed it." So just say and be present to this sentence one more time: "If I live to be 100 years old, I will have 'wasted' ___ years of my life in negative, unsupportive thoughts and emotions."

How does that feel? Ideally there is "fuel" there for change—the feeling that the "cost" of that much negativity in your life is too high, and the burning desire to day-by-day, moment-by-moment rewire your inner game for higher happiness and your outer game for higher success.

Let us take the average percentage–that is, that 70% of humanity, or 70% of our entire human species, is "wasted" in negativity every single day. Sigh … yet … this is the number that fuels us every day, the hope of dropping this number for us and our fellow human every day and permanently rewiring, raising the success score every day.

Imagine a world, or your world, with less negativity, less arguing, less worry, less "turning people off," less missed opportunity, and instead "turning people on," more "yes's," more opportunities, solutions, and satisfying results. Imagine dropping your percentage by even 10 or 20%, that is 10 to 20 bonus years for you, for the people you care about, interact with, do business with ….

Many people who have worked with us have dropped that number by 30, 50, some as high as 70 percent, adding 70 positive years to their lives! Now that is a good return on your investment, and in fact a good rewiring of your investments, because for every part of your "inner game" thoughts and emotions that you rewire, there is a direct correlation to your "outer game" results.

How to "Cash In" and Rewire

How did we "cash in" on past or recent experiences? Realize, now, that "cashing-in" is simply one of dozens of techniques that we have employed in a whole system of rewiring for higher success and happiness. Having said that, "rewiring" can be a fun and fruitful practice none the less.

At this point it is probably valuable to give you brief highlights of our challenging experiences, so that you can either more closely relate and/or realize that our perspectives come from direct experience and direct break-throughs.

Colin, my business partner, witnessed physical abuse when he was three years old; later, the teachers told him he was stupid, and then came the alcohol, the drugs, the drug dealing–and then climbing up a 150-foot cell tower, ready to jump and take his life. Suicidal depression. Luckily, he is still with us; he has a huge contribution to make in this world.

In my case, I experienced the first (and last) abusive business relationship of my life. It started with a man who appeared to be successful, who appeared to care about the planet, and appeared to want to build a sustainable business. Then enter myself, stage left. It seemed to be a perfect fit, for one of my dream contributions is planetary restoration through sustainable business solutions.

Unfortunately, appearances and reality could not have been farther apart. The six-figure-debt that my business partner racked up in my name was dwarfed in comparison to the bullying of myself and every prospect, client, and potential joint venture partner I ever brought to the table. With our suppliers, he would temporarily chum up to them, buy tens of thousands of dollars of materials, then flippantly not pay them back, nor generate his promised sales results, despite his raging ego as being a world-class salesman. All this left me frozen at my laptop, watching the credit card debt rack up, borrowing more money every week to meet payroll and cover his vast array of "business" spending, all with his well-spun illusionary dream of a planetary business and his promises of hitting his sales targets "next week."

Can you relate to going to bed and waking up in fear, so anxiety ridden that it feels like something is going to break in your body ... and for me, heading for my first (and last) ever nervous break-down.

And so followed hours, days, weeks, and months of "pay-out"–of lost time, lost money, lost health, wasted anxiety and rage, lost prospects, lost revenue, until I chose very consciously to win, until I chose very consciously to stop "paying-out" and start "cashing-in." Among the 27+ reframing, rewiring and success techniques that changed our success trajectory permanently, one in particular is relevant to this "Cashing-In" and "Reinvesting the Gold" conversation.

Reinvesting the Gold - a 3-step process:

1. Clarity to See Top Win: "If I were to earn a million dollars as a direct result of this 'challenging' experience, what key area would I take 100% responsibility for?"

2. Courage to Shift Direction: Drop the old story and free the energy to refocus on your new million dollar strategy–"From 100% responsibility, what is my new best action today to contribute to my million-dollar strategy?"

3. Commitment to Be Successful: Declare daily, "I think and take action that reinvests the gold into my life and livelihood and generates exponential passive returns."

Instead of perpetuating worry and waste, examples of your actions as a result of "Reinvesting the Gold" may be to close the business, consolidate your debt, tap into your true purpose and talents, train with millionaires, and launch your new endeavour with strong passion, direction, and demand for your services.

"Cash in" every day. Become wealthier every day. Rewire every day. Step closer to your dreams every day. Live some of your dream life every day.

Rewiring 4 Success - Principles, Practices and Profits

Chunking up from this particular million dollar "Reinvesting the Gold" practice, let us take a look at rewiring for success overall. You can slice the success pie many different ways. One framework that we find valuable is looking at success versus failure. More specifically, look at success versus failure Principles, Practices and Profits (or losses in the case of failure).

In our "Successipedia" ©, we have identified 38+ Success vs Failure Principles.

To the credit of many success experts, they often simplify the road to success into a few key nuggets or fundamentals or principles, such as "Define your dream, and get a burning desire for its achievement."–Napoleon Hill. The pro of this is that it offers you a quick jump-start, and if you apply it, then also an early win. There is great merit in this. AND as we went deeper, road-tested more, threw out what didn't work, dug for the missing pieces, we found that there are a number of aspects to "complete" the story or the roadmap of success. This is why we created "Successipedia–a Living Reservoir of Success Principles and Practices." We give the whole Successipedia to participants the very first week of the "Rewired4Success" Program © where we run through a complete "Success Cycle" and you can access a copy right now for yourself at www.rewired4success.com/successipedia

One distinction that you may find valuable when interacting with any success principle is not just to say "yes" or "no," √ or X, "I do that" or "I don't." Instead, rank your percentage on the failure side of that principle and your percentage on the success side of that principle, adding up to 100% every time. We get all our clients to rank their % failure and % success habits next to each and every Principle. For example, the Success/Failure Principle of Focus: Most people hear in their head a 0 or 100 answer, either "I'm focused" or "I'm not focused." In reality, though, rarely are we 0 or 100% of anything. To reflect on your accurate percentages, as opposed to judge 0 or 100 definitively, creates an invaluable mirror for yourself across any set of success principles. Then you can see where your real strengths are, as well as your biggest leverage points of which principle to put more into practice over, say, the next 90 days.

Under each Principle are optimal Practices to maximize your success. Some of the key Principles that we train our clients up on are getting their "Why" or motivation clearer, then setting a particular kind of Sweet Spot Goal, defining their Track to Win On, creating a Daily Success Plan, learning to Reframe and Rewire when your inner "monkey-mind" hijacks your thoughts and emotions, and Focusing back on your Sweet Spot Goal with higher Excitement and Belief. Optimizing both your inner and outer game, both your future dreams and your current action are key in the balance of attaining success.

Finally, you may learn from living these Success Principles and Practices that "Profits" come in all shapes and sizes. They come in whatever form that you focus or set your intention on–Financial Profits, Relational Profits, Health Profits, Love Profits, Happiness Profits: whatever the "Pro Fit" © is that you set out for yourself.

Success is not just a "drive-through" experience; it is the entire highway and the country roads of your life. Enjoy the ride, choose your best route, take in the scenery, stop to enjoy the sights and experiences along the way, yet also ensure you set and reach your key destinations.

Hopefully this time we have spent together you will never say was "wasted" and instead was "winning" time, if nothing else to come to the realization and hopefully the motivation that you need to reduce your "wasted" years and increase your "winning" years, starting now. Keep in mind to commit with greater passion to your own permanent rewiring through practices such as the million-dollar "Reinvesting the Gold" process and finally to realize success is a vast territory of success principles and practices leading, if implemented, to great life profits, profiting yourself, those you are contributing to, and the world around you in infinite possible ways!

To Your Rewiring and Success!

Heather Ramsey and Colin Campbell

Founders–Rewired WorldWide

Visit us at: www.rewired4success.com

About Heather Ramsey

Founders of Rewired WorldWide, Heather Ramsey & Colin Campbell have mentored and trained with some of the World's Top Leaders in Success Mastery. Featured on Fox TV, the Nikki Clarke Show…Rewired WorldWide is one of those rare enterprises that integrates you - the whole human with the whole "Success Cycle" © - to ensure your ever increasing highest possible success & happiness.

Heather has trained over 1000+ people in the art & science of facilitation at the Executive Business School of York University and the University of Toronto. She has led such international experiences as the World Council, and has made significant contributions to "Greening Business," working with executives to build sustainable business strategies. Her appointment to the Minister of Energy's Advisory Council, led to doubling both the renewable energy & conservation quotas.

Now Heather is living her mission of Rewiring 1 Million humans for higher success & happiness! Write or call Rewired today at contact@ rewired4success.com for your free Private 30min "Success Check-Up", to begin your 'Rewiring for Higher Success' - and put "Achieve" in the subject line!

www.rewired4success.com

1-888-310-7703

About Colin Campbell

Colin started off his career as a carpentry apprentice, and soon realized he was born to be successful in business. He quickly carved a new path for himself, tripling his top sales lead generating results for a renewable energy company.

He then applied these winning strategies to build Operation Feel Good, training professionals on the link between happiness & results. This led to the launch

of Rewired WorldWide, where entrepreneurial-minded people like you get trained and coached on how to put all the pieces of the "success puzzle" together – achieving higher Outer Game results & success, while rewiring your higher Inner Game happiness – permanently!

www.rewired4success.com

1-888-310-7703

How to Engage Success

By Steve Beckford

Introduction

In order for companies to achieve sustainable growth and profits, both the company and the employee interests must be mutually aligned to achieve a common goal. Achieving a common goal is far easier said than done, as both parties are motivated by self-interest, which creates conflicts within the short run, ultimately jeopardizing the future success of the corporation in the long run. It is because of this conflict within the organization that we have decided to pursue this study in order to solve the principal agent theory.

Our hypothesis: Is it possible to create a business model in the workplace that solves the Principal Agent Theory? If so, what are the common denominators shared by several highly successful organizations that have solved the theory in various sectors? Moreover, once we have identified the key factors to solve the principal agent theory, the question is, how many resources should a company allocate to a specific area in order to gain the maximum benefit?

In order to further explore and drill deeper into the solving the Principal Agent Theory, the areas of exploration consist of examining the organizational models of Google, Disney, and Southwest. In addition, we have studies and scientific research based on Robert Cialdini's 60 years of studies on the science of persuasion to validate where or not we can initiate proven tactics that will aid us in solving the Principal Agent Theory.

The Google Theory

The major motivational tactics used by Google are centered on employee freedom and flexibility (Google, 2013). This aspect can be applied to any organization in order to match the goals and objectives of upper management and employees. Google has successfully implemented this into their organization, which explains one of the reasons why they are the leading innovative firm in the world.

If employees are given flexibility in respect to working hours and location to perform their tasks, it is likely that they increase both productivity and quality of their output, which creates the perfect environment to solve the principle agent theory. This bridges the gap between employee efforts and the vision of the company. As a result, overall performance of the company will improve, creating a family culture where positions in the hierarchy will not matter in terms of interpersonal interaction.

In addition, open discussion allows employees freely to suggest innovative ideas to upper management because communication barriers are eliminated (Google, 2013). This leads to employee efforts being in sync with the company's goals and objectives, creating a win-win situation for both parties.

Selecting the "right fit" for the company

It is often believed that employees make up the organization. Individuals who can complement each other by leveraging strengths and weaknesses will have a higher possibility of achieving a stated goal.

Google has successfully implemented this notion into their recruitment function. They hire only people who they think are smart and determined and favour ability over experience (Google, 2013). This statement alone shows that Google is not willing to hire any Joe on the street, but is looking for people that possess a specific processing ability. People who can think critically when faced with difficult situations on a daily basis are ideal (Duboi, 2013). In essence, this leads to having people that can align themselves with the company's vision.

Based on this information, Google tries to eliminate the conflicts of interest between employer and employee from the initial phase of recruiting. This means that by the time a potential employee is given a job, he or she is already in tune with the company's mission and vision. The recruitment criteria itself is sufficient to solve the principle agent theory.

The Walt Disney Company
Organizational Culture

Believing in magic is the main theme that Disney wishes to deliver to its guests. In order to implement this experience, employees play a major role because they are the backbone of Disney that strengthens this belief. A strong organizational culture is, therefore, important because it allows employees to perform at their maximum potential, which ultimately benefits the organization. Not only does Disney create magical moments for its guest, but they also make employees feel special. Whether a member of the cast of characters or a simple caretaker, every employee is referred to as cast member. All cast members are taught and come to believe that they are performers on the world stage. Essentially, Disney's objective is to hire people that find joy in delivering on core values, rather than finding people that can simply do the job (Maanen, 1999).

The expectancy theory is used to explain how cast members are inspired when working at Disney. According to Victor Vroom, people are motivated to achieve the goals with the highest expected payoff (McShane & Steen, 2012). If cast members understand the attractiveness of the outcomes, they will put in more effort, which improves performance. In addition, negative qualities are reinforced through the Traditions 101 training program. This training program is run by cast members who work and spend time with new cast over several days to immerse them in the culture of the organization (Maanen, 1999). Disney has created a culture for their staff where they feel that they are valued as an individual and are a vital part of the team.

This solves the principle agent theory because cast members are able to align valued outcomes with the overall vision of Disney. In order to convince the public that magical moments can happen, cast members need to portray the roles of Disney characters effectively. In doing so, they promote the fantasy ambiance of Disneyland, which makes guests buy into the theme of magic. The organization is able to achieve its goal (Maanen, 1999) through employing the service profit chain model. Cast members deliver great services since they are satisfied with their jobs due to Disney's strong organizational culture. As a result, they are motivated to perform well, which not only increases customer satisfaction and loyalty, but also encourages organization profitability and growth.

Develop Worker's Skills and Potential

Training and education motivates staff and makes them more productive and innovative. Disney realized early on that a successful organization needs to implement strategic training in order to continually encourage the staff to provide magical experiences to guests. It offers training programs that allow cast members to develop their career professionally and build leadership skills (Disney Careers: Learning & Development).

Disney provides cast members with a supportive environment that enables them to advance further in their careers. At Disney, cast members have the opportunity to become an ambassador (Disney: Ambassador Program). These people are the face of the organization because they represent all cast members in the public. This position is very competitive since only one to two people are selected each year. Therefore, cast members who want the position perform their duties exceptionally so as to prove that they are the most deserving of the position.

This solves the principal agent theory because cast members who are well trained are more satisfied and motivated. The focus that Disney puts into each cast member is paid back through their efforts to create magical experiences for guests. Well-trained cast members are more competent and have better control over their jobs. They have the ability to answer questions and solve problems, which provides stronger customer service and encourages guest loyalty.

Southwest Airlines

Leadership plays a huge role in the success of every company; it is the process of influencing people to perform assigned tasks willingly, efficiently and effectively. Enabling people to feel they have a say in how they do something results in higher levels of job satisfaction and productivity. Leadership is one of the single most important factors that can make a business organization successful; it enables a not-for-profit organization to fulfill its mission. The absence of leadership is equally dramatic in its effects. Without leadership, organizations move too slowly, stagnate, and lose their way. A strong leader leads employees in alignment with the company's mission. (Kuhlmann, 2010).

Leadership: Herb Kelleher

A strong leader leads employees in alignment with the company's mission.

"The Amazement Revolution" involves Building a customer service culture that creates customer and employee loyalty through seven steps. One of the role models in this strategy is Herb Kelleher, founder of Southwest Airlines. Kelleher believed in an employee-first approach, which at the time was very controversial. Herb Kelleher put an enormous amount of emphasis on culture and the customer experience. He realized that the culture could serve as a constant no matter who was in charge, and southwest corporate culture persisted even after he stepped down as CEO (Lucier, 2004) (Hyken, 2014).

Employee Benefits and Perks

The company rewards their staffs through financial, promotion and non-financial rewards, which meets four of the five levels of Maslow's hierarchy of needs (Security, Affiliation, Esteem, and Self-Actualization). Southwest has never had a major layoff, never cut salaries, and has always paid employees generously. Southwest is a conservative, cautious company that doesn't take risks with employee's jobs or security. For that reason, its employees are extremely loyal and are willing to make sacrifices when necessary. This contributes to solving the principal agent theory because by offering employees benefits and perks allows Southwest to keep employees long term and align them with company goals (Sunoo, 2005).

Employees Benefits and Perks include:

Free flights on Southwest Airlines and discounts to hotels, theme parks, and car rental companies

Profit-sharing plan: Reward employees with a portion of the company's profits (Contributed 7.96% of employees' salaries into their profit-sharing accounts).

Employee Ownership: 13% of Southwest is employee owned.

Comprehensive health and wellness package: Medical, Vision, Dental, Life Insurance

Herb Kelleher promised all workers (front line employees to corporate) that if they kept profits up for five consecutive years, they could wear jeans every day of the week (Non-financial reward).

Perfect attendance program: Company gave away Ford Explorers to demonstrate the $1M in savings in sick leave pay.

Optimax
Optimize Employee Performance

The external (environment) and internal (character) stressors are the elements which prevent an employee from balance; however, there are three key elements of life–SELF, FAMILY and WORK–that the system focuses on (Hill, 1925). By understanding these key elements individually, we can then bring our employee in alignment before they come in alignment with the company purpose, mission, and vision, thus solving the principal agent theory (Optimax Human Performance Inc, 14). It is important to note that these three areas of life cover 24 hours of day-to-day activities. Each one of these three elements impacts on the others, and a problem with one will affect the other two. We see this when imbalance in our work life impacts our family situation or when a strained personal relationship causes problems at work (Sports Conflict Insitute, 2014). Character impacts on all three elements, but despite popular belief, we do not build character, nor can we change character. What we can do is to optimize all three areas. We can have significant influence under the condition that we understand our character (Optimax Human Performance Inc., 14). To understand character, we have to know our strengths and weaknesses and be able to identify and prioritize our passions, thus enabling us to solve the principal agent theory.

Robert Cialdini's 6 Principles of Persuasion

Robert Cialdini is an experimental social psychologist who coined the six principles of influence; however, we will be discussing only reciprocity and social proofing. Mr. Cialdini began researching the psychology of compliance because he was easily persuaded into donating to charities, subscribing to magazines he would never read, and purchasing event tickets that had no relation to his work. As a result, he submerged himself into the world of compliance professionals such as salespeople, fund raisers, and advertisers who utilize the technique most. Upon completion of his research, he proposed six categories of compliance with the ability to stimulate a preferred response: reciprocation, consistency, social proof, liking, authority, and scarcity (Cialdini, 2009). These are the six principles of persuasion that offer insight in solving the principal agent theory. If an organization utilizes these principles, it will better motivate staff in all aspects of their lives.

Reciprocity

Cialdini (2009) points out that people are likely to say yes to people they owe. This act of reciprocation is defined as "the embedded urge to repay debts and favours, whether or not help is requested" (Solomon & Tuten, 2013). It is imperative when using this persuasion tactic to be the first to give, by shaping the gift in a personalized and unexpected way (Cialdini, 2009). If a company were to offer incentives above and beyond general benefits, the staff may feel obligated to return the favour, thus aligning themselves with the organizational goals. For example, certain organizations employ emergency assistance funds to aid employees during times of distress. This act of kindness is personalized to the situation and is not a generic benefit company's offer. Through reciprocity, managers can build personal relationships that are both positive and productive (Cialdini, 2001, p. 75).

Social Proof

Social proof indicates decisions are made by observing others (Cialdini, 2009). Social norms such as stopping at a red light and waiting in line to enter the bus are examples of the principle in action (Tuten &

Solomon, 2013). Depending on the goal of the company and the roles of the employees, the exploitation of social proof deviates. This is an important factor in solving the principal agent theory because when workers are more committed to their organization, they are less likely to deviate from the expectations because they are more invested in the membership. Activities such as company sports teams and events allow staff to feel they are adding value to a membership, thus maintaining the vision of the company.

Statistical Analysis

The statistical analysis consisted of a sample size of 125 average everyday workers. Every person filled out surveys which lead us to the following five key areas required to increase performance.

These five predictors are:

Impact - showing/proving and making your employees feel that work that they are performing has high impact on the company and possibly the world

Perks/Benefits- includes all the free benefits that an employee might receive (health benefits, gym memberships, vacations, etc.)

Corporate Culture- making your employees feel like home, love being at work, creating a community as well as aligning your vision with theirs

Efficiency Training- providing your employees with training on how to work effectively, balance their lives, give leadership courses, and any other self-improvement courses

Flexibility/Opportunity- Providing employees opportunity to grow within the company as well as have an ability to shift from one position to another

Testing

All of these predictors are important, but in order to receive a numerical number for each predictor, a marketing research analysis was run, and the result will help a company determine which areas are more important and where the company should invest next in order to maximize ROI from the employees as well as solve the principal agency problem.

The chart below shows the plotted data of all predictors with respect to the overall perceived score of the company by the average employee. Outliers exist which prove that there are special cases of people either not caring about a certain predictor for an unknown reason or feeling overly attached to a certain predictor, but the analysis could be taken further. Even though there is a certain weight that each predictor contributes to the overall score, each one of them has a possible error variance. This means even though Impact and Benefits/Perks betas are the same, it might be safer to invest more into one than another, due to lower probability of an error. Once standard error is included into consideration of the predictor weight, importance of each of the factors can be determined.

Importance of Predictors:

Impact: 33.9%

Perks/Benefits: 23.7%

Corporate Culture: 19.8%

Efficiency Training: 16%

Flexibility/Opportunity: 6.6%

Below is the visual representation chart of the importance of each of the predictors.

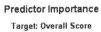

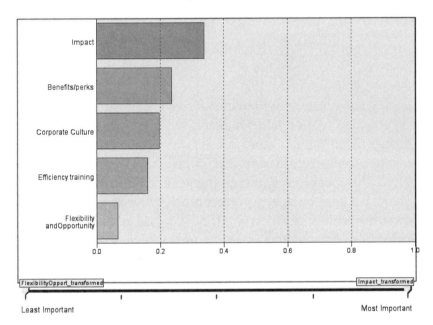

Conclusion

As a result of this study, the weight and importance of each of the predictors was determined. It is also concluded that results are significant, and average employees will follow this pattern with very little deviation. It is safe to assume that the best place to invest your money is in Impact predictor since even though it has the same value as Benefits and Perks, the probability of variance of the results is lower than with the Benefits and Perks. Another reason would be cost. Impact predictor is relatively affordable by any corporation to invest in, in comparison to including health benefits and gym memberships into employee's package. To obtain your copy of this 50-page detailed report, please email me at steve.beckford@gmail.com.

References

(n.d.). *Disney: Ambassador Program*. Retrieved from http://publicaffairs.disneyland.com/community/ambassador-program/

(n.d.). *Disney Careers: Learning & Development.* Retrieved from http://disneycareers.com/en/working-here/learning-development/

(n.d.). *In About Southwest: The Mission of Southwest Airlines.* Retrieved from http://www.southwest.com/html/about-southwest/index.html?tab=5

Chinsky, D. (2012, May 26). *Leadership Fitness.* Retrieved from http://instituteforleadershipfitness.com/2012/05/peak-performance-and-the-ultradian- rhythm/

Cialdini, R. (2009). *Influence: Science and Practice.* (5th ed.). Pearson Education, Inc.

Dubois, D. (2013, September 11). Google, the Network Company: From Theory to Practice. *INSEAD Knowledge.* Retrieved from http://knowledge.insead.edu/leadership- management/organisational-behaviour/google-the-network-company-from-theory-to-practice-2602?nopaging=1#PUQhE5mMD6cQBYXS.99

Jackson, L. (2013, July 23). The Real Secret of Google's Corporate Culture. *Corporate Culture Pros.* Retrieved from http://www.corporateculturepros.com/2013/07/the-real-secret-of-googles-corporate-culture/

Kuhlmann, A. (2010, April). Culture-driven leadership. In *Ivey Business Journal* . Retrieved from http://iveybusinessjournal.com/topics/leadership/culture-driven-leadership#.Uzi3Pyh1G-I

Lucier, C. (2004, June 1). Herb Kelleher: The Thought Leader Interview. *Strategy & Business.* Retrieved from http://www.strategy-business.com/article/04212?pg=all

Maanen, J.V. (1999). *The Smile Factory: Work At Disneyland.* Retrieved from http://www.analytictech.com/mb709/cases/smile_factory.pdf

Makovsky, K. (2013, November 21). Behind The Southwest Airlines Culture. *Forbes.* Retrieved from http://www.forbes.com/sites/kenmakovsky/2013/11/21/behind-the-southwest-airlines-culture/

Optimax: About Optimax. (n.d.). *Optimax : About Optimax.* Retrieved from http://www.optimax.org/sitemap.asp

Our culture. (n.d.). *Google Company.* Retrieved from http://www.
google.ca/about/company/facts/culture/

Paik Sunoo, B. (2005, June 1). How Fun Flies At Southwest Airlines.
Workforce. Retrieved from http://www.workforce.com/articles/
how-fun-flies-at-southwest-airlines

Research & Publications. (n.d.). *Sports Conflict Institute.* Retrieved
from http://www.sportconflict.org/team_member/dr-peter-guy/

culture-to-rival-southwest-airlines-ideally-before-you-leave-for-your-
next-lunch-break/

Tomer, M. (2011, September 5). Corporate Communication. *Google
Portal.doc.doc.* Retrieved from http://www.slideshare.net/Sam-
petruda/google-portaldocdoc

(2013, May 14) Southwest Airlines Releases Fourth Annual Integrat-
ed Report on Triple Bottom Line of Performance, People, And
Planet. *Southwest Airlines.* Retrieved from http://www.swamedia.
com/channels/Southwest-News-2013-May/releases/southwest-air-
lines-releases-fourth-annual-integrated-report-on-triple-bot-
tom-line-of-performance-people-and-planet

About Steve Beckford

As a Presidential Scholar, Steve graduated from University with a Business degree, obtaining a double major in Entrepreneurship and Strategy and Global Management. During University, Steve operated as a Marketing Director, Consultant, and an Intelligence Analyst. In addition, he is a Personal Trainer and is passionate about motivating and helping individuals achieve their personal goals. Steve believes that you are massively more than what you think you are!

Steve is known to turns facts and observations into theories, strategies, and concrete plans to meet established goals. Quick to identify inefficiencies, fallacious arguments and poor decisions, Steve's tendency to take on leadership roles stems from a desire to steer people and projects toward a positive outcome. Steve stands for the tools not only inspiring you, but giving you the steps and systems required for success and ultimately, teaching you how to live life on your owns so that you can spend time with the people that matter to you the most in life.

How to Achieve Financial Freedom under 40

By Anna Maccani

Have you ever wished you could just walk away from your boring or monotonous job? Do you daydream about long vacations on a sunny beach in the tropics? Or maybe a skiing vacation in the Swiss Alps? Maybe you just want to be able to send your kids to any university they want? Well, you are definitely not alone.

Ever since I was a teenager I have been fascinated with personal growth and wealth. As I've gotten older, this desire has only magnified. I really craved it though after I attended Anthony Robbins *Mastery University* courses. I could literally taste the margaritas as I relaxed on a spectacular white-sand beach. Then, after receiving coaching by Robert G. Allen, there was no holding me back. It really made me realize that the whole idea of simply working hard my entire life to obtain financial independence and then retire at 65, was just not cutting it for me. This widely accepted "social norm" definitely doesn't fit "my" dreams. I want it all sooner than that.

I have reached my goal. I have found my passion. I love what I do and it makes me money each and every month. So, I have no intentions of retiring—not just yet. My goal now is to help so many people obtain financial independence. And it all starts with a few fundamental principles of simply understanding how your money, debt, and savings work. You might be aware of the principle of *Spend Less, Save More, Make More*. The issue is not that you don't know WHAT to do. It is more likely you don't know HOW to do it. And this is where I come in. I am going to give you a few easy-to-follow steps that if you actually give them a chance and stick with them over the long term, may provide you with all the financial freedom you could ever dream of!

Now, the concepts I am about to give you are by no means "earth shattering." They are, however, fundamental principles you *need* to follow if you want to change your current financial situation—NOW. So here we go.

How to Plan Your Financial Independence –Daily.

The ONE thing I want you to remember from this chapter is that **the faster you become financially independent, the faster you can finally choose how you *want* to spend your time.**

For me, *Freedom 55 or 65* is just too far off. How about *Freedom under 40?* Sound good? I bet it does.

Did you know that historically, one of the fastest and safest ways to create financial freedom is through real estate? Forget about everything you were brought up to believe about real estate investing. It is not just for the wealthy or people with fancy degrees. It does not have to be risky when done properly. With proper mentorship, you can build a portfolio of positive cash-flow-generating assets that can reduce risk of market fluctuations and help you become financially free!

EXERCISE:

A. Get a clear picture of your financial health. What are your debts? Your income? Your savings? What are your monthly expenses? Obtain a clear picture of your starting point.

B. How much income do you actually need to cover all your monthly expenses? Add up all your expenses and you will get a good picture of what is really happening with your income.

C. What type of income would you like to generate to replace your income from work?

D. What consistent actions do you need to take to help replace your current income and cover your expenses, savings, investments and entertainment (yes, you get to have a "Fun & Rewards" budget!).

E. In his book "Secrets of the Millionaire Mind" T. Harv Ecker reviews the Mason jars system for —Savings, Mortgage, Fun, Investments, Education, Emergency Fund, Giving Fund or whatever works for your situation (just make sure you cover all areas of spending and savings) and begin to "deposit" money into these daily. The goal is for your habits to change, change your consciousness, and align the Universe Energy with your goals. It's the system that is important, not the jars. Think and visualize the actions of putting more and more money into each jar and becoming financially independent.

F. Magnify and increase your goals, monitor your progress, evaluate and be open to new opportunities coming your way that may help you with Step E.

G. Most importantly, think about who you can reach out to *today* to follow them about creating your financial freedom?

Back to Basics.

Now it's time to get down to the actual concepts that will help turn your financial direction around, ultimately leading you faster to financial freedom.

1. Spend less

Have you ever gone to the grocery store intending to get some milk and walked out with over $120 in groceries? Walking down the aisles you probably saw the new chips being advertised, and before you knew it, you've dropped them into your basket.

Part of your new money mindset, however, needs to be "spend less" where you can. So, maybe instead of buying that La Rocca bakery cake for $29.99, which is 10 times more expensive than actually baking a cake for $2.99 at home, you opt for the less convenient but financially responsible choice!

How about your next car purchase?

Have you ever considered what the cash difference is when you use premium gas vs. regular unleaded gas? Well, it's about 30 cents/litre. If you drive 600km/week, at 10 liters per 100 km, that adds up to $60-100 per month, or $1200 per year! Look at where else you are "leaking" money. Some examples of areas you can spend less include:

A. Be Brand Flexible—look where you can spend less for comparable non-brand items.

B. Use no-fee ATMs and monitor your bank charges.

C. Keep a daily log of your expenses and keep to your budget. Prepare a budget if you don't have one. Not sure how? Google "budget templates."

D. Pay for things with CASH. If you are using credit cards for points, pay off your balance in full each month. Think of your purchases in <u>after-tax terms</u> i.e., that $80 pair of jeans suddenly becomes a $110 pair of jeans etc.

E. Make your next car purchase one that takes the cheapest gas for long-term savings. Ask the dealership if the current vehicle can use regular gas. Often this is the case even though the manufacturer says premium gas only. Consider the maintenance costs of your future car.

F. Buy items in bulk to get a better price, but only if you will use them.

Being frugal does not necessarily mean sacrificing your quality of life. It just means being economically aware! Once you start to live this way, you will have a hard time going back.

2. Save more

Mary was a single mother. Raising two children was not an easy task. Yet she knew that financial security and having a backup bank account was a necessity. Not only did Mary watch her expenses, she used the savings from daily expenses through proper budgeting, sales and specials and put that money away for a "rainy day." She invested her money wisely. Over time, these small amounts ($5 here and there) began to grow, and multiply. With the power of compound interest and time, she found herself with a substantial amount of money she never dreamed was ever possible in her situation. Albert Einstein called "interest compounding" the eighth wonder of life. "He who understands it makes it; he who does not, pays it". Mary followed these simply steps to SAVE MORE money, and her financial dreams came sooner than she ever thought possible.

All beginnings start with a "decision" AND an immediate "action." For instance, you may choose to make coffee at home instead of spending $6.50 a day for a cup from your local branded coffee shop. By doing this, you are choosing to save $6.00 a day, which you can eventually use towards a down payment on a house. Now let's count: 2 cups of coffee/day at a branded shop at $6.00 x 365 days = $4,380 after tax. If you are at a 30 percent tax rate, you need to make approximately $6,738.40 in pre-tax income just to cover your daily habit. In two years that's $8,760! It may be enough for a down payment or a home with a tenant, depending on your location home prices. That's huge!

Think about other areas in which you are simply letting money "slip" through your hands. Why not put that same $6.00 daily in your "Savings Jar"?

Suggestions:

A. Open another 2 low-fee bank accounts and set up monthly fixed forced savings—one for emergencies, such as roof repairs, car repairs; the second one for a dedicated savings fund, which you will use to invest into your future positive cash-flow generating assets.

B. Save more by reducing your housing costs. Could you have a tenant paying you additional $1,000/month that can go towards your mortgage repayment?

C. Learn how the interest on your credit cards and mortgage works. Based on a minimum payment each month, how much in interest will it cost you to carry your current balances?

D. Watch your electronics. There are many providers that offer Family Plans and reduced rates, or company or group discounts. As well, do you absolutely need the newest gadget or can you go another year with your old model?

E. Talk to your mortgage lender about changing your mortgage to a bi-weekly payment to speed up your repayment and reduce mortgage interest expense.

F. Consolidate any debt and get rid of high interest credit cards. Get a 3-4% percent home equity line of credit instead. That's a huge savings alone.

G. KEY: Create a power team of trusted advisors. Find a great accountant and tax lawyer. Invest time into family, estate and business planning. Knowing how to save on taxes using appropriate tax planning techniques may save you thousands of dollars in the long run.

3. Make more money—increase your income

Tom was a very hard-working young man. He was madly in love with Jane, and he knew if he wanted to build a life for them he would need to increase his income. He not only took extra courses to improve his education, but he studied and followed people that were already financially successful. By creating new sources of income, he was never financially dependent on one "job."

Tom was patient. He knew that it may take some time for this new income to materialize, yet he consistently dedicated time and resources to build multiple streams of income. With the advice of a trusted mentor, he used his current income and his good credit to start investing in real estate. Once he acquired a few properties, the cash-flow and equity growth allowed him to expand his real estate portfolio even more. By creating a thriving real estate portfolio, as long as his properties produced positive cash-flow, he was able to ride out market fluctuations.

After owning properties for over 25 years, Tom and Jane had completely replaced their regular income. They used the cash-flow to invest into other businesses to diversify their income streams even more. Tom and Jane are now financially free!

Suggestions:

A. How can you exponentially double, triple or even ten-fold your current income? Think outside the box: For example, how can you leverage the work of other people to secure passive repeating monthly income?

B. How can you become more efficient so your productivity and income go up? What _systems_ can you leverage to increase your productivity, efficiency and results?

C. What is the next source of income you can focus on and create through passive or active investments? Some examples include photo licensing, blog writing, parking fees, storage unit rentals, etc.

D. Find out what you are _passionate about_ and learn _how to monetize it_. You will never need to "work" another day in your life.

4. How to Manage Your Money while Leveraging Other People's Time and Money.

We all have the same 24 hours every day. It's what you choose to do with these hours that make the difference. Successful people utilize and plan their time for the future in order to have more time and money for the things that matter the most. Successful people also use "leverage," or use other people's time or money to grow their investments.

For example, instead of doing yard work for 3 hours each weekend, can you hire a student at a minimum wage? Give them the opportunity to earn money and use that time toward things that will increase your income.

EXERCISE:

A. Spend 15 minutes daily for 7 days to review your budget. How can you reduce your expenses by 2, 5, 10, 20 percent and put that money toward a bigger goal? If you don't know how to do a budget get a professional to help you.

B. How can you make your money grow faster at higher rates—not 1-2 percent, but 8-9 percent, or 15-20 percent?

C. Think big, yet safe to preserve your capital. Where can you generate these returns, locally? Maybe through international real estate investments, joint ventures, or by using the services of skilled professionals that really know the market and can spot a gem you can flip?

D. Review your financial balance sheet and income statement on a regular basis: your assets, debts, savings and equity, active and passive income. Watch them grow.

E. Evaluate what actions you need to take to purchase your first, 5th or 50th property?

F. What actions can you delegate to advisors, property managers or employees to gain the time you need to focus on other income-generating projects?

G. With the extra time, plan what your next source of passive income will be. Complete daily affirmations and visualize the success you ARE ALREADY RECEIVING from this next source of income.

H. What steps need to happen in order for your next source of income to materialize?

I. Now plan, review, and repeat steps A through H. And enjoy the fruits of your labour.

5. Set Goals.

Have you ever wondered why 3 percent of Harvard MBAs make 10 times more than all the other 97 percent combined? According to *Mark McCormack*, author of What They Don't Teach You at Harvard Business School, in 1979, 13 percent of the class that had goals, were earning, on average, twice as much as the 84 percent who had no goals. Even more staggering, the 3 percent who had clear, written goals were earning, on average, 10 times as much as the other 97 percent combined! Evidently, having clear written goals for your future and making plans to accomplish them, is what helps to make people successful.

The moral of the story: **goals matter.** It's no accident your boss asks you to complete your goals for the upcoming year or a performance review for the past year. But what about the rest of your life—outside of work? Don't you think YOU deserve more? Why not set clear goals and actions followed by an annual performance review for your personal life? Get Started Today!

EXERCISE:

A. Write down your objective. Example, "How do I make $1,000,000 by the time I'm 40?"

B. Write down 3 goals that support your objective. For example 1) Hire a coach; 2) Determine 5 potential streams of income and; 3) Research, evaluate and implement these new goals.

C. Write down 5 strategies for reaching each goal.

D. Gratitude - Be grateful each and every day for what you have: your health, the people you love, and the life you have. Focus on the positive to multiply the positive. HINT: <u>"What you focus on expands"</u>. Continue to work on your mindset.

6. Surround Yourself with powerful mentors.

Joseph knew that if he wanted to make the PGA championship he would have to work harder than ever. He also knew that hard work is not enough if you are not going in the right direction. From an early age, his parents invested in the best coaches—for golf, physical development and mental toughness. One for each critical area of the game. Success is easier to follow when you are following mentors who have been there and done it before you—AND those who have been successful at it.

I look at things a little differently than some people. I don't consider myself to be a *perfectionist*. I am a *progressionist*. Progress creates motion, motion creates action and results, results create confidence and desire to do more. Bottom line is get yourself a coach who has done what you want to do and then follow in their footsteps. If you implement only one critical idea per month, that is 12 fantastic new ideas per year. If each area of your life improves just by 5 percent, think of the progress you will make in the months and years to come.

EXERCISE:

A. What field do you want to master? Where can you find solid mentors for that field? Research first to make sure you are spending your money wisely.

B. Who in your field is a role model, master or mentor you can reach out to? How can you contribute to their success as well, creating a Win-Win situation for everyone?

C. Connect with your future coach and sign up for systematic coaching classes.

D. Follow the 1-3-5 model to accomplish more (see my eBook for details).

E. Find networking events and seminars you can attend in your desired field. Attend, network, learn, implement, review, revise, course correct and continue to grow.

F. Help other's achieve their goals. Let "the law of reciprocity" work in your favour.

G. Believe in your dreams and continuously visualize your success and growth.

What Does All This Mean?

In they latest national bestseller, *The One Thing*, Gary Keller and Jay Papasan talk about the concept of setting goals and focusing on the ONE thing that matters the most. If you could only set your goals once in your life, how big would you dream?

"What you think about, you bring about." So **DREAM BIG!**

And remember: Never, ever, ever give up. Big success is made of small daily tasks and accomplishments. Focus on your priorities each and every day, hour, minute of the day as "Time" is a very precious commodity. I will leave you with a powerful quote by the late Zig Ziglar, Motivational Speaker:

"When you do the things you need to do when you need to do them, the day will come when you can do the things you want to do when you want to do them."

About Anna Maccani

Anna Maccani was always fascinated with Personal Growth. Her passion is to help others grow and transform their lives and businesses. After completing a number of years in the corporate world as a CPA/CA (Chartered Professional Accountant) Anna walked away to satisfy her inner calling of helping people get to the next level in their lives. She is currently one of Top 10 Real Estate Professionals with Keller Williams Real Estate Associates Brokerage in the Toronto Area.

She runs the "Maccani Advantage" Real Estate Team and is a Luxury Agent and Global Property Specialist working with individuals, families and real estate investors. Anna focuses on transforming people's lives and helping them achieve financial and personal independence through real estate investing, coaching, and creating multiple streams of income. She also supports her local community and business owners through community events, charitable causes and educational training.

Thank You.

A *special thank you* to the people who expanded my mind and inspire me every day to be more and contribute more to others: Anthony Robbins, Robert G. Allen, Sunil Tulsiani, Peter Mazzuchin, Scott Harris, John Maxwell, Joel Bauer, T. Harv Eker, Robert Kiyosaki, Gary Keller, Dianna Kokoszka, Mary-Anne Gillespie, the late Napoleon Hill and Jim Rohn. Finally the biggest thank you to my Parents (Barbara and Walter), my Parents-in-Law (Gilia and Giulio), and my husband Silvano for their never-ending love and support.

Special Gift For You.

Anna is giving away a complimentary 30-minute coaching session for a limited time. To learn more about Anna Maccani and how your goals and dreams can become a reality or to obtain a free copy of her eBook, feel free to connect with Anna at www.MaccaniRealEstate.com or www.FreedomUnder40.com. And she invites you to connect with her on Facebook, Linked-in, YouTube, Twitter and Pinterest.

HOT MARKETING TOOLS FOR PROFITABLE REAL ESTATE INVESTORS

By Kotty Kihara

If you're already a real estate investor, then, like me, you've probably read many books, purchased programs and taken courses on how to be a successful Real Estate Investor (REI). Today I will focus on what most new and experienced investors struggle with—and that is building the business and marketing side of their REI enterprise.

Marketing is one of my favorite parts of any business because it's the heart of a company. It pulses and beats when you get the phones to ring, when you start getting leads in the door, when you communicate with your prospects, and when you promote your product and services. The systems to help close the deals and propel your REI business into the stratosphere start and end with marketing.

You may have learned about conventional methods to generate leads—giving out business cards, using signs, making cold calls, placing newspaper ads, mailing letters and even post cards. Although these work to some extent, today there are more effective marketing strategies to attract deals and investment prospects.

But before we get into the details of the various tools and tactics, I want to emphasize that the most important ingredients for succeeding in any business are: *passion, drive* and *determination*—building a business does not happen overnight. It takes time and hard work, but if you have the motivation, and if it's done properly, you will be able to make your dent in the industry.

Why is Marketing Important?

- It lets people know *who you are*: Name and brand recognition is crucial.

- It lets people know *what you do:* The products and services you offer.

- It attracts clients and makes them join your list (investors, buyers, sellers, etc.)

- It makes the phone ring—it generates leads! **This is the single most important factor for business survival.**

- The more leads you generate, the more sales you will close—and the more money you will make!

7 Keys to Effective Marketing for Real Estate Investors

1. Define your target market—the people you want to reach with your message and that will fit your business model.

2. Determine your area of expertise—the products and services you want to communicate and promote.

3. *How* you market to your target audience is key to developing and maintaining a profitable business. Effective marketing tactics will attract investors, qualified buyers and sellers.

4. Be consistent in your marketing tactics to generate a steady flow of leads.

5. Make it easy for your prospects and clients to *find you* and *reach you.*

6. Know Your Market. Understand the supply and demand of a market to determine the most profitable areas (wholesale, flips, etc.) and stay on top of trends such as the unemployment rate, mortgage rates, new construction, migration, etc. This allows you to plan for the future.

7. Develop a Niche Market. There are numerous ways to invest in real estate, so find a way that sets you apart from the rest. Learn as much as you can about a specific type of investment such as residential, commercial properties or even flipping rundown properties for quick sales. Whatever you decide to specialize in, make sure you become an expert in that area.

Marketing is putting together systems to get the phone to ring, get investors, buyers and sellers to find you, and get the leads in the door so you can close them. If you do this consistently, you will quickly earn your place in the REI industry.

Target Markets

It's important that you define your *target audience* early on. Don't try to tackle everyone at once with a "one fits all" message because it *will not* be effective. Your message needs to speak to the people who need a quick and effective solution to their problems.

Example of target markets:

- People who need to sell their house fast

- Houses in foreclosure

- People who are tired of dealing with their property

- People who want to buy a house but cannot get financing

- Investors that don't want to do the work—where you can do all the heavy lifting

7 Ways to Create a Great Message

The message you chose to send to people is important—you want to impart a message that will get your target market to contact you!

1. Create a message that catches people's attention. Have a compelling headline. Your message must resonate with the customers you want to attract. Some examples are: *"Great cash flowing properties, ROI 12% on passive investment"*

   "Amazing properties—Gross Rents $25,000"

2. Your message needs to be clear. People need to know *right away* what you are offering.

3. Your solution to their problem should be prominent and plausible. It's about what you can do for your investors and clients.

4. Your message also needs to be clear about *how* people can reach you. Whether it's by phone or email. Make it easy for people to know how to reach you quickly.

5. You need a "Call to Action." Give people a good reason to contact you RIGHT AWAY! Examples:

"Call me now if you want to take advantage of this great opportunity."

"Call me now and I will cover the closing costs!"

6. Be consistent with the frequency of your messages and campaigns. Consistency should be once a week, biweekly or at least once a month to be effective; otherwise people will forget you. Sporadic deals will never give you the consistency you need to meet your business objectives.

7. Get creative! Do things in a way that sets you apart from all of the other businesses. Today, people are more open to things done differently, which leaves the door wide open to coming up with something unique and memorable to get your message across.

How to Deliver Your Message

Consider the most effective way to get your message out. Whatever medium you chose, it should tie in with your market and your message. For example, you wouldn't want to advertise in a newspaper or site where there are no real estate advertisements or people specifically looking for what you are offering.

There are many effective mediums like email marketing, mobile marketing, videos, social media, etc.

The key is to *leverage technology*! The Internet is your new best friend. It will cut down on wasted and inefficient time. It will save you money. And it can provide you with consistent and effective ways to generating leads, which translates into deals!

The Modern World Lives Online

There are thousands of investors looking for good opportunities and motivated buyers and sellers looking for someone to help them. Make it easy for these potential customers to find you by appearing *everywhere* online.

The World Wide Web has significantly transformed the REI business. The Internet provides endless possibilities on how to market to your target audience. It can give your business immediate attention, create networking opportunities, generate consistent leads and rapidly propel your real estate business to the top.

You can use the Internet to present a credible image of both yourself and your business. It's also great way to create viable business contacts.

The best part about using the Internet to market your business is that you can create immense visibility without spending a lot of money.

If You Don't Have an Online Presence, You Don't Exist.

Benefits of Putting You and Your business Online

- Availability: Being online means being found everywhere by investors, buyers and sellers who are looking to connect with you.

- Networking opportunities: These include Facebook, LinkedIn, Twitter, YouTube, Google+ and About.me, just to name a few.

- Credibility: These days, if you don't have a website, people don't trust that you are a legitimate business.

- Communicate with potential customers in a timely and effective manner–through your website and Facebook.

The REI business is a very competitive industry, so you need to be constantly evolving with the times. Below I will give you great marketing tools you can incorporate into your tactics to generate those leads and help you achieve greater success!

Top 7 Online Marketing Tools and Tactics

Website

If you want to build your REI business, you need to have a website. Today, having a web site is more important than having a business card and as important as having a cell phone.

Here are 7 benefits of having a website:

1. People can find you easily in the search engines when looking for someone like you.

2. Drive people to your site so they can learn more about you, your products and services—and the solutions your business provides to help people fix their problems.

3. Increase visibility by getting your brand out there.

4. Capture leads for your business while you sleep! Your business can be open 24-7- 365 days of the year. I will share my squeeze page link with you so can see an example and be inspired by it www.HighProfitProperties.ca

5. You can send potential investors to your website to show them what your company is about and learn more about the great investment opportunities you offer.

6. A website provides an inexpensive form of advertising. Today there are many website templates available through companies like Godaddy, WordPress, Google and Wix that you can use to build your own website without issue. You can also hire a professional to create a great site. Whatever you chose, make sure your website looks professional, conveys trust and markets your REI business effectively. A poorly designed website can have a terrible effect on your business and your credibility, so if you don't have experience in website design, I recommend you get a professional to do it. As an example, you can check out these websites: www.needtosellmyhousefast.com, www.SpaceInvest.ca.

7. A website can offer you the opportunity to network with other businesses. For instance, you can offer a directory of complemen-

tary businesses such as insurance agents, mortgage brokers, etc., and they can reciprocate.

Keep in mind that having a website will not automatically generate leads. You will still need to promote your website through other online channels such as social media, press releases, eBooks and networking in order to generate steady leads for your business.

Google

Google search engine has 3 billion local searches every month, so you most definitely want to increase your visibility on the biggest search engine in the world.

This can be done with **Google AdWords** campaigns in which customers can quickly find you when searching on Google for the things your business offers.

Google AdWords campaigns are a great tactic to gain online visibility and attract more of the right visitors to your website and generate sales. These are also affordable because you pay only when people click on your ad to visit your website.

Google Alerts allows you to monitor and get notifications on all **content** activities related to your business on the Internet. Those activities can be on websites, news articles, forums, blogs and videos. For example, when people type in "Looking for income properties," or "Need to sell my house fast," you will get an email so you can jump on the opportunity to help those people and land yourself a deal.

YouTube

YouTube is the second biggest social media site in the world. One of the most effective ways to get noticed on the Internet is to make powerful videos about your business, products and services. You can use a regular camera or your phone to record your video. Just make sure the quality is reflective of your business.

1. A video can easily convey your message to clients that matter to you and have an effect from any other form of media. It's a more

direct and genuine way to connect with your target audience. It engages people and allows you to build trust with potential investors, buyers and sellers.

2. Creating a connection with your prospects can be more important than giving them literature to read. People prefer to watch an engaging video instead of reading 1000 words of data and sales pitches. There is no better way to connect with your prospects than with face-to-face video conversations on what interests them.

3. A video is also a great method to showcase the products and services your business offers. It can make you stand out from the competition by providing explanations on why people should work with you, what makes you different and how you can provide clients with great results.

4. You can register your own Youtube channel—it's easy to do. Just register, pick a name, and you're good to go. You can make detailed videos on properties you are selling. Buying a home is not just a numbers game. Potential homebuyers want to know what the house looks like from the inside out. They even want to know what the neighborhood and surroundings look like. If the house is to their liking and the numbers fit, they will contact you. This saves you time and weeds out customers that simply don't fit with a particular property. By viewing the home first, people will already know whether they like what they see and want to see more. This gives you a better chance to land the deal.

5. Video testimonials are a great way to show potential customers that your business provides a needed service. They can also show potential customers that you have a good track record and help build credibility for you and your brand.

6. Having a YouTube video will help your business show up on search results and give you multiple page results on Google and other search engines.

Social Media

Facebook is the number one social media site in the world. People spend literally hours chatting with friends, checking out local businesses and what their friends have to say about them. Facebook pages show up when people are searching for your business on Google, giving you a chance to show your **Facebook fan page** on the search results in addition to your website.

LinkedIn has close to 100-million members who use the site to find other businesses and business owners to work with. LinkedIn is one the best places to be found online. It is an effective networking tool that allows you to connect with other Investors, private lenders and potential customers. It may sound obvious, but it's very important that you have a nice profile written and a good picture.

About.me is a great place where you can create a movie poster about yourself for free. When people Google you, your About.me website will show up, on the first page sometimes, and people get to read about you and your business.

Google + is another effective way to create a business page for your company. It can help you close more deals. You can also put your YouTube videos and LinkedIn information on Google+, which multiplies the reach.

Email Marketing

Email marketing has one of the highest returns on investment of any marketing media. It is a great way to deliver your sales message and reach out to new potential customers.

Building a list of prospects for your REI business is vital. A list of investors, buyers, sellers, moneylenders and joint venture potential partners is essential for your real estate business growth.

Here are a few ways to build your lists:

- Find people doing what you are doing, create a list and see how you can joint venture with them.

- Give away a free gift. Show it on social media so people can go to your website to get it, give their name and email address and join your list.

- Use Google AdWords or place ads in newspapers and in free sites like Craigslist, Kijiji, and eBay and give something away of value, such as an eBook, a video or a report.

You can build massive email marketing lists that you send out all at once, or they can be tailored to a designated group of people. You can also send individual lists for a specific type of property or personalized feel that includes the names of your customers.

You can use an auto responder—a simple yet effective marketing tool that allows you to build lists of names and email addresses and then automatically sends a series of emails to your target market on a regular basis. It can also automatically deliver property information upon request or deliver your sales messages at a number of predetermined times after you have identified your prospects.

Some of the main players are:

- *AWeber*

- *MailChimp*

- *Constant Contact*

- *iContact*

The benefits of automating your marketing system:

- Drive traffic to your website, video channel or blog.

- Continuous marketing without hiring people.

- Generates leads and repeat sales.

- Helps you build relationships with clients.

- Cost savings and time efficiency.

- Measures response rates and results easily.

- Allows you to brand yourself with all the e-mails.

With the rapid growth of mobile devices, the popularity of email marketing is only going to increase.

Search Engine Optimization (SEO)

This is the process of getting traffic search results on search engines so when people search for certain services, your website or video will show on the first page of search engines such as Google, Yahoo and Bing.

SEO can boost your sales exponentially. Good SEO is about making sure your website has great content—key words matter, title and links matter in search rankings. Get a professional to set it up for you in the right way.

Some good companies are:

- Boostability

- Digital Current

- ThinkBIGsites.com

Craigslist

Craigslist has over 700 local websites in 70 different countries. It's one of the largest and most popular buying and selling platforms in the world. And it's free!

You can run your real estate ad campaigns to inform people about your products and services or give away a gift to drive traffic to your landing page, which will help you build your list. You can also track your ad statistics to help you determine which ads get more responses.

Now it's your turn to use these marketing technics and online tools, and watch your REI business grow like never before!

Before I say goodbye, I want to give you my eBook, *Cash Flow Investors*, to take with you on your real estate investing journey. To receive it right now, go to www.SpaceInvest.ca/cfi

About Kotty Kihara

Although Kotty Kihara was raised in Montreal, Canada, she has lived in many parts of the world, including Peru, Alberta, Los Angeles and Europe. She has been in sales and marketing for over 20 years and has worked for the largest telecomm company in Canada as a Project Manager and Marketing Associate Director for 15 years. Kotty dove into real estate investing in 2006, and since then it has become her passion. Although she enjoyed working for different companies, she wanted to put her real estate investing and marketing expertise to work to build a business that not only stimulated her, but also helped other people obtain financial freedom. Since then, she has grown her REI and marketing consulting business and has helped many people make money in real estate investing and grow their businesses. She believes that REI is one of the best and most profitable businesses in the world.

DO YOU SEE IT?

By Dinesh Bharuchi

This chapter is an excerpt from my book, G.A.M.E of Wealth. Here you will learn key concepts in Goal Setting: What millionaires do without even knowing it.

If it weren't a critical step to your success, why would we give it its own chapter? What do you want? What are you passionate about? What makes you feel great when you're involved? If you think this part is a waste of time, please ask for a refund because you are definitely in the wrong section. The defined goal is to provide a means to create a specific outcome. Your goal must be clearly defined if you really want to achieve it. *This is step 1 in the creation process.*

You need to set goals, but there is a definite method to setting them. Which method works for you will depend on what feels right. Always remember to follow your feelings when it comes to goal setting.

There are three types of feelings, but only two of them have creative influence in your life. Keep in mind you are now connecting feelings with goals, an important nuance in the creation process.

Having a neutral feeling about anything is neither creative nor destructive and therefore will not impact you in your creation process. This is rare, however, as almost everyone has some feeling about almost any subject matter, consciously or unconsciously. Having a negative feeling about your goal along with the intensity of the feeling, will most certainly impact the speed at which you will achieve your goal. Having a positive feeling about your goal along with the intensity of the feeling, will most certainly impact the speed at which you will achieve your goal.

So it's clear both negative and positive feelings about your goal affect the speed at which you achieve your goal. Your feelings either slow the process or speed up the process. The stronger your negative feelings, the slower the creation process, and the stronger your positive feeling, the faster the creation process. You need a very strong positive WHY! *This is step 2 in the creation process.*

Your feelings can originate from your ego's desire or your heart's desire; ego-based feelings ultimately lead to conflict and chaos. You will know when your feeling is ego-based because you will feel physically weak and need to justify your decision. Heart-based feelings lead to understanding and cooperation. You will know when your feeling is heart-based because you will feel physically strong and have no hesitation.

Your feelings directly impact your personal power. Your personal power is what you use daily to accomplish tasks that lead to your goal. This is not the tasks themselves, but the confidence in moving forward with each step. *This is step 3 in the creation process.*

Now isn't that interesting? Your personal power, negative or positive, has a direct correlation to the success of your goals. Keep in mind that personal power has nothing to do with being arrogant or obnoxious. Personal power is all about stepping into who you are and not being what others want you to be. You have rules you live by, integrity, and you have a moral code of conduct. You have a clear understanding of change and that you must be part of that change as long as you are true to yourself.

Immediately the thought of many successful people who seem to be careless in their lives will come to mind. Successful people who abuse their power and who are arrogant or obnoxious seem to exist everywhere. What makes them successful is that they are congruent within themselves. They believe that what they do and how they behave is their right. Therefore they are in their personal power. Their feelings about their wants and desires are in line with their value systems, and therefore they achieve their goals. History tells us of people who rose to power and led with an iron fist. They were all congruent within themselves. They believed they were in the right and that they had moral authority to behave the way they did. There is a Karmic response to every action, but that is another topic in and of itself. What's important to know is you are the creator, and it's all about your feelings and personal power or congruent nature.

A good friend once mentioned all the things he wanted from life. Asking him what he was willing to give up in return for all these things brought about an intensely strange look. Yes, you could just see it all over his face. You mean you have to *give something up* to get what you want into your life? This was a hard concept to grasp for my friend, as no one had every said this before.

So there's a house that's amazing, and you see yourself living in it. How can you create this as a goal and achieve it? It's all about following the process. Be aware there is this unseen give and take. The better words are *give and receive* to describe this unseen force. It's like the law of gravity: We can't see this thing called the law of gravity, but we can see the effects of it. Same thing is true for the law of give and receive. You cannot see the law of give and receive, but you can feel its positive or negative effect in the life you live. There is always an exchange, and this universe is based on this unseen give and receive law. Up/Down, Right/Left, North/South, Hot/Cold, Positive/Negative, Give/Receive are just a few ways to understand the law of Give and Receive, or as another way it is known, the Law of Opposites. These opposites exist, and this is a fundamental truth in our existence: You must give something to receive something. In order to reach your goals, regardless of the size, you must do something. There is action required, and if you follow each step correctly, it will feel like effortless action, but there will be action nonetheless, or the Give element. You must do something to get something. You can never win the lottery if you never purchase a ticket. Action will always be required. *This is step 4 in the creation process.*

So how does it work and what does this have to do with your Goals and making more money or getting the house of your dreams? When you have a clear understanding of giving and receiving, you will have a clearer understanding of how you attract your goals into your life. What exactly are you giving, and how does this impact greater earnings or your dream home? How this process impacts greater earning will be described in full in the complete book, "G.A.M.E. of Wealth." For now, we continue to focus on setting goals. Giving has very specific requirements and will, in most cases, require you to rewire your brain. OK, relax–it's simple, but just not easy. Most people give in hopes that they will also receive from the person at a future date. This is conditional giving. You simply entered into a mental contract that states: I have given him or her a gift, a kind gesture, a piece of good advice or something that displayed an act of kindness. He/She is now beholden to me and therefore must reciprocate the same level of goodwill or greater. If this does not happen, then I will be hurt. This is a mental contract that ties your emotional stability to another person's actions or inactions. If you are ever hurt in this manner, you are conditioned to experience pain as a result of your mental contract(s).

This is the beginning where reconditioning the mind is necessary. So what does this mean? You start immediately by setting up new rules in your subconscious. The function of this chapter is not to get into deep psychology of remapping your thought for success, but I can tell you it is something that is part of your absolute success. When you give, as explained above, you have shot an arrow. The power of the arrow is purely based on your thought process at the time the arrow was launched and previous mental conditioning. So what is the correct state to have the maximum power when launching the arrow? Your actions must be pure and without hidden motives. *This is step 5 in the creation process.*

The second you have broken any of these conditions, you have established a contract, and your arrow is weakened; so is the outcome of your goal. The result will be hurt, anger or simply a sense of imbalance and weakness. You have to remember that how you feel is entirely up to you to decide regardless of external circumstances. So what do you do? You must feel good about everything you do. When giving, you must not have any expectations in return except the absolute understanding of your worth. Do it from the heart or just don't do it. Ask yourself the following question every time you're looking for an answer. "Is this decision for my highest and best good?" Wait for the feeling to guide you in making the best choice and follow it. *This is step 6 in the creation process.* It will be an immediate response. If you think about your response, you just gave your ego permission to add its two cents, and the result will most likely be a bad choice. This is a learned process, and you will need to do this all the time to perfect the positive impact of following your initial feelings.

How about that dream home as a goal? What exactly do you need to give? The law of giving and receiving does not state what you need to give from your heart. Holding a door open for someone or helping an elderly person cross the street, helping at the local food bank or making a donation to a worthy cause are all acts GIVING. Creating a system that allows people to achieve a new level of financial success is also an act of giving. You may ask how this is giving when there is a price attached. When the perceived value of what is received is greater than the cost, it is also an act of giving. The law will continue to tally these acts, and they become your positive balance. You must remember never to think about it in this way; otherwise you are connecting the law directly to a contract and it becomes null and void. *This is step 7 in the creation process.*

Continue to build your positive bank balance with the law of giving and remember always to feel good. In a time, not in our control, we will receive in accordance with what we have given, and it's tallied against your desired goal. The thing is, the law actually gives a bit more than what you give, so over time, you will be further and further ahead. Now understanding the rules and not acting because of the gain is the trick. You can manifest or create anything you want simply by following the goal-setting process that feels right for you.

Achieving your goals is directly related to the nature of your giving. It's that simple.

So what are your goals, and how do you define them? Goals can be in the form of a dream home, a car, a vacation, a stereo system, meeting a perfect mate or perhaps having a large surplus bank balance. In every case you must be as specific as possible. Use each of your five senses when you think about each goal. The sixth sense is your emotional state. Begin listing, in writing, each of your goals. Now, for each goal you will describe each one in some level of detail along with incorporating each of the five senses along with the sixth sense. By writing them down (and please do it with a blue pen), you will have started the manifesting process. Read your goals and feel the feelings of receiving and having now what you are focused on in your goal.

Life is so much fun when you know how to play the G.A.M.E. of Wealth.

Defining your goals and starting the creation process:

Step 1 – Clearly define your Goals. Be specific, but leave a bit of room.

Step 2 – Make sure you have a very strong "Why" when defining your goals.

Step 3 – Personal Power or confidence to move forward with each step.

Step 4 – Effortless action.

Step 5 – Your work must be pure and without hidden motives.

Step 6 – Understanding the right feeling.

Step 7 – Give without expectation.

Successful people know what they want and take action in the direction of their goals.

Love and Gratitude,
Dinesh Bharuchi – Internet Marketing Coach & Online Educator

About Dinesh Bharuchi

Dinesh Bharuchi is an internet marketing coach, online educator, and happily married father of three. He is a graduate in Electrical and Electronic Technology with over 25 years of internet experience, 10 years of project management and 5 years teaching experience. He walked away from a lucrative career to venture into the online business arena. Dinesh is now one of only 20,000 people globally who receive a payment directly from Google every single month because of his marketing expertise. He has created multiple streams of income through various online marketing methods including selling products, selling services, and selling nothing. His passion is now to help existing online business owners and start-ups to reach their goals through www.InternetTrainingSecrets.com.

You are invited to register for access to the free training videos. Each video is designed to help you become computer savvy and prepare you for financial freedom by creating your very own online business. Successful people know what they want and take action in the direction of their goals. All readers of this chapter are encouraged to email Dinesh@ InternetTrainingSecrets.com for a free 30-minute consultation on your current online presence or online business goals.

THE HOME STAGE ADVANTAGE

By Nicky Lehwald

Introduction

First, I would like to congratulate you on making the choice to make changes in your life, for that's what this book is about–changing and transforming your life. While most of the profound change you can do is from within, your environment also plays a very big part in supporting you in both your willingness to change and in helping you to sustain the changes you make. As you go through this process, remember that FUN is the operative word. We are going to make change FUN!!

In this chapter, my primary goal (aside from fun) is to help you begin to feel confident in decorating or designing your home so that you can create a space that fulfills you, inspires you, supports you and most of all, helps you to create a home that you love coming home to. In this chapter, I will also share with you a few simple rules to help you achieve these goals, the most important of which is: Unless you love it, don't bring it into your house.

Rather than ramble on needlessly, I'll give you as much information as I can in one chapter in order to help you achieve your goals and help you win! Let's get this party started!

Step #1: Less is More (aka de-clutter, de-clutter, de-clutter)

Ok, I'll be honest with you: Here's where most of my clients have their biggest challenge, de-cluttering. I can almost guarantee you that you have too much stuff; most people do. I too have collected too much stuff in the past and didn't realize how much I had until I had to move about a year ago. I could not believe how much stuff I had! A lot of it was stored in cupboards, closets or in the basement and garage, and I hadn't seen or used it in years. I was equally amazed at how free I felt when I got rid of all the things that were covered in dust or that I forgot I had. I felt like the weight of the world had been lifted off my shoulders and I felt lighter somehow. It felt amazing! So how do you decide what to get rid of?

Sort, Sift and Separate

First, create three different areas or boxes to sort things into: 1) Things to Keep, 2) Things to Donate and 3) Things to Throw Away or Recycle.

1.) Things to Keep

The basic rule here is if you haven't seen or used it in more than 6 months, then you should just get rid of it. Now I realize that some of the things have sentimental value, but you have to be careful with this because before you know it, *everything* has sentimental value, so you end up keeping it all and getting nowhere. Be really diligent with yourself, and it may even be helpful to have a friend or significant other help you through this process to ask you this question, "Do you need it or do you want it?" When you're truly honest with yourself, you'll find most of the time that you don't *need* the item (especially if it has an inch of dust on it). Then you think, "But Aunt Martha gave that to me, and I don't want to hurt her feelings by getting rid of it." My advice is get rid of it. Do you really like dusting it anyway? Probably not, because it's covered in dust! In fact, there's so much dust on it, you can't even tell what it is without wiping it off! I think you get the picture.

2.) Things to Donate

There are going to be those items that you know right away that you don't want to keep, i.e., the clothes you still have in the closet with the really big shoulder pads in them or that are covered in sequins, the high school or college books you haven't read in eons (and probably didn't even open), or the mounds of "extra" towels or linens you have in case you have a family reunion and they need to stay over. Let's face it–nobody dresses like Madonna did in the 80's anymore, and if she can move on and change her look, so can you! Besides, Halloween is coming up, and the local Salvation Army or Goodwill can make some money selling your stuff as a prize-winning costume! Ok, so I know I'm being a bit of a smart aleck here, but consider that I have seen many closets and heard many excuses from clients as to why they keep the things they do. It may sound ridiculous, but when it comes to "cleaning out your closet," I have seen people literally start to hyper-ventilate. There is no need to have anxiety over cleaning out a closet. Consider that you could potentially be helping somebody else by donating your slightly used items to charity of your choice (i.e., Goodwill, the Salvation Army, Habitat for Humanity, Women's Shelters, churches, etc.) or even bring other people joy because they either want or need the items that you had forgotten about in the closet.

3.) Things to Throw Away or Recycle

While this may seem obvious, I will mention this briefly. These items include those that are broken, severely damaged, worn out, thread bare, stained, or have been used as a chew toy by the dog. No, you don't need it as a rag to clean the car. And after all, how many Tupperware containers that no longer have lids do you really need?

Move forward in baby steps...

Give yourself permission to do it in baby steps and do it in small chunks. The goal here is to set this up like a game and to set the rules so you can win. For example, if you are starting by cleaning out your garage, start in one corner and set an achievable goal for accomplishing it (e.g., sorting and organizing the garden tools). Do not feel you have to do it all in one day or even have that expectation of yourself. Most people fail to achieve their goals when they take on too much at once and then, when they can't accomplish everything they planned, feel overwhelmed and have thoughts of "this can't be done" or "this it too hard to do"; before they know it, their goal of de-cluttering never happens. Keep in mind that it's taken you years to collect the things in your home, so allow yourself some time to go through your house; be gentle with yourself and set realistic goals so you can win. As you accomplish one small goal at a time, you will keep yourself inspired to keep going. I promise it gets easier as you go and even starts to get fun as you start to let go of these things. Before long, you'll wonder why you kept all this stuff in the first place.

Focus on one area until you are finished.

The easiest way to begin sorting through your things is to go through one room at a time or even just finish what you've started. Even if you have to give yourself an entire week to get through a room, do it. Set aside a specific time or times to accomplish your goal and stick to it. If you set aside an hour, then do it even if you don't feel like it and you end up just sitting in the room for an hour. It's unlikely you'll be able to sit there and not pick up even just a few items to sort through. Again, I realize initially it can be overwhelming, especially if you have a lot of clutter, but remember Rome wasn't built in a day either. Just move one stone at a time and stay focused on that one room or area before you move on to the next one.

The "Only Touch it Once" Rule

I can tell you from experience that this one may take a little practice, but it is such an incredible time-saver, it is well worth becoming efficient at. Essentially the premise behind this rule is that once you pick something up, decide where it goes and then leave it there, so that you're not picking it up and moving the same item several times. This especially happens a lot when you're clearing paper or receipts off of a desk. First decide if you need the document, and if so create a file for it and place it directly in the file holder or cabinet. You can try this method as well when you are sorting into your three groups.

NOTE: If your first impulse is to put the item in the donation or throw away pile, follow your gut and leave it there. Do not second-guess yourself and think of reasons to keep it. Go with your first instinct and avoid listening to the voice in your head that says, "No, wait, I might need that for …." Do yourself a favour: Just put the bag (or statue or sweater or shoes or class notes from high school) down and walk away.

Step #2 – Design Your Space

Now that your space is clear, it's time to decide what you want the room to feel like and what its purpose or function is. Is the room for relaxing, working, eating, or sleeping? If you struggle with figuring out what your style is, get a few decorating or design magazines and mark the pages of the rooms that you like, even if it's only one piece of furniture that you like, the window coverings or even just the color of the room. After going through a few magazines, you can usually get a sense of what works for you and what doesn't. Take notice of how the colours and the general look of the rooms in the pictures make you feel. This is a key to designing a space that you will love.

Live Your Life in Different Colours

Keep in mind that dark colours visually bring the walls in and make the space look smaller; lighter colours visually push the walls out and give the room a feeling of more space. If you really love dark or vivid colours, consider painting only one focal wall in that colour and use a lighter, complimentary colour on the rest of the room. You can then bring that colour in with accessories or artwork to give it balance. I do not recommend painting ceilings other than a flat or eggshell finish (for kitchens and bathrooms) white. The goal is to have the ceiling essentially disappear. If colour is put on the ceiling, it tends to make the room look like a cave and can make it feel claustrophobic, not to mention that if at some point you decide to change the colour of the room, you'll more than likely have to paint the ceiling again too. Semi-gloss and gloss paints tend to reflect light and also make any imperfections in the walls and ceilings more noticeable.

It is a good idea to find one piece of furniture, artwork or accessory that inspires you and select your colours based on that. A colour wheel (available at art supply stores) is a very useful tool in helping you to decide what kind of colour scheme you want to go with and also gives you valuable information about the tints and hues of colours to make the selection process easier.

Window Treatments are not to be Forgotten

Window treatments are also very important to a space, although they tend to be under-rated. Natural light is always best for showcasing paint colours and for our well-being. Recently, California shutters have become very popular, and while they are great for privacy, there are some downsides to them that many people do not consider. Shutters tend to cut down dramatically on the amount of natural light that comes through the window. They can get very dusty and are tedious to clean. When swinging them out to open them fully, they stick out into the room or take up a lot of space to the sides of the windows or sometimes can't be opened completely due to obstruction by furnishings or even bulkheads/valances above the window.

Drapes and blinds can achieve the same result as shutters, but have the advantage of being able to be pulled aside to allow more light in. In addition, drapes can be used as an accessory to add colour and texture to a room and also help to act as a noise buffer, and they also take up less real and visual space. An added benefit to blinds and drapes is that as more and more décor and design stores appear, there are larger selection of economically priced window treatments to suit any budget.

To Tantalize and Surprise, you must Accessorize

The key to creating the *wow* factor in any room is to accessorize with splashes of contrasting colours with items such as throw pillows, artwork, area rugs, candles, vases, small statues or other interesting knick-knacks. Even if you are going for a monochromatic look, you can get your accessories in varying tones of the same colour and still create visual interest. While less is more, you want to find pieces that inspire you, are one of a kind, or make you stop and take notice. Just allow yourself to play, be creative and have fun. You can always return it if it doesn't look quite right in the space.

When selecting artwork, allow yourself to be inspired or moved by a piece. Don't just buy it because it could work in the space, or from the other perspective, don't leave behind a beautiful piece of artwork just because the frame or matting doesn't quite match your style or the look you are trying to achieve. Mat colours can be easily changed to enhance the artwork, and frames are quickly transformed by spray painting them or using distressed painting techniques.

Step # 3 – Light Your Way

Lighting is crucial for any space. You must first determine what type of lighting you need in the room. Do you need task lighting for spaces like the kitchen (you can't chop onions in the dark) or office? Or do you want soft lighting for spaces like the dining room or family room? A light fixture can make or break the design of the room, so take some time to find a fixture you like and make sure it provides the type of lighting you require.

As an example, most people expect to see a chandelier in the dining room, but how often have you seen a small crystal chandelier in the bedroom? Add a dimmer switch, and suddenly you have created a romantic, secluded retreat from the world.

Table lamps and floor lamps also provide different types of light. If you choose a *torchiere* type floor lamp (where the light shines up towards the ceiling), it provides ample lighting for a room as the light reflects off the ceiling, especially in those rooms that have no other light source. Table lamps tend to direct more light towards the table tops and floor, which gives a more ambient, softer kind of light.

A Word about Light Bulbs

Compact fluorescent light bulbs are being phased in, due to being more energy efficient, but wherever possible, I would highly recommend either using 60 watt incandescent light bulbs or finding an alternative to these mini fluorescent bulbs. Firstly, they quite literally alter the colour of paint on the walls, especially the cool white bulbs. You may have a beautiful warm colour on the wall, but these bulbs will wash the colour right out so it looks dull and lifeless and can make it look putrid. There is a reason they don't use these bulbs in restaurants; for example, this lighting can alter the colour of your food so it looks like it has gone bad. Imagine a thick juicy red steak that on your plate looks green. Would you want to eat it or go back to that restaurant if it did?

Secondly, they contain mercury, which we have already been told is a neurotoxin and is highly toxic for the brain, spinal cord, liver and kidneys. Why would you want to put them in your home or later have them end up in landfill sites?

Thirdly, and perhaps most importantly, they have a negative effect on our well-being. Just like the fluorescent tube lighting, these compact fluorescent lights operate at a frequency that has a negative effect on our brain wave patterns. These differences in frequency can cause headaches or even migraines in people. In addition, the light they provide is not as bright as that from incandescent light bulbs. This is especially important for areas where task lighting is required, as insufficient lighting can also lead to headaches.

Fortunately, other lighting alternatives to compact fluorescents are being introduced. Many of the new LED light bulbs are comparable to the incandescent bulbs, and while the LEDs may have a higher price point than incandescent bulbs, they also have a much longer life span and are also energy efficient, so they can help you save money in the long run.

Conclusion

Whatever your design tastes or style, you can have a home that you love to come home to and that supports you in who you are and your well-being. It's true that change and personal growth comes from the inside out, but unless your outer environment supports you and your inner game, it will be harder for you to achieve your goals. When you let go of the clutter and create a space that is free for energy and ideas to flow, everything just works better. I wish you every success and happiness on your journey and life path. Namaste.

About Nicky Lehwald

Nicky Lehwald is a dynamic, fun-loving entrepreneur, interior designer, decorator and stager. She has owned and operated her own business, BNC Designs, since 2007. She has helped hundreds of clients to prepare their homes for sale and/or re-decorate their houses to help them create their dream home. Her clients often make comments like, "It looks like a brand new house," or "You have created my dream home!"

Her results speak for themselves. Over 90% of the homes she has helped to transform and stage have sold over asking and within a week or two of being put on the market. Many of her clients who have had staging done have said they wished they had done the work before considering selling their homes so that they could have had time to enjoy it, and they often hire her to redecorate the new homes they are moving into.

Nicky has a natural talent for creating spaces in fun and exciting new ways and often uses décor items in unexpected ways. She believes in empowering people to have the confidence to decorate their own homes. Her only rule ... "If you don't love it, don't put it in your home."

OPENING YOUR DOOR TO FINANCIAL SUCCESS

By Philip Hoy

Have you ever dreamt of owning a beautiful home in one of the finest street locations either in your local town, city, or somewhere else in the world? What about owning multiple properties? I am sure that many of you are wondering how this can be achieved in today's economic climate, where it feels that it requires two or more incomes to be able to afford one property. It takes time, but it *can* happen.

To quote Robert G. Allen, "Don't wait to buy real estate. Buy real estate and wait."

As a consumer, real estate offers you a shelter, a place to live with the potential for future price appreciation and equity growth in the property; however, as an investor, real estate offers not only shelter for the tenants residing at your property, but also the potential for you to gain wealth by having your tenants essentially pay for your investment property through the rental income collected. The property price appreciation and/or equity growth enables the investor to utilize these funds to purchase additional properties. Repeat this process again and again, and you'll notice that your dreams of owning that special property or whatever it may be can come true.

In this chapter, I would like to share my insights and key considerations that you as an investor must be aware of in order to become successful in real estate investing. They are as follows:

The Investor Mindset

"Don't make what you do about the money" – quote from the famous redneck millionaire, Jim Shead

Do you have the right mindset as a real estate investor? Why are you interested in real estate as an investment vehicle when there are other ways to invest to make money? Are you willing to dedicate time, commitment to managing your business? What is your business plan? Are you willing to make a difference as a real estate investor?

Discussions on "mindset" seem to be the very first topic raised by mentors. Some of my mentors, whom I am truly blessed to know and continue to learn from, are Robert G. Allen, Jim Shead, and Sunil Tulsiani. They not only helped me obtain clarity in my mind and business, but also to give back and make a difference in the communities that I invest in. Ensure you understand the reasons why you want to invest in this business.

Education

"If you do what you always done, you'll get what you always got." – quote from the famous redneck millionaire, Jim Shead.

One of the best ways to learn about real estate investing is to join a local RE (Real Estate) club, an RE association, or hire and learn from a mentor. My journey into real estate investing commenced approximately four years after the great United States housing crash. Foreclosures and auctions were aplenty. The savvy marketers were out in full force promoting great opportunities to purchase properties at up to 70% discount from the previous highs. I took notice and educated myself on how to purchase US properties. I learned about why and how the crash happened, the buying opportunities as an investor, demographic changes, the migration of baby boomers, millennia and echo boomers, setting up and structuring my business, developing a Power Team, financing, taxation and many more tidbits.

I absorbed as much information provided by my mentoring group as I could and took action by purchasing my first two US properties through my business entity. You too can do what I did, and perhaps in a much shorter time period than the six months it took me to make my first purchase. Remember, education is key to making informed decisions.

Creating your Business Plan and Structure

Wikipedia defines a **business plan** as a "formal statement of a set of **business** goals, the reasons they are believed attainable, and the **plan** for reaching those goals. It may also contain background information about the organization or team attempting to reach those goals."

The business plan and your business structure is your roadmap. It will enable you to keep focus on your short and long-term goals and the returns that your investments are projected to target for a defined period of time. This plan becomes an important tool as you seek financing for your investments.

The structure of your business needs to take into consideration whether you need to create Trusts, Limited Liability Companies, Limited Partnerships, and/or Corporations. Before you venture into your first property, ensure your business structure is in place. Speak to accredited tax accountants, tax lawyers, etc., on the best way to arrange your structure in the most tax-efficient manner.

Creating your Power Team

Teamwork enables you to accomplish your RE goals much quicker. It is important, as you build your Power Team, that you have key members who understand your goals and needs. The relationship must be a win-win so that everyone is compensated and paid for their participation. Key members of your Team include: realtors (Bird dogs), title companies, Escrow companies, Insurance companies, RE lawyers, financial lenders, home inspectors, tradespeople, property managers and accountants.

Understanding your Exit Strategy

There is a likelihood that not all of your property deals will be the same each time. One aspect that you should always ask yourself is, "What's my exit strategy for this property/investment?" In the event that I need to access cash immediately, do I sell or re-finance? It is important to have thought it through should circumstances change and you are required to execute your exit strategy.

Financing the deal

Whether it is your personal finances funding the real estate, institutional or private money lender funds, it is important to have this arranged ahead of time so that you can have access to it immediately to lock in your deal. As the saying goes "The one that ties up the property first wins."

Finding the Deal

"There's never a wrong time to invest if you chose the right strategy." –quote from Sunil Tulsiani

Instead of jumping all over the map, focus on one geographical area for investing when you are first starting out. The reason for this is that you will need to replicate your Power Teams in the other locations if they are not from the same town or city.

Once you locate a property and it makes good financial sense (the rate of return on the investment meets your criteria), tie the property up so that no one else can take it from under you while the due diligence is being performed. Place clauses such as:

"Subject to" clause–"Buyer agrees to purchase the property subject to...." This is your escape clause should any of the following conditions not meet your criteria.

Inspection clause–"Buyer agrees to remove the clause regarding the property condition within 7 days of the signed contract after completion of a home inspection for which they are satisfied with."

Due diligence clause—normally 14 days to complete. Due diligence means taking caution, performing calculations, reviewing documents, walking the property, etc.—essentially doing your homework for the property BEFORE you actually make the purchase. If there are too many issues with the property—and that means too much potential risk and cost—then you can cancel your purchase agreement and look for a better property.

Special stipulations–contingencies.

While there are many other clauses that you can likely use, just remember to include the critical ones that will enable you time to complete your due diligence.

Negotiating the Deal

Remember to "listen" and understand the situation of the seller. Although you want to obtain the lowest price for the deal, remember to make it a win-win. Trying to understand the seller's situation and determining whether you can help that seller may be the one aspect that tips the scale in your favour, especially if there are others who want the same property.

Closing on the property

Once you are satisfied that the property is a good investment, the next step is to close the transaction so that the property changes hands over to you and your business. In the USA, the closing activity can vary with the use of title companies and/or real estate lawyers. Ensure that you have purchased adequate insurance coverage for your investment properties.

Repairs

General maintenance and upkeep is important to retain tenants in your properties, maintaining property insurance, and equity appreciation. Keeping handymen and ladies in your Power Team or with the property management team to perform repairs on your properties makes smart business sense.

Finding suitable tenants

Advertising and screening for suitable tenants can be an exhausting and time-consuming activity. It is best to leave this with knowledgeable people within your Power Team (i.e., Property Management team) to perform this function. This becomes even more important when you are an out-of-town investor like me. I left it up to the pros, which enabled me to focus on what matters the most–search and evaluate other good deals.

Managing the properties and portfolio

Sure, you can do this yourself; however, would you *like* to receive calls at any hour of the day and night to fix things? This is where the value of the property management team really shines. They not only collect the rental cheques, deposit the monies into your business account, look after the maintenance on your property, but can also perform other administrative activities (for a nominal fee) such as paying your property taxes, generating rental and expense summaries.

Searching for a reputable property manager is worth your time and effort. They are an essential and vital partner within your Team that can make or break the ongoing success of your returns on your investment.

Replicating your system

You have now taken the leap and have purchased your first investment property. Now, re-examine all of the major steps that you had to take to make it happen, including the landmines which you faced and resolved. This is your system! If you were capable of doing this once, do you think you can repeat this for another property? Remember that the key to creating long-term wealth in real estate is to continue, replicate, and purchase more investment properties.

Protecting yourself from economic downturns

Every investor understands that unexpected downturns can occur in any investment sector. To minimize this risk, the successful RE-investor may invest into multi-unit properties (i.e., duplex or 4-plex units) to decrease the tenant vacancy concern, or pay down debt more quickly to own the property free and clear.

Annual Reports, Licenses, Tax Filings

Depending on where you are conducting your real estate business, ensure you understand the rules for filing your annual reports, renewal of business licenses, and filing your personal and business tax returns on time. Ensure that you document and keep all of your receipts as proof of business expenses. Your professional and certified tax accountant plays an important role here to ensure that all pertinent deductions are used, the tax filings are properly done, and that you do not overpay in taxes.

Paying it Forward

You're now an experienced real estate investor. Do you remember how you felt a few years ago when you didn't know the first thing about real estate? Is this as good a time as any for you to contribute back to your community? Imagine teaching others to invest successfully from your proven system? Consider paying it forward.

About Philip Hoy

Philip Hoy is an active real estate investor. He currently owns properties in Canada and the south-eastern United States. Philip attributes his passion for real estate investing to the trainings provided by Robert G. Allen, Jim Shead, and Sunil Tulsiani of Private Investment Club.

Philip continues to invest in USA properties and providing affordable renovated homes for his tenants to live in. With his real estate investing successes, he plans to pay it forward by mentoring others within his community so that they too can enjoy the rewards that real estate investing can bring.

In his spare time, Philip enjoys spending time with his wife, Marie-Claire (author and entrepreneur) at their second home situated by the water on Lake Ontario. Philip and Marie-Claire currently reside in Toronto, Canada, but divide their time between the two properties.

THOUGHTS ARE THINGS

Your 5 Step Guide
To
Bringing ONLY Good Things into Your Life

By Roman Turlo

Would you be surprised to learn that you CAN have everything you want—right now? No matter what circumstances you find yourself in, you can change your future in this very moment. Does this sound too good to be true? Of course it does. Because that is how you, and the majority of the world, has been conditioned to think.

But this does not have to be your fate! With a very simple mindset change, you can truly have everything your heart desires—for real. Just follow this five-step process and I guarantee you will begin to see extraordinary changes in your life almost immediately.

1. MAPPING

Your Starting Point

Start by identifying where you are right now. If you are not clear on your starting point, you'll have little chance of getting where you want to go. Besides, knowing where you are will assist you in determining the optimal, easiest and most joyful path toward inner peace and tranquility of the mind.

Ask yourself if you are you currently living each day stressed, worried about finances, your health (or that of a loved one)? Do you spend your day watching the clock, trying to pack everything you have to do into one seemingly too-short day?

Take some time to figure out where you are now, especially in the world of thought and feeling. You are where you are—and that's okay, because you cannot actually be anywhere else.

The important question is, "Where do you want to go?"

Dedicate some time to reflect on what you are currently experiencing in your emotional realm. What is your predominant state of being? Are you happy? Are you stressed? Are you anxious or in fear of losing something? Identify your mood. Determine how much time you spend in your typical "mood." Have people around you labeled you as being a certain way? If so, ask them why.

Now that you have done this, what are you actually *feeling*? For some, this might be a little challenging because you have spent much of your life describing and explaining why you are the way you are. As well, you likely spend more time enrolling others in their point of view than looking at your own. As a result, you have little time to envision where you want to go.

The bigger question now is, "Do you really want to continue to feel this way?" What are you getting from your current attitude? We all get something from our actions or we wouldn't continue to do what we do—good or bad. Is the result of your current state of mind positive or negative? Decide!

Now decide how you *want* to feel. You really do get to choose. Just like how you would look up an unknown city on a map, look at the *Emotional Guidance Scale* I have provided and choose where you want to be. Moving up the scale is possible, like climbing up a tree, but you must do it one branch at a time. And like climbing a tree, you will never get to the top in one motion, so enjoy each step along the way.

Remember, where you are *now* is not an indicator of where you can be. If that were the case on the physical plane, no one would be travelling anywhere.

So how do you change the way you feel? *You change the way you think!* Change the thoughts you offer yourself and others. Have less resistance in those thoughts. Soften them—make them more positive. To do this, you will need to become aware of every thought you think.

The next step toward serenity is to monitor your thoughts daily, if not hourly or every minute.

2. MONITOR

Your Emotions are your Guide

Be super vigilant at monitoring your emotions. And, stop blaming others for your thoughts and feelings. Then you can pinpoint where you are on the *Emotional Guidance Scale (EGS)*. You can then tell if you are on or off course—much like a thermostat that tells you it if it's too hot or too cold in your house.

Ask yourself the following questions:

1. What *is* your typical emotional temperature?

2. Are you happy satisfied and fulfilled?

3. Are you depressed and isolated?

4. Are you raging hot and out of control?

5. Are you open and allowing or perhaps loving and at peace?

Much like the GPS in your car, your emotions are accurate indicators of how you are doing, where you are, and how well you are lining up with the *real you,* not just how you have come to see yourself. Get to know your "true self," not your "false self."

The emotions we feel (happy, sad, frustrated, angry etc.) are all "controllable." Only **you** are in charge of what you feel. Too often people put the responsibility of their feelings onto others.

The following are common misnomers that are often deeply ingrained in our psyche.

1. Your emotions were never intended to be a reason for you to continue practicing your dominant feelings and then using these feelings as a way to justify why you criticize or punish other people for their actions or feelings.

2. Your emotions are not the reason why you should continuously engage in the "blame game" and dwell on what has happened in the past or on what someone else has just said to you, or about you.

3. Your emotions are not intended to rationalize why you are where you are in life or why you will most likely stay there.

4. Your *state of being* is a valuable asset. It must be monitored and protected. Any emotional upset means that you have opted out of being YOU—being in harmony with YOU.

5. Your *natural* state of being resonates peace, love, joy, and empowerment. Many people believe they have to work hard to earn these higher-level vibrational feelings. And those outer conditions—something outside of themselves—create their inner state of being. Perhaps something in the physical plane is not quite working out or measuring up. But nothing is further from the truth.

6. Your *state of being* is totally your responsibility and *your* business. Other peoples' states of being are strictly *their* business. Trying to make others happy, especially when you are not, is like paddling upstream. Eventually you will become exhausted. So do *not* make other people's business your own. From now on, when interacting with the people in your life, just resonate happiness and see what happens. If someone criticizes you in the middle of your joyfulness, then decide what you will focus on.

Simply *notice* their comment! Even if you are caught a little bit off guard, you can still just sit back and notice what gets stirred up in you. What buttons are being pushed in you? *Be* with those feelings. This will be hard at first because we are so conditioned to "stuff" our feelings or, for a lack of a better word, "vomit" them onto others with no regard. When you can simply allow yourself to feel, whether good or bad, you can then objectively determine if that feeling is necessary and why. And even if you determine the emotion is justified, perhaps anger, you need to understand, *that* feeling is only going to hurt you. If the feelings you consistently have are anything but positive—joy, happiness, gratitude or love—you will never reach a point of true serenity in your life.

Your full presence. your pure and objective observation, will make a huge difference in what you ultimately experience. How you consciously experience yourself is of great value.

Imagine what it would be like if you could actually **choose** to totally opt out of reacting to anything, no matter what is happening around you.

Being aware that *you* have a choice allows, you to **monitor** your state of being. If you notice yourself being happy and later notice yourself dipping into a lower vibrational feeling (a negative emotion), you will know that your hands are still on the steering wheel and how to adjust in order to stay in the middle of your emotional road.

For most people who get 'triggered' by the actions of others, the spark and the downward spiral tends to be automatic—usually igniting in a millisecond and it quickly cascades out of *conscious* control. A co-worker, for instance, can make an off-hand comment that you take to mean something (that it may not even actually mean) and you switch from being happy to angry before you even realize what has transpired.

Your goal is to bring your thoughts from the unconscious realm into a conscious domain because when you are conscious you can actually *interrupt* the ensuing sequence of events.

If you hammer a nail and accidently smash your thumb, you get immediate feedback and become aware of your mistake. Would you not then pause, reflect, and recalibrate your next action, making every effort not to do it again?

On the mental plane what you want to get good at is being able to recalibrate your t*houghts,* which have a feeling component to them that then influences your actions.

Thoughts *are* things.

Once a thought gets focused into existence; it vibrates. The universe has no choice but to respond to it, bringing to you more of the same vibration.

Thoughts are hard to isolate and identify at first. Over time, they are obscured by the veil of habit and attachment, something that has been cultivated over many years. We have conditioned ourselves to believe our thoughts are *normal*—part of our personality . . . your *personal-ity bity.*

I once told a friend about how someone deliberately scratched the length of my car while it was parked at the mall. I mentioned I wasn't upset. She looked at me in disbelief then immediately proceeded to tell me something must be wrong with me. She actually got upset because *I failed* to get upset. She felt I wasn't dealing with "reality." But what she failed to understand and what the majority of people on this planet fail to understand, is that *our current condition need not be our future reality.*

It's never the outer conditions that create your mood—it's the very specific and very personal perception and interpretations of those conditions. It's what we take them to mean.

The bio-chemical receptors in your brain have formed a familiarity—sometimes an addiction to certain feelings. It actually craves the satisfaction that comes from the "food" (our reactions) that we feed them.

Much like a "sugar rush" that comes with eating sweets, you have certain receptor-sites in your brain that have been conditioned to receive the neural peptides associated with specific feelings.

You can't make these sites disappear, but you can start feeding other sites. You can become addicted to *better* feeling thoughts. Eventually the neglected negative thoughts will "taste" terrible and dwindle away.

In order to do this however, you must then take the next step, which is to modify your thoughts.

3. MODIFY

Reach for and Transmit Higher Vibrations

Elevate your *Point of Attraction* to its highest frequency. As you can see, Joy is at the top of the EGS and depression is at the bottom. There are a lot of emotions in between—some obviously better than others. Feelings like frustration, doubt and pessimism are somewhere in the middle.

How Do Emotions and Feelings Work?

If you transmit a frequency such as frustration into the world, you will receive the vibrational essence of it right back. This is the *Law of Attraction*. While the law is as old as the ages, it has really only made it into the minds of the general public in the past few decades. Whether you can see it or not, everything on this planet is vibrating. Your thoughts (thought feelings) also send a vibration out to the world. Image 2 tuning forks. Striking only one of them will automatically activate the 2nd one. Much like a tuning fork, your thoughts will activate a vibration – attracting more of the same thoughts.

The world is constantly bringing into existence, people, things and situations for you to experience. We live in an expanding universe–an expanding world–and you are an expanding being.

To keep it simple, some things make you feel good, and some things make you feel bad. For others, the same thing that makes you feel bad may *not* make them feel bad. It is all about interpretation.

For example, if eating lousy food makes you feel bad, then don't eat it. But if that same lousy food makes a starving person feel good, then they should eat it.

Clearly, it's not the event or circumstance that determines how you feel. It's what we say to ourselves about that event that determines how we feel. And chances are you have been saying the same thing for many years. The majority of the thought patterns we have were developed before the age of seven! So, the commentary is *thick*—it has a lot of *momentum*.

The good news is that although you cannot control the outside world, you can *modify* what you choose to say to yourself about it.

Your thoughts (usually unconscious) *ignite* how you feel. So why not consider adjusting your thoughts. Reach for a better thought and resulting feeling. Yes, a better *thought feeling*. The thought actually comes first, and then the unnoticed (but well-rehearsed) feeling, a microsecond later.

<u>How do you do this?</u>

1. Practice bringing awareness to your patterned response.

2. Practice slowing down the sequence.

3. Practice creating a noticeable gap

Within this gap, you can now insert a better *thought feeling.*

Most people go through life believing it is a two-step dance. In other words, perhaps someone says something you don't like and you get angry. The typical view is that an *outside action* created an *inside reaction.*

The two-stage model is:

1. Outside *action*

2. Internal *reaction.*

But consider a possible three-step dance. Someone says something to you, you then have an immediate imperceptible thought about it (opinion), and then you have your reaction based on your view or opinion.

So the three-stage model looks like this:

1. Outside *action*

2. Your *thought* about that action

3. Internal *reaction*

Now look closely and see that in the last stage, what you are now reacting to is **your thought**, not **their action**. When you can do this, you are no longer powerless and at the mercy of what others are saying or doing.

Let's add an empowering fourth step.

Someone says something to you. You have a thought about it. You then have a *replacement* thought about the first thought, and you now respond to your new and improved better *thought feeling.*

The four-stage model now looks like this:

1. Outside *action.*

2. Your automatic *thought* about that action.

3. Your new and improved *thought* about that action.

4. Your internal *reaction.*

Before, in the two-stage model, you were *unconsciously reacting* to your internal state, now, in the four-stage model, you are *consciously choosing* a response.

And the good news is that this sequence doesn't have to be inserted immediately. You can wait a few seconds in the gap, and see for yourself if you are immersed in the emotional quicksand and that you still have choice.

When falling from a tree you have the choice to launch out your arm, reach up and grab the closest tree branch. This would be called *relief;* and usually happens quickly. Do do not wait too long because the emotional weight— that downward momentum—will soon be too great to overcome. Fortunately life gives you a fair time lag!

This reminds me of when I was a child and I used to play a game with my bike. I would put my bicycle upside down and slowly spin my back wheel. I would then carefully insert a stick in between the moving spokes and watch in amazement as the whole wheel just suddenly grinded to a complete stop.

I then tried the same experiment with the wheel spinning quickly. On those occasions, the stick simply bounced off the spokes, having no chance to stop the wheel.

So how does this relate to you? When your *vibrational momentum* is high, outside influences have little chance of affecting your momentum? So, if you're feeling really good, and your wheel is spinning with velocity, something "bad" can happen and it will not have a noticeable effect. Conversely, if you're not spinning with much power and velocity (feeling bad), even a tiny "twig" in your day can *throw you off* or *stop you* and create upset.

Now that you know how to recognize, evaluate and modify your thoughts, it's time to learn how to maintain them.

4. MAINTAIN

Always Feel Good

Stay awake! Be a night watchman of your emotional state 24/7. If you "dip" into a lower vibration, be totally present, recognize it and reach for a better *thought feeling* and then do what makes you feel good.

So how do you maintain this equilibrium and balance this alignment? How do you align **yourself** with **you**? By feeling good. When you're not feeling good, just admit you're not feeling good. Realize that life is always about constantly and consistently realigning of yourself with your "true self." When you don't feel good, distinguish your *set point*, recalibrate and reach for a better *thought feeling*. There are no answers outside of you, so stop looking for them.

What you *say* to yourself, *believe* about other people and your emotional reaction is an indicator of the degree to which **you** are misaligned? Failure to own your thoughts and feelings will only allow them to persist—and show up later with even more velocity. Eventually, they will receive the **attention** they want via ruined relationships, constant irritation or poor health. Why wait for the crash? Don't you properly maintain your car? You put air in the tires, gas in the tank, oil in the engine, fluid in the brake line, etc. It's your responsibility to maintain these levels and then be sensitive to the dashboard indicators. If these levels drop and you fail to recognize them, eventually there *will* be a problem. When maintaining your car, it's better to catch things early. It's far easier to fill up the gas tank before you run dry.

So, in the same way, look at your *emotions* as indicators. Know your emotional levels. Know where you are on the EGS. Constantly identify your *Emotional Set Point* so you can have an idea of what *thought feeling* you wish to reach for.

The final step in achieving ultimate tranquility and peace in your life is to learn how to become a master manifestor.

5. MANIFEST

What do you Really Want?

Always remember it's NOT what you don't want. Never focus on what's missing or what's wrong. Do not invest any vibrational currency there; you will be disappointed with the dividends. Just like the magnets, "what you think about, you bring about."

A better prescription is to focus on and offer love, forgiveness, appreciation, gratitude and joy—you will be amazed at what you will get in return.

About Roman Turlo

Roman Turlo is a lifelong student of "discovery and expansion." He began his career as a high school geography and physical education teacher in 1980.

In the early 90s, he embarked on a spiritual path, studying, practicing and tutoring Eastern philosophy and meditation. The subsequent training and disciplined practices of body, mind and spirit created a solid foundation for future endeavors. Awareness training, proper use of the senses, stillness practices and unity consciousness, all reinforced that serving others is the gateway to experiencing one's true nature.

In 1999, he became a photographer—a passion he could no longer suppress. He left teaching (and his pension) behind and opened a photography studio. He then began nurturing his entrepreneur spirit and started focusing on real estate investing, creating a net worth of millions.

Starting in 2008, he underwent extensive leadership training with Landmark Education. And in 2012, Roman fully immersed himself in the *Law of Attraction*, attending workshops around the world and eventually facilitating his own programs including his own revolutionary system called the *Serenity Code — Your Pathway to Happiness*.

Roman is offering readers a 45-minute consultation. He can be reached at: www.thoughtsAREthings.net

How to Become a Successful Real Estate Investor when You have Little or No Experience

By Wendy Yap

Alliances have become an integral part of
contemporary strategic thinking.
—*Fortune Magazine*

Two bulls, one young and full of enthusiasm and the other older and wiser, see a herd of cows. The young bull says, "Let's charge down this hillside and have our wicked way with a couple of those cows."

The old bull replies, "No, how about we stroll gently down this hillside and have our wicked way with all of them."

You're probably thinking, "What? Did I miss something?" Are you asking yourself what does this story have to do with making money in real estate? Well, read on, and I promise that I will make everything clear.

I think many people look at real estate investing as something unobtainable for many reasons, mostly money—but experience is a big issue as well. After all, it's not like buying a BBQ at the local Home Depot. Yes, you might "hmm and haa" over which one to pick (some people take their grilling pretty seriously.) You may even do a little research in consumer magazines (or not), But ultimately, if the BBQ doesn't work, you can return it to the store, and even if it turns out not to be the perfect one for you, you are not out a whole lot of money. A house, apartment or condo, on the other hand, is a little scarier—there is no way you can return those, and if they are not suitable, well, it's still going to be yours.

So, I get it. I understand why people have reservations when it comes to investing in real estate. But the truth is that real estate, as an investment, is probably one of the safest investments you can make. And with all the help and guidance other real estate investment advisors are willing to give you, lack of experience should not be a concern either.

I also have some tips below that are perfect for new investors who really have no idea what they are doing.

What Do You Need?

Are you tired of sitting on the sidelines, watching as the prices of real estate climb? Are you tired of being afraid to jump in because you don't know what to do or how to do it? Well, those days can be over—today. What you need is to find someone to help you— you need a "partner." And not just any kind of partner. You need a *Joint Venture* (JV) partner. Someone who knows what they're doing and is willing to help you invest your money wisely.

A Joint Venture is simply a strategic alliance between two or more people. It allows each party to pool their strengths such as money, knowledge, experience, and connections. Ultimately, it minimizes your risks. Remember the saying "Two heads are better than one"?

What Can a Joint Venture Provide?

Anytime you pool your expertise and resources, you increase your chances of success. JV agreements can bring many things to the table including:

- Access to capital

- Increased technical expertise

- More resources

- Networks

- Greater capacity for growth

- Access to established markets and distribution channels

- Increased chances of success and minimized risk

How Does a Joint Venture Work?

So how does my story at the beginning of this chapter relate to this? Picture the two bulls actually having a joint venture agreement to invest in real estate together. The younger one is enthusiastic and energetic (i.e., he has the funds), and he has his own idea about how to go about it. The older one calls upon his experience and suggests an alternate plan that will produce better and more productive results.

Each bull is contributing to the "joint" venture by pooling their strengths. The young bull shares his money, and the old bull his knowledge. Together they yield more successful results for both parties. Alone, they would still be sitting on those sidelines.

A joint venture is not a partnership in a legal sense because there is no transfer of ownership. A joint venture is an agreement for a particular purpose and usually within a defined timeframe.

Joint ventures have existed for centuries. In the US, they date back to the late 1800s when railroads were the investment of the day. Since the late 1980s, joint ventures have become more popular as a way to gain an advantage in today's competitive market. You may think that joint ventures are only for big corporations, but this is not the case. Two individuals can also form a joint venture.

Types of Joint Ventures

The process of partnering is a well-known, time-tested principle. There are three basic types of joint ventures in real estate: Corporations, Co-ownerships, and Partnerships (either general or limited). Trusts are also used on occasion, but they are not as common.

Joint venture corporations are generally created with a larger specific investment project in mind. Each joint venture partner holds shares of the corporation, and the joint venture will be governed by a shareholders' joint venture agreement. The corporation is rarely used in real estate joint ventures simply because of its negative tax implications.

In the co-ownership model, participants hold a direct interest in the entire property. You will enter into a co-ownership joint venture agreement. Each co-owner is taxed separately and will have the flexibility of being able to determine his or her own discretionary deductions, such as capital cost allowance.

Partnerships (especially limited partnerships) are generally the preferred form of joint ventures in real estate because of the flexibility it affords both individuals. When you enter into a partnership joint venture agreement, you need to be clear in your documentation that it is not a legal partnership–the reason being so neither party has responsibility for the debts of other participants.

So, let's assume you have decided a joint venture is the way you want to invest in real estate. The critical aspect of a joint venture does not lie in the process itself, but in its execution.

We all know what needs to be done: Specifically, it is necessary to join forces. It is easy, however, to overlook the "how's" and "what's" in the excitement of the moment. All mergers, big or small, need to be meticulously planned and executed following a strict agenda in order to reduce any risk and improve the chances of success.

Strategic alliances are built on trust and similar goals. It's a matter of working together in a give and take manner. The goal should be win-win for all parties. Self-serving attitudes are not in synch with the essence of a joint venture. A joint venture concept is only effective when there is a true willingness to move forward together.

First Things First

Obviously, your first hurdle will be to find your JV partner. If there's a specific type of real estate you want to buy, or a particular area of the country that you want to invest in, you will want to find a JV partner with those areas of specialization. As in any relationship, it's important to find a partner that can provide what you need, whether that is expertise, money, time, or something else.

Suppose you have some extra money put aside that you'd like to invest in order to bring in some extra monthly income, and you've chosen real estate as your vehicle to do that. First, let me say yes, you made a smart decision. More people have become millionaires through real estate than through any other investment method. The problem now is you don't know anything about investing in real estate, so you will look for a JV partner that has the knowledge and experience that you lack. You will want to listen to your partner's recommendations when it comes to what type of property to buy and where to buy it. This will reduce your risk and provide the results you want much faster than if you were to go it alone.

You'll also want your JV partner to have more than just expertise in joint ventures. Ensure that he or she has an established process set-up with a proven system in place when dealing with joint ventures. Again, it's all about reducing risk and increasing profits.

Questions to Ask a Potential JV Partner

It can be hard to find the perfect JV partner. You will be trusting this person with your money or trusting his or her expertise. Let's face it–there's a lot on the line, so to avoid any potential problems down the road—you will be spending a fair amount of time with this person— you should ask for what you need up front. In order to do this, you will have to figure out exactly what it is that you want from your partner going into the partnership.

The best way to figure out what you want from a JV partner is to put it on paper. By that, I mean make a typical pros and cons list. Start with what you know you want from a partner. For instance, maybe you want a "hands off" type of partner—someone who is willing to put up the money and then allow you to do the rest, without constant interference. Maybe you want someone who is able to do more than just one deal and therefore would need access to a lot of money. So, in this case, you are not going to look for someone who only has a few thousand dollars to complete one deal.

On the other hand, maybe you do need someone to guide you through the process, step by step. So, in this instance, you would not want someone who just wants to be a silent investor.

The point of doing this exercise is to establish clear criteria for what you want in a JV investment partner. Once you know this, you can confidently ask the right questions, saving everyone time and avoiding misunderstandings.

Possible questions might include:

- How much control do you need in a JV investment?

- How quickly do you need to get your money out of the investment?

- How many JV investment deals have you done in the past?

- Are you currently active in any other JV deals?

- What are you looking for from a partner?

Questions like these can help you quickly weed out investors that are not suitable to your long-term goals. If you know exactly what you are looking for going into the process, you are less likely to end up in a partnership that is uncomfortable for all partners, a situation that rarely ends well.

Now What?

So now you've found a JV partner that you trust and want to work with, is willing to contribute the resources you're looking for, has similar expectations and timelines to your own, and has proven processes and systems in place to reduce risk.

Well, the second step is to discuss the nitty-gritty details of what you both want to accomplish with the partnership and what type of ownership structure you want to implement.

There are several options when it comes to the structure of a joint venture. Simple is usually best.

Some factors to consider:

- Does either party consist of a husband and wife?

- Do all participants have to contribute equally?

- Is the venture capitalized by way of equity or debt by each participant?

- Who makes or how are capital calls made?

- Are profits to be split 50/50?

- Are expenses to be split 50/50?

- Are the parties involved companies, individuals, or a combination?

- Where is the financing coming from?

- Is this joint venture for a currently owned property or to purchase a new property?

- How are profits and losses allocated for tax and accounting purposes?

Be proactive and also discuss possible "what if" scenarios. For instance, what will happen if one of you backs out or wants out later on after you've already bought a property together? What if one of you cannot live up to your commitments?

All of these "what ifs" should be covered in a legal agreement that will carefully list which party brings which assets (tangible and intangible) to the joint venture table—as well as the objective of this strategic alliance.

The Importance of Clarity and Communication

A couple was celebrating their 40th wedding anniversary at their favorite restaurant. After the meal, the husband gave his wife a gift—a very old antique gold locket on a chain. Amazingly, when his wife opened the locket, a tiny fairy appeared. Addressing the astonished couple, the fairy said, "Your 40 years of devotion to each other has released me from this locket, and in return, I can now grant you both one wish each— anything you want."

Without hesitating, the wife asked, "Please, can I travel to the four corners of the world with my husband, as happy and in love as we've always been?"

The fairy waved her wand, whooshing it back and forth in the air sev-

eral times, and magically, there on the table, were two first-class tickets for a round-the-world holiday.

Stunned, the couple looked at each other, unable to believe their luck.

"Your turn," said the fairy and looked at the husband.

The husband thought for a few seconds, and then said, with a little guilt in his voice, "Forgive me, but to really enjoy this holiday of a lifetime, I yearn for a younger woman. So, I wish that my wife could be 30 years younger than me."

Shocked, the fairy glanced at the wife, and with a knowing look in her eye, waved her wand . . . and the husband became 93.

Be clear! If you don't understand something, make sure it is clarified. Make sure misunderstandings like this don't happen to you. Have a proper Joint Venture Agreement written up.

The Property

Next up? Now you need to decide on a specific property to collaborate on. Is your joint venture partner providing the knowledge and experience? Then you are probably relying on him or her to provide you with information and recommendations. You'll want to make sure you are supplied with some sort of prospectus on the property before making your decision about whether or not to buy. A good prospectus will include details and photos of the property, a property comparison, a breakdown of the numbers, a recommended plan of action, exit strategies, and more. Your partner should be able to get you the answers to all your questions concerning the property and the purchase.

I cannot give you specific details on what to look for in a property at this point—only because there are so many different types of properties and which one you want will depend on your long-term goals. Do you want small or large sums of money? How soon do you want the money? Do you want ongoing income? Once you establish the pros and cons of each, you can make an informed decision. And once you have a goal in mind, someone like myself can give you all the necessary information on what type of investment property to buy.

The Agreement

It is crucial that the joint venture agreement clearly define how the costs and benefits of the joint venture will be shared by each partner. At a minimum, the joint venture agreement should include the following sections:

- A description of what you want to accomplish

- Identification of the parties involved

- An account of the initial investment from each party

- A description of any other contributions such as specific contacts, property management, etc.

- How additional funding will be handled (if required)

- How profits and losses will be allocated for tax and accounting purposes

- The term of the joint venture (i.e. how long will the contract be in effect)

- An explanation of how the joint venture will be managed (who will take on what roles)

- How dissolution, liquidation, withdrawals and transfers will be handled

- Dispute resolution (how the parties will resolve any issues to the satisfaction of all involved)

Liability

This agreement must be detailed and completed before any money passes hands. Of course, it's always recommended to have all legal documents reviewed by a lawyer.

When an agreement such as this is created, it becomes the basis of the relationship moving forward and should deal with all potential issues (taxes, income, expenses, death, divorce, duties and disputes.)

So, there you have it—one way that you can make money in real estate when you don't have the required knowledge or experience.

Now, go out there and use joint ventures to build your wealth. I believe that wealth encompasses much more than money. Money is only a tool to get the things that really matter in life— love and family, treasured friends, good health, being of service to others, and most importantly, having the time to enjoy it all.

As part of my service to you, I am offering a free copy of my eBook detailing five different approaches to making money in real estate when you don't know what you're doing. It provides more in-depth knowledge on joint ventures as well as other strategies that will reduce your risks and guarantee profits when investing.

Go to www.realestate-wealth.com/5 and get it now.

About Wendy Yap

Wendy Yap is known as a business owner and a real estate investor, but she is also much more: She is a wife, a mother, a daughter, a sister, an aunt, a friend, a neighbour and a volunteer. She has a passion for real estate and has been involved in the market in one form or another for over 20 years.

Wendy provides well-managed, profitable real estate investments to her investors that have predictable cash flows, ultimately mitigating any risk for the individuals who have limited time or expertise to invest on their own.

Wendy has invested thousands of dollars and hours into learning what to do to minimize risks and maximize returns for her investors. She built a large network of investors and experts associated with real estate. In doing so, she has paid her dues and made mistakes, but she has become the successful real estate investor she is today by learning from those mistakes. She currently participates in select mastermind groups for both personal and business growth, and her passion has led her to volunteer with Habitat for Humanity, both as a founding Board member and out in the field as a crew leader.

Wendy has been involved in property management for many years and has dealt with residential, commercial and industrial properties in some capacity. She has personally owned single family homes, student rentals and rent-to-own properties and has overseen full rehabs that have been flipped for big profits. Currently, she own properties in both Canada and the US, and she is in the process of developing a private vacation community in the Caribbean. Wendy has also been involved in numerous successful joint venture agreements.

Wendy also belongs to many real estate investment groups across North America. Her new book, which will be available next year, will cover a multitude of strategies for making money in real estate—for those with money and little expertise, or expertise and little money.

She is currently offering group coaching and one-on-one personalized mentoring to aspiring real estate investors, especially those that have not yet bought their first property, and is always on the lookout for good joint venture partners.

To contact Wendy, email her at Wendy@realestate-wealth.com

THERE'S GOLD LYING ON THE STREETS OF THE USA

How to Successfully Invest in
the American Real Estate Market

By Anil Kumar Walia

I think we are all born with special and unique talents or attributes. Whether or not we discover and use these abilities is ultimately up to the individual. My gift, as I see it, is that I have an intuitive understanding of real estate. Essentially, I understand the underlying dynamics of the business, and this knowing has allowed me to own 28 properties in as little as three years.

I was born and raised in Hoshiarpur, Punjab, a small town in India. My parents knew the importance of a good education and at a very young age, they instilled me with a lifelong yearning to learn. I was always a curious child and where others would see a car, for instance, I would want to look deeper. I always wanted to learn how things worked, what made them tick. This love of learning led me to engineering, which seemed like a perfect fit for my inquisitive mind. And in 1975, I graduated as an Electrical Engineer from Punjab Engineering College (PEC), Chandigarh, one of the most esteemed universities in the country. Life was mine for the taking.

As I look back, I think it's funny how life steers us in various directions, all of which ultimately lead us to our destined path. Along that journey however, we are given numerous choices, and it is those choices that define where will finally end up. My choice was the Indian Navy. I was selected by the Navy during my pre-final year of the Engineering. . While I loved my country and was happy with my growing career in the military, I craved more. I needed to fill that need to learn, so I continued my education and eventually completed a Masters in Engineering (M-Tech). In 2000, I also finished a Masters in Business Administration (MBA). I think it was my quest to continue learning that also opened the door to real estate for me.

While real estate in India and real estate in North America are two very different things, the common principles are the same. I started by buying and selling land, and eventually I bought and sold a few houses and apartments. And for the most part, these investments were very profitable. I loved what I was doing. However, like most lessons in life, it is usually the ones that hurt the most that give us the most useful information. And the same is true for me. My biggest and most important lessons came from the investments in which I lost money. Obviously, I didn't want to make that same mistake again, so I dissected each of these deals to see where I went wrong. I looked at the different variables of each bad deal and took away an invaluable lesson that has helped me in every deal I have done since. I now look at every situation as a lesson, especially the bad ones, as these are the gifts that will bring you success in the future.

Investing in Canada

I came to Canada in 2004, after retiring as a ranking Commander in the Indian Navy. As you can imagine, immigrating to a new country is always difficult, or at the very least stressful—simply because everything seems so new. I immediately applied to numerous positions as an engineer but nothing much transpired. It was tough and disappointing but it made me realize that I needed to pursue what I knew best, and most of all, my passion—real estate investing. I think anyone who wants to be successful, needs to concentrate on what they are passionate about. This is a primary key to success.

I decided the best way to enter the REI market was to educate myself. And I did. I got my real estate license in 2005. While my goal was always to *invest* in the market, I also knew that to do this I needed to understand the intricacies of the real estate business in Canada. So while I was learning the 'ins and outs', I continued to sell homes as a real estate agent.

I also managed a job as an engineer in February 2006, but only to get laid off in December, 2008.

When I finally jumped into the investment market in 2009, it was as a *passive* observer. Education and information is imperative if you want to succeed. I knew that then and I will tell you that now. So I watched more experienced real estate investors, and learned from what they were doing—both the good and bad. I began lending money to other investors for private mortgages to help them do the investing as I watched and learned. I issued first and second mortgages to numerous borrowers using the real estate as collateral. At the same time, I kept my eyes and ears open to investment opportunities.

One of these opportunities came in the form of tax sale properties, and I jumped in, head first. Things were great and my investments were doing well, but then something happened that changed my focus—the US real estate market crashed. While this was a horrible thing for people who were losing their homes, it provided a great opportunity for knowledgeable people like myself, to pick up properties for little to nothing—literally pennies on the dollar.

I quickly learned that buying properties in Canada is like looking for a small fish in the open sea whereas investing in the US is like finding a large fish in a small pond. There is no comparison. Gold is lying on the streets of US, and it is up to you to pick up.

Investing South of the Border

Again, education is the key to success in REI. I cannot stress this enough. I did almost three years of research into the US market before investing a single dollar. I attended seminars, hired mentors, took courses from several REI gurus. I spent close to $40,000 on research. I could clearly see this was an opportunity of a lifetime and I wanted to make sure I did it right. So when I felt I was ready, I had to decide WHERE I was going to invest. The US is a very big country. There were and are countless variables to consider when choosing a property to invest in, including such things as population, economy climate, culture, school zones etc. all of which can make a huge difference in whether your investment will succeed. I decided the best way to make this decision was to physically go to different cities to see and experience the pros and cons of each.

In August 2009, I flew to Chicago for five days and then took off to Atlanta for another five. I spent almost every waking hour just looking at potential properties. In September, I went to Los Angeles. In January 2011, I flew to Indianapolis for two days and in July and August 2011, I spent some time in Las Vegas. I even spent some time in Detroit, Buffalo and Cleveland to explore the market there. I did my due diligence and more.

Then, in November 2011, I finally chose Orlando, Florida as the place I would jump into the market. After looking at all of the other cities and comparing the pros and cons, Florida, and especially Orlando, seemed to have inherent advantages over the countless other cities I had looked at.

After doing a further final analysis of the city, I bought the first house for around $180,000, and in 15 days after closing the deal, it was rented for $1800/month. It was amazing. This opened my eyes and I looked at other similar opportunities in the area. Even better, I saw that the housing prices were appreciating in the area, which of course encouraged me to buy more. Today I own 28 properties (single family homes) in the US, together worth about $4.5 million. And of those , 27 are currently rented and producing positive cash flow of approximately $400,000 (gross.)

You have undoubtedly heard the saying by Thomas Bertram Lance, "If it ain't broke, don't fix it?" Well we have made a very successful and viable business model in which we are able to create positive cash flow and huge appreciation while still managing the financing that allows us to finance our future acquisitions. It's a win-win-win situation.

And now I'm going to let you in on a few of my secrets.

Real Estate Deconstructed

Did you know that about 77 percent of investors who have at least $1 million in assets, own real estate?

For centuries, real estate has either been used as a means to generate a high net-worth, or as a vehicle for holding accumulated wealth. And today, the US market continues to grow stronger as economic growth slowly rises, especially in Florida, which remains the country's foreclosure epicenter. As of December 2013, over 300,000 homes were in some stage of foreclosure or owned by banks. This is almost 25 percent of all the foreclosures in the country.

Renting a home instead of buying has always been attractive to people at any stage in their lives. It provides a wide range of options that may not be available to most people, without the responsibility and cost of owning. With the 2008 housing crash, the advantages of renting increased, while the obstacles to homeownership rose. With so many people being laid off or losing their jobs, incomes dropped and the ability to own a home, or hold onto one, also fell. Renting became the only viable option for many people. And although the economic climate is changing in the US, the number of people renting is still at an all-time high.

Beyond these reasons, there are several reasons real estate remains such an amazing investment opportunity.

1. *Leverage:* Real estate debt, or *leverage*, can be structured far more safely than using debt to buy stocks by trading on margin.

2. *Tax free cash flow:* Because of depreciation and mortgage interest deductions (if you leverage your capital), your cash flow can be tax-free. You may not have to pay any taxes on the property until you actually sell it, at which time you will pay capital gains tax.

3. *Finite:* The need for residential, commercial or industrial real estate grows with our expanding population. People will always need homes, office space etc. Economics 101 teaches us that price of any product/commodity is based on its supply and demand. *Supply=Demand.* The beauty of real estate is that the supply is typically somewhat limited while its demand continues to rise. This characteristic makes real estate, at the very least, a good inflation hedge, if not a great tool to accumulate wealth.

4. *Tangible*: You can visit your investment property, you can speak with your tenants, and the banks consider it equity. Because of its tangibility, you have a certain degree of physical control over your investment—if something is wrong with it, you can fix it. You can't do that with a stock or bond.

5. *Durability:* Unlike a bond, which has a fixed maturity date, real estate does not normally mature i.e. a building can last for decades or even centuries, and the land underneath it is practically

indestructible. In many parts of the world, it is not uncommon for investors to hold property for over 100 years. This durability allows you to sell your property whenever you want. As such, real estate can be a great source of passive income—you can purchase and hold the property as long as it continues to make good investment sense.

8 Reasons to Invest in US Real Estate

Canadians are the largest foreign investors in the US residential real estate market. They make up about 25 percent of all foreign purchases. Since the US real estate crash in 2008, residential real estate investment has provided a lifetime opportunity to build long-term wealth. This is especially true for Canadians for the following reasons:

1. Investors can look to a rebounding real estate market as fixed-income yields remain historically low and equities rise.

2. The Canadian real estate market is strong, which allows Canadians to take their equity from their Canadian properties and invest it in US real estate.

3. Almost all age groups (apart from seniors) in the US have shifted toward renting. The largest increase is in people in their 30s, which is up by close to 9 percent over an eight-year span.

4. The Canadian dollar is much stronger compared to its historical value.

5. The US is the world's largest economy and the demand for real estate is very solid.

6. With its proximity to Canada, it is easy to move in and out of US.

7. The US and Canada share similar ideologies and rules. The US real estate market is similar to Canada's market.

8. U.S. commercial-property has risen in value by 8 percent in the past year. Further, since 2009, it has risen by 71 percent. These improving fundamentals speak well for the future of US real estate investment.

Where Should You Invest in the US?

With all the research I have done, I believe that Orlando and Kissimmee, Florida offers one of the best opportunities for investment in the US. This is based on the following:

a. Inward immigration into Florida has been steadily increasing with the retirement of the baby boomers. Orlando is considered the #1 market for second homes.

b. Orlando is ranked the #1 tourist destination in the world, with approximately 57-million visitors on a yearly basis.

c. Orlando has taken some very constructive steps to diversify its economy. While tourism continues to account for the majority of the city's GDP, Trade/Transportation and Healthcare are growing.

d. Land is limited in Orlando and zoning laws are inflexible compared to other places in the US.

e. Prices in Orlando/Kissimmee have declined approximately 43 percent since the credit bubble burst, allowing a lifetime opportunity to enter into this real estate market.

f. With many homeowners having to foreclose, rental demand in the city is high.

How Do You Analyze a Deal?

Step 1: Locate an area where there are plenty of jobs, limited supply of land and low property prices. As mentioned, I believe that Orlando and Kissimmee, Florida offer these fundamental elements. Use www.city-data.com and www.fhfa.gov to help you in your research.

Step 2: Within the selected city, then locate a zip code with good demographics. I use zipskinny.com to point out the area with the demographics that suit my planning. You will want to look at such things as education statistics, marital status, household income, occupation, race and age for the residents of a particular zip code. You can then compare these demographics with those of other zip codes and find the best possible combination.

Step 3: Search properties through a Real Estate Agent. Look at few real estate deals to confirm the average selling price of houses (I recommend purchasing single family homes with 3 bedrooms and 2 bathrooms) and their respective rental potential. I follow the 1 percent rule to ensure that rent per month for a particular property is at or more than 1 percent of the purchase price of the property. While, sites like zillow.com are a quick way to determine if the property is priced appropriately, the best way to confirm the price of the property is to get it appraised by an appraiser or get a real estate agent to do a Comparative Market Analysis (CMA).

Step 4: Make sure all the numbers make sense. I sometimes use www.finestexpert.com. Just copy the address of the property and paste it into Finest Expert. You can then adjust the numbers and confirm the actual cash flow you will generate.

What is the Best way to purchase Real Estate in US?

I believe everybody needs to specialize in their business. One person can't possibly do everything well. It's better to use your strengths where they will benefit you most and find other people with the strengths you lack and are looking for and let them do what they are good at. As such, building a team of professionals to help you in your business/investment endeavors is paramount.

For real estate investment, you will need a *very good* (and I emphasis, very good) team, including:

a) A real estate agent

b) A home inspector

c) A reliable and trustworthy contractor/handyman

d) A property manager

e) A chartered accountant and a Lawyer

f) A good Mortgage Broker

My part in the business is that intuitive knowledge of the real estate market that I mentioned early on. I have developed the skills to acquire properties at an attractive value and I let my team help me in the other aspects of the investment.

If you want to purchase a lot of properties in US, then you will need to develop deep relationships with investment banks, private equity firms, lenders and lawyers to source and find new opportunities.

I believe it is extremely important to focus on the following three criteria when analyzing current opportunities in US real estate:

1. Buying quality assets at prices that are below replacement cost

2. Acquiring only properties with positive cash potential

3. Targeting areas with limited supply and growing demand

The Final Word

I believe the 3 keys to success are:

1. To get a good education and then work hard to implement your education in your chosen field.

2. If you are making a good salary, you should develop an investors' mindset. Use your savings (including any equity in a home etc.) to find positive cash flow investments,

3. Learn from people who have already done what you want to do.

I have always made sure I continue learning and educating myself, no matter how old I get. Sometimes the best way to learn is to partner with a successful investor and learn by being a passive observer.

I strongly believe that education is the most important and first step to real estate investing, so, I am willing to provide 1 hour of free consultation to anybody who wishes to learn from my experience. I can provide you with the knowledge and confidence to enter the real estate investment arena and help you take the first step to your financial freedom.

About Anil Kumar Walia

Anil Kumar Walia is a former Engineer and Commander in the Indian Navy. He has been investing in real estate for 30 years. He started investing in India and then, after immigrating to Canada in 2004, he obtained his real estate license. He began investing in the US in 2011 and now, he owns 28 properties, 27 of which are rented. His initial investment was modest and now, 2.8 years later, his real estate portfolio is currently worth $4.5 million. He believes the US real estate market is "gold," and his goal is to help anyone who is interested in investing to learn the ropes. You can contact Anil at waliaak@yahoo.com for a free 1-hour consultation.

HOW TO MAKE THE LAW OF ATTRACTION WORK FOR YOU—NOW

By Mary Ann Miano

Have you ever wondered why you sometimes get something you really don't want or need in your life? People often tell me, "I didn't ask for THAT!" But I disagree.

Unless you have been living under a rock in the last decade, you have probably heard of the *Law of Attraction*. If not in the sense of how it affects your everyday life, I have no doubt you know how it relates to magnets—"like attracts like," which is a basic grade school concept.

So how does the Law of Attraction relate to you and your current life situation? Well, the two are inextricably connected. In the same way that a magnet attracts like things to itself, so do all of your thoughts and actions. In other words, good thoughts and actions attract more good situations and opportunities into your life. And bad thoughts and actions attract more bad situations into your life. It really is that simple. Let me explain.

At some point every child has dreamed about what they want to be when they 'grow up.' When I was growing up it seemed that most little boys wanted to be policemen, fire fighters or even cowboys. The little girls wanted to be princesses, ballerinas or "mommies." I, however, always dreamed of being a school teacher. Even back then, I knew I wanted to help young children transition from home to their first day of school. I had a need to instill in them a love of learning and a love for school.

Like most people in my generation, growing up I had no concept or knowledge of the Law of Attraction. And yet, it was still at play in my life right from the beginning. That is the beauty and danger of this basic law of the universe.

I was a shy child. I had very little self-confidence. So at school, when the other children picked teams, I would always pray, "Pick me, pick me." But I was always picked last or at the very least, next to last. Little did I know I was creating a self-fulfilling prophecy, with no knowledge of what that even meant. All I knew was that everything I *didn't want* always had a weird way of materializing in my life.

My parents immigrated to Canada in the 1960's. And as far back as I can remember they imparted in me a deep love of learning. I was taught that in order to succeed and win the "prize" in life, you needed to get a good education. So, I went to school, worked hard at my studies and eventually earned a Bachelor of Arts and my Teaching Certificate. I was on my way to realizing my dream. Or so I thought!

Energy and the Law of Attraction

The Law of Attraction at a very basic level states that everything is energy. Basic physics agree. So, with this principle in mind, the Law of Attraction states that thoughts are also energy. And because we know that energy can be attracted or repelled, so can the repercussions of our thoughts. That being said, our thoughts can attract physical things, people, situations and circumstances—both positive and negative. In fact, your thoughts are attracting these things in this very moment! So, what are you thinking about?

Ancient Law

Buddha said, **"All that we are is the result of what we have thought."** The *Darby Bible Translation* tells us that Job, of the *Old Testament* declared, **"For I feared a fear, and it hath come upon me, and that which I dreaded hath come to me."** The common denominator is that both Buddha and Job understood the eternal workings of the Law of Attraction. However, unlike the enlightened Buddha, Job, like the majority of people today, suffered the unfortunate and often dire consequences of not using this law to his advantage!

So what I didn't know or understand as a child, or even as a young adult, was that the more I tried to repel or push away what I didn't want, the more, in fact, I was attracting it to me. I can recall throughout school when the teacher would ask us to give some insights on any given subject and I'd fervently pray, "Not me." And guess what? You got it. I was invariably called upon to give a response—each and every time.

In fact, I have talked to so many people who are aware of the Law of Attraction, but swear it isn't working for them. Yet, what they don't understand is that when they attract something they don't want into their life, the law is in fact working—just not in the direction they may want! You see, the Law of Attraction doesn't hear the words "don't, not, or no" (as in "I don't want that," or "That's not what I want." or "No more of this!") The Law can only respond to your feelings (your vibrations/ energy) about any given subject or feeling. If thinking about a certain situation causes you to feel upset or anxious, for instance, the Law of Attraction sends you MORE upsetting situations to make you feel even more anxious.

The bottom line is we are where we are because of our past thoughts.

EXERCISE:

Try and sit still for a moment (even just 2 minutes) and simply not think about anything. Clear your mind completely. Do it right now. Okay, was it hard? Did you find the more you tried NOT to think about anything, the more random thoughts would simply pop into your thoughts. I am willing to bet that you were not able to do this—at least not without conscious effort or practice.

As humans, we are always consciously or even subconsciously thinking about something. This isn't necessarily a bad thing if all you think about is happy, joyous thoughts. The problem is that we usually think more about things we don't want, than the things we do want. Have you ever heard the saying, "what you think about, you bring about?" It is so true. It doesn't matter if you want or don't want something, you'll ultimately get what you think about most.

Now take a look at your present situation as a whole. Are you generally happy in life? Do you currently have a lot of stressful situations happening? Whatever your current situation, it is the result of your past predominant state of mind. And in the same token, what you are thinking now is creating your future even as you read this!

EXERCISE:

Okay, now try the above exercise again over the next few days. Try to simply sit back, detach from your mind, and just observe your thoughts for a day or two. Notice how you feel when you think those thoughts as well. Do you mostly think about the things that you worry about? Things you don't want to happen? Things you are afraid of? Or do you mostly think about pleasant and wonderful things? A simple barometer of your thoughts is your feelings. If you are unable to control your thoughts at first, be aware of your feelings. Your feelings perfectly indicate what your predominate thoughts are. For instance, if you feel happy, your thoughts must be good thoughts. On the other hand, if you feel anxious, sad, angry, frustrated (any negative emotion), you're not thinking positive thoughts.

A simple way to change your thoughts when you notice a negative feeling is to try and smile and consciously hold your smile for one minute. By doing this, you are forcing yourself to think happy thoughts. Why? Because it is impossible to think bad thoughts when you have a genuine smile on your face. So, go ahead and try it. It works! So, in the future when you notice you are not feeling positive, just put a real smile on your face for an entire minute and you will feel your emotions switching.

The Past is the Past

The definition of past is: *gone by in time* and *no longer existing*. So, the past is gone. Unless you have a time machine and you can magically send yourself back a few days, years or even decades, you can't change it. If you dwell on something from your past that was unpleasant, you are not feeling happy now. And by feeling unhappy now, you are creating further unhappiness in your future. The only thing that truly matters, and the only thing you can actually change, is what is happening *now*. By having a predominantly happy and positive state of mind *in this moment*, you're creating your happy and positive future. Through the *Law of Attraction* you can attract whatever you want in your life: happiness, wealth, perfect health, love and wonderful relationships.

The flip side, however, as you now know, is that you can also attract things and situations that you don't want, and you are actually doing it subconsciously all the time. Because you are energy, you are like the magnet you studied in science class. And like the magnet that attracts like objects, you are doing the same. The difference between you and the magnet, however, is that you CAN control what you ultimately attract. As humans, we were given FREE WILL. This is the greatest gift of all. It means that everything we do in life is a choice. *We either choose to do something or we let something be done to us.* This is a hard concept for many people to understand at first. Often I find people look to outside forces to blame for their situation simply because it is hard to believe that we would bring unhappy situations into our lives on purpose. But if you can grasp this one concept alone, you will have the key to everything you want in life. Nothing will be able to stop you because you will have the ability to change it—through different thinking and actions. Only you can control your body, and only you can control your mind. There is no one else to blame. *No one can MAKE you feel something.* It is a choice to feel, whatever that emotion or feeling may be. It's all up to you.

Your mind can be your best friend or your worst enemy. The good news is that the Law does not demand 100 percent of us, meaning if your thoughts, the majority of the time, are positive, you will still be able to make drastic positive changes in your life. We are, after all, human and as humans we are not perfect. And the Law understands this. So just make sure your predominant thoughts are positive and you will begin to see massive changes in your current situation. The minute you see things changing for the negative, however, you will know you have tipped the scales, and your predominant thoughts must be negative. Once you are AWARE of your thoughts however, you can make the necessary adjustments.

5 Ways to Change Your Thoughts and Actions to Bring Positive Situations into your Life—

1.) **Become aligned with your Goals**. You must be in alignment with what you do want. To be in alignment with your desires is not always easy. Let's say you have a desire to attract $20,000, but you are flat broke and almost everything in your environment screams poverty. You may be wishing and hoping that things change but everything in your being feels more like $10 than $20,000. In fact, when you think about it, you have no idea how $20,000 would even feel like. You just know that is what you want. The trick to the Law of Attraction is that you must not only imagine what you want, BUT you must also FEEL what you want, as though you already have it. Your objective should be to find a way to begin to feel like you are worth $20,000. So, go window shopping. Look at all of the expensive clothes you want. Try some on. Feel what it is like to have cashmere on your body. Go to the electronics store, play with the newest gadgets. Get a feel for what it would be like to own them. Look at cars, drive by expensive houses and neighbourhoods etc. The point here is that you need to actually feel what it would be like to have that $20,000 right now. Do you remember when I said that the Law of Attraction cannot discern between what you want and don't want? Well, the same is true with what you already have and what you don't have. If you feel like you already have something, you will be emitting that energy and ultimately attract more of that energy. This is the first and most crucial step to activating the Law of Attraction.

2.) **Become Focused**. Being unfocussed is another hindrance to manifesting what you desire. In order to get the universe to move what you want into your physical reality, you must begin to hold a clear and steady focus of what you want all times throughout the day. This ties into the above step. You need to feel what you want 24 hours a day.

3.) **Intention**. –In order for the Law of Attraction to work quickly and be aligned with your desires, you must truly believe you are getting what you want. Setting an intention is like making a conscious decision about what you want to attract to yourself. If you believe, without a doubt, that you are getting what you want (or even better, that it is already here), you are essentially sending out a signal to the universe that you want this situation to be pulled into your life. If you have even slight feelings of doubt, these doubts will work as a barrier, blocking the situation from coming into your life. This is one of the biggest reasons why people don't get what they want. Instead of looking at what they are doing wrong, they simply say the Law of Attraction doesn't work. So, if you are not attracting what you want, take a look at the above three keys objectively, without any feeling, and see where you may be falling short and the course correct.

4.) **Understand the Universal Laws.** The Law of Attraction is one of several laws that can assist you in manifesting what you desire. There are other laws that can actually cancel out your intention if you are not aware of them or how they work. Manifesting your desires requires that you learn all the necessary parts of the basic laws of the universe in order to achieve great success in manifesting what you want.

5.) **Surrounding yourself with like-minded people.** This is by far one of the most difficult things to do in order to successfully apply the Law of Attraction. You see, other people's beliefs and doubts can greatly hamper your ability to manifest what you want. These people can be family members, co-workers or friends. The universal Law of Attraction moves on vibrations and energy and those include the vibrations and energy of those people and situations you choose to be aligned with. Other people's vibrations can have a great effect on your own personal vibration. Remember "like attracts like."

One of the best ways to shift your energy and manifest what you want faster is the use of positive affirmations. Affirmations have been used since the beginning of time. You use affirmations every day—you just aren't aware most times. Every time you tell yourself you can't do something, or you are not smart enough or good enough, that is an affirmation—just not a good one. If you tell yourself you are amazing, you did a great job, you are perfect the way you are, these, too are affirmations—ones that will ultimately bring you what you want in life. The trick is consistency and again, intention and belief.

How to Use Affirmations

Here are three ways to use affirmations for positive results.

1. The first step to using the affirmations is to become very clear about what you want. In order to become clear you need to write

out all the details that you would like to see and experience in the situation or object of your desires. The clearer you are about your intentions, the more power you give to your affirmations

2. Write a clear positive affirmation in the first person stating your desire as if it is already complete. Never make statements such as, "I wish I could be"… "or someday I can have" . . . "or I don't want to do…." These three statements will either never bring you what you want because your desire is always in the future or it will bring you what you don't want, as I explained above. Your affirmation must be created with power and faith in order to fully shift the Law of Attraction in your favour. You must absolutely omit any words that tie you to something you do not want. If you want to stop thinking in a negative way, it is best to state, "I now think and feel in the most positive way. My thoughts are happy and positive every moment of the day."

3. Feel the affirmation. Feeling adds the power to your desires. Feelings generate an internal energy that allows your whole being to absorb your statement.

Many people find it a bit hard to really create success with their affirmations and this is because of *stuck emotional energetic patterns* that are difficult to change. There are many incredible techniques that can shift affirmations and make the attraction process even easier and more effective without the mindless repetition.

How deeply are you willing to go to see positive changes in your life?

You can have wild success or unbearable failure when trying to apply the Law of Attraction to manifest your desires. You can change this roller coaster by learning to apply some small changes.

Are you applying the Law of Attraction correctly? If you are like most people, you are most likely quite frustrated. You want to manifest changes faster. You want to manifest money faster. You want to manifest new friends or relationships but for all your hard efforts something seems to me missing.

You may be thinking, "If I can have, do or be anything I want, then why can't I see the results?" This is a common frustration with most people who are new to the Law of Attraction.

The pain of failing again and again at applying the Law of Attraction can cause anyone to give up. Many years ago, when I first learned of the Law of Attraction, I went through the very same frustration until I learned what is at the heart of the secret to manifesting greater results.

The Secret to the Law of Attraction

The secret to manifesting anything you want in life is the amount of energy you put into your intention and your thoughts. Energy is abundant in the universe. You are constantly being influenced by energy all the time. Every degree of energy affects your ability to manifest differently.

Although most people who learn of the Law of Attraction think exclusively of changing their thoughts, they are unaware of the role energy plays in the equation.

The more sensitive you become to the intention of your energy, as well as the energy in your environment, the easier it will be to align yourself with the energy of what you want to manifest in your life.

If the energy within you is out of alignment with where you want to be, then you simply cannot manifest what you truly desire.

The Law of Attraction is an art that must be understood at its very core. Learn to become still and ask yourself, "How am I feeling at this moment?" Although you may be thinking of what you want, your feelings may not be in alignment with your desires.

As you become more aware of the tone of your energy, you can slowly learn to increase your energy to become a magnet for what you want. When you can master this, the Law of Attraction will become an incredible tool to manifest what you truly desire.

As long as the Law of Attraction has only the "DON'T want" script, it is restricted to orchestrating that script over and over. You must give the Law of Attraction some NEW MATERIAL to work with. So, change your thinking and you will change your life.

About Mary Ann Miano

Mary Ann Miano lives in Niagara Falls, Ontario, in the Niagara Peninsula where she is a retired elementary school teacher with over 30 years of teaching experience. She continues to be a life-long learner, so upon retiring from teaching, she immediately embraced another of her passions—Real Estate Investing, which she currently does alongside her husband. Mary is now an experienced landlord, having acquired and maintained rental units and apartment complexes for many years.

Mary is offering readers a complimentary ebook at:

www.mianoinvestments.com/loa

She can also be reached at: mmiano51@gmail.com

ROI Secrets

By Peter Mazzuchin

Rule of 72

If you were to visit Mount Everest for the first time, what would be the most effective way of learning how to climb this mountain? I think we can all agree that going it alone would obviously prove foolish. After all, it is the highest mountain in the world! Did you know that almost 10 percent of Mount Everest climbers have actually died trying to conquer this natural wonder? As well, over 50 percent never even reach the summit. It's truly a monumental feat that requires expert advice and training. Leveraging the experiences of those who have already scaled this mountain successfully is imperative. Not only can it save your life, from a practical standpoint, it will save you a huge learning curve, protect you from potential disaster and reduce your chances of failing. It's just common sense! Unfortunately, 'common sense' isn't always commonly practiced in mountain climbing or real estate investing.

What does this have to do with the Rule of 72? Everything! The Rule of 72 is a mathematical formula that works each and every time without exception. This rule is an accurate way to determine how many years it will take to double one's initial investment principal. To calculate, first divide the rule number (72) by the interest percentage per period, which will give you the number of years required to double your original investment.

So, 72 ÷ return on investment (ROI) percentage per year, x (times) the original investment amount in dollars = the number of years it will take for your original investment to double in value. For example, if you invest $100,000 into Canada Savings Bonds paying 2 percent per year, then (72/2 percent) = 36 years for your $100,000 to double in value to $200,000. Regardless of your current age, isn't 36 years just a little bit longer then you'd like to wait to earn that $100,000? If it is, keep reading, if not, reconsider the example of the most effective way to climb Mount Everest above.

So, now that I have your attention, let me show you a better way to invest your hard-earned dollars . . . and turn those same dollars into "easy-earned" cash.

The Magic of Mentorship

I knew that if I wanted to learn how to invest wisely, I needed to look to those who have already done this. So, years ago, I attended *Millionaire School*. This course was taught by millionaires and multi-millionaires. One of the things they shared is that they consistently focus on doubling their portfolios **with at least 10 percent ROI**. So, plugging this into the Rule of 72 formula, 72/10 = 7.2 years for the original investment to double in value. Wow! Just by targeting a minimum 10 percent ROI you can shave off 28.8 years to double your original investment. Does this sound too simple? Well, as a theory, yes, it is simple. Is it easy? It depends on how you look at it.

The issue is not so much that it is difficult to find a 10 percent ROI, it is that most people think that investing in 10 percent ROI properties is too risky. But the truth is that it doesn't have to be especially risky as long as you have a trusted investor and mentor who is willing to coach and guide you through the process, just like those climbers who hire a Sherpa to guide them up the mountain.

How Do You Do It? A Real Investor Example

Let's take first-time buyer, Jake*. He bought a condo for $291,000 and lived there for 8 years. Jake originally put down 10% ($29,100) plus had closing fees of 2% ($5,820). So Jake's original investment was $29,100 + $5,820 = $34,920. It was eventually sold for $487,000. He made a gross profit of $196,000 ($487,000 - $291,000). If you then subtract his selling (Realty) expenses of 5.65 percent on $487,000 you get $27,516. Then subtract $800 of legal fees that were incurred on the sale. After subtracting initial closing fees of $5,820, that left him with $161,684 profit versus the initial investment of $291,000. So his total ROI is over 50 percent ($167,684 ÷ $291,000 = 463.53 percent). If you then divide that number by 8 years, his ROI is 57.94% per year. That's not the full story. We must also take into consideration that the mortgage principal was paid down $63,693 for the 8 years he lived there. Then, his true ROI would be higher. The $63,693 mortgage principal debt pay down was calculated based on the 3.25 percent average interest rate Jake paid on his initial mortgage over the 8 years, using a standard 25 year amortization period. This is easily seen using a standard amortization table.

Jake also rented out 2 of the 3 bedrooms so we must also consider that he had some positive cash flow. He received $400 a month in rent from each of those 2 bedrooms. Since Jake was kind, he never raised the rents and collected $800/month x 96 months = $76,800. This, of course, reduced the total monthly carrying costs (mortgage principal & interest, condominium fees, property taxes, insurance & utilities). In a truly 100 percent investment, he would have rented out the entire property, including the third bedroom, for another $450 plus utilities. Property taxes for Jake averaged $2,004 a year. In terms of capital improvements over the 8 years, he invested about $3,000 and the majority of that was for staging and improvements just before he listed it for sale. Jake did this under the savvy direction of his competent Realtor® and Staging Consultant. Guess who was the competent Realtor® who emphasized these minor capital improvements would have a great ROI when done effectively? History proves this point with Jake and many other sellers like him, no doubt.

He also had condo fees of about $200 per month (about $2400 for the year). We also need to factor in Contents and Liability Insurance of about $30 per month x 96 months = $2,880. Jake's utilities averaged $150/month x 96 months = $14,400. Jake's total monthly payments were $1,489/month. His mortgage Principal and Interest payments averaged $1309 per month. Jake paid the utilities (heat, hydro, water) which averaged $150/month. So after his rental income of $800/month Jake only paid $689/month ($1,489 Total Expenses minus $800/month Rental Income) net to live in a nice 3 bedroom newer condo townhouse in South Etobicoke!

After all of Jake's income and expenses are accounted for on the ROI Spreadsheet herein, he ended up with a Total Net Profit of $121,181.

After dividing that by the original investment of $34,920, then dividing it by 8 years, Jake's Net Annualized ROI% turns out to be a Sparkling 43.38%! So, it dramatically exceeds the 10% ROI baseline established by the Multi-Millionaire Mentors of mine!

Further, Jake benefited from several tax deductions because he was able to a) write off the interest against his income (which reduced his income tax owing); b) he was able to write off the negative cash flow against his other net income; and c) he could also write off the repairs.

Jake, at a 30 percent marginal tax rate, gets a 30 percent tax credit for all eligible expenses on Qualifying Real Estate such as this investment property. So if Jake's operating expenses were $10,000/ year, then Jake could write off 30 percent of the $3,000 against his other taxable income! In addition, if Jake was married or had a common-law partner in a lower marginal tax bracket, he could lower his marginal tax rate and reduce the amount of income taxes he would otherwise pay. There are numerous additional tax benefits for Jake, which he and all savvy investors can receive to increase their cash flow, defer or lower income taxes! This makes the investment even sweeter! ☺

We must not forget that the property will also continue to increase in value. The Capital Appreciation Forecasted Rate on the property is approximately 3 percent per year, and that is being very conservative.

The spreadsheet on Jake's property is shown on next page.

Chart A "ROI Spreadsheet":	
Jakes* Condo Townhouse, Toronto, ROI Spreadsheet	($)
Purchase Price	291,000
Original Downpymt 10% of Purchase Price =	-29,100
Original Closing Fees $291,000 x 2% =	<u>-5,820</u>
Original Investment Total =	-34,920
Average Rental Income was $800/month x 96 months =	76,800
Debt Pay Down of Mortgage Principal after 8 years is =	63,693
Net Capital Appreciation after 8 years was:	
Sale Price	487,000
Minus Realty Fees on Sale ($487,000 x .05 x 1.13 hst) =	-27,516
Minus Legal Fees on Sale ($708 x 1.13) =	-800
Minus Original Purchase Price	-291,000
Minus Closing Fees on Buy @ 2% =	-5,820
Minus Maintenance Fees after 8 yrs.($200/month x 96 months.) =	-19,200
Minus Property Taxes after 8 yrs ($167/month x 96) =	-16,032
Minus Capital Improvements and Staging	<u>-3,000</u>
Net Capital Appreciation after 8 years =	123,632
Therefore, Total Profit after 8 years was:	
1. Debt Pay Down	63,693
2. Rental Income @ $800/month x 96 months =	76,800
3. Minus Mortgage Pymts @ $1309 x 96 =	-125,664
4. Minus Utilities (Heat, Hydro, Water) @ $150/month avg. x 96 =	-14,400
5. Minus Insurance (Contents & Liability) @ $30/month avg. x 96 =	-2,880
6. Net Capital Appreciation =	123,632
Total Net Profit after 8 years =	121,181
ROI % on Original Investment is $121,181/$34,920/8 = $34,92	43.38%

*Jake's real name was changed to protect his privacy.

CMHC Premium was added to Jake's Mortgage so he could enter the Real Estate Market before he had 20% down!

Another benefit we need to consider is that if he was able to refinance the property (after 8 years, the appraised value was $487,000). Suppose Jake refinanced 80 percent of the property, which is $389,600. Then imagine he used that money to buy another identical property for $487,000.

Even if we just look at the rental income of $1250 per month (plus utilities), less the condominium fees of approximately $200 a month, you can see that this is truly an amazing opportunity. Where do you think Jake will end up in 10, or 25 years? In less than 25 years, he will own the property free and clear. Don't forget that over time, the rent will have also gone up from the original $1250 as you can typically increase the rental rate by 3 percent each year. That mirrors the average annual Consumer Price Index or Cost of Living increase over the past 40 years.

As you can see, when you take all of these factors into consideration, owning a positive-cash-flowing property is a gift, and it just keeps on giving. By using the original property to grow his portfolio, Jake ends up being able to combine the ROIs of each investment. For example, if he's making just a conservative 10 percent on each property and the original investment was $291,000, after 8 years he's earning 10 percent on $974,000 (i.e. $487,000 x 2). That means he is now making $97,400 per year on just 2 townhouses!

So what do you do when you're presented with an investment opportunity of under 10 percent ROI? Ignore them! Just do what millionaires and multi-millionaires do: Target investment properties that are forecast to achieve ROIs of at least 10 percent ROI. Focus on what expands and grows your investment and ignore the rest. It's really quite liberating and saves you treasure chests of time!

Quite frankly, real estate has one of the most phenomenal advantages—it has legal financial leverage . . . and conservative banks provide it. Why would banks offer so much leverage on real estate compared to every other investment? It's because they realize the value of the investment. Everyone has to live somewhere. Most people, last time I checked, would rather live in a nice, warm, safe and secure home they own versus being homeless, living under a bridge or on the streets. And as I gaze at the serenity of my own backyard, I can write this chapter and have peace of mind at the same time. So not only does real estate have all the tangible benefits I mentioned previously, it also has other intangible benefits like providing a particular lifestyle, heightened peace of mind and a sense of tranquillity—which is a dwindling luxury in today's rapid–fire, highly congested world.

Investing in real estate is quite easy to accomplish, especially if someone else is willing to give you most of the financing. If so, how many positive-cash-flowing properties should you own? The correct answer is, of course, as many as possible.

Why Real Estate Should Be Your Primary Investment

Investing in real estate is probably the most desirable and the best-yielding investment there is. Given that most people become financially free through some form of real estate, be it just purchasing a home for themselves or investing, big or small, versus any other investment, there is zero reason why you should not at least test the waters. If I have learned one thing from my wealthy and knowledgeable mentors, it is that risk is a state of mind. If you have done your proper due diligence and you have learned from those that have travelled the road before you, nothing should hold you back.

For the most part, investing in properties can be very "hands off." But if you want to appreciate "property management" then go ahead, manage a property. If you don't have the time, which is really our most precious resource, then it makes sense to hire professional property managers to manage your properties. Either way, you'll quickly realize that owning investment properties is more than worth it.

You should, however, ensure that any property you buy is a true positive-cash-flowing property in order for it to be a *savvier* investment. Why? Because if the market ever does turn, as we all know it sometimes does, then you'll never be in the position where you have to sell your property simply because it will always make money. It's independent. Yes, you do have to factor in maintenance, repairs, vacancy, property management fees, capital expenditures and, of course, financing. However, at the end of the day, if you have a true positive-cash-flowing property, (they are rare, yet they do exist) a downturn in the market won't matter because the property will still make money. It's a wonderful way to drive more freedom.

Coveted single family homes should yield in the neighbourhood of 7 to 10 percent ROI. That being said, keep in mind it's not what you pay: *it's what you net*. You must compare apples to apples. Often what happens is people try to compare *cumulative ROIs* instead of *annualized ROIs*, which is really misleading. They're not comparable. One investment may take place over 10 years. The other investment may take place over 2 years. Comparing the two simply won't make sense. When people promote cumulative ROIs, they are practicing the art of deception as a friend of mine pointed out because a 180 percent ROI sounds fantastic, but if it's over a 20-year period, it's really just a 9 percent ROI, annualized. So that's the way it should be compared. Every ROI should be annualized for you to have a true comparison. Denominator and the holding period should be the same. It's the gross revenue less all the expenses, including vacancy, contingency funds, capital expenditures, property management, etc. ROI is only realized once the property is actually sold or refinanced. I say refinanced because it is actually a healthy way to gain greater wealth as you can defer paying the capital gains tax you must pay once you sell the property. That in itself is a huge advantage that other investments like stocks, bonds or regular interest income cannot offer. As long as you own the property, you can defer paying your capital gains tax. It's like the Canada Revenue Agency (CRA) is giving us a tax-deferred loan with a zero percent interest rate— for life. If you could go down to your local Canada Revenue Agency Bank and borrow money at 0 percent for as long as you own that real estate, would you? Of course you should!

So, why aren't more Canadians Investing in Real Estate?

Does it surprise you to know that only 6 percent of Canadians invest in real estate outside of their principal residence? I find that number to be shockingly low considering all the benefits investment properties can bring. If it's so great, why isn't everyone doing it, you ask? Think about it. There are a lot of great things in the world that the majority of people never do or take any action toward achieving. Does that make those things more or less worthy? Obviously more worthy . . . for the people who take action! It's the people who take action, with the guidance of those trustworthy mentors that have been there before them, who actually get ahead faster and more effectively. It isn't rocket science. And come to think of it, I have yet to meet a rocket scientist that was a millionaire or a multi-millionaire.

So, if you are looking to kick your financial stress to the curb and realize your dream of financial freedom, you need look no further than real estate. Everybody wants it and everybody needs it. Like the singer Billy Squire sang "Everybody Wants You!" It's a win-win situation for everyone. And what can be better than winning all around?

About Peter Mazzuchin

Peter Mazzuchin, Author, Realtor®, and grateful father of Brandon and Lauren. He has been actively investing in Real Estate since 1986. After receiving his degree, he worked in the banking industry for 10 years. As a bank manager, Peter saw that far too many people were consistently living month to month and were financially stressed. He decided he didn't want the same fate so he started researching the 'ins and outs' of real estate investing. He quickly realized it was an effective way to alleviate financial stress, increase security and pave the way toward financial freedom.

In 1992, Peter left the banking industry and began working with a real estate developer. His first investment was a tax advantaged, positive-cash-flow condominium that he was able to purchase sight-unseen with only 10 percent down. The property has since been paid off multiple times by his 'residents' (tenants he treats with respect).

Peter believes that everyone should win in real estate investing and some of his clients refer to him as the ***Spiritual Real Estate Investor***. He further believes that investing in real estate is "exponentially expandable," because it is a legacy you can leave to your family, children, friends or favourite charities, who can, in turn, do the same with their wealth, knowledge and sphere of influence.

Peter's focus is on helping Canadian investors invest in higher return properties in Canada or the U.S. He has a vast network of Realtors®, lenders, contractors, property managers, lawyers, insurance specialists, suppliers, landscapers and tax advisors. To date, he has helped countless investors relieve their financial stress and reach financial stability, some even achieving financial freedom.

His goal is to help at least one million people. He says that each person has a sphere of influence of approximately 150 people. So, if you divide 1 million by a 150, you actually only need to help 6,667 people to affect 1 million individuals. To accomplish this he's founded the Actus Real Estate Investors Club. Visit: www.ActusREIC.com.

In his "**Inspire It Forward**" quest to help people reach financial freedom, Peter is offering a free e-book, which you can download now at **www.roisecrets.com**.

Please share these secrets to help others.

Thank You!

GROWING MONEY WITHOUT SPENDING YOUR OWN: HOW TO PROFIT FROM REAL ESTATE

By Sadhana Sabharwal

What do you want out of life? More income, security for the future, a better lifestyle?

You can have it if you want it–if you take action and *make* it happen.

I'm a single mother with three sons, and I have a full-time job at a law firm–so I don't have a huge amount of time to spend on other pursuits. Still, in the past four years, I have invested in eighteen different properties–including single family homes, duplexes, fourplexes, a five-plex, sixplex, and, most recently an eight-unit building.

Most importantly, I am realizing positive cash flow from most of these buildings.

Eighteen properties may sound like an awful lot for one woman who didn't have a lot of financial resources at her disposal to begin with. Luckily, though, I worked with a group of elite people who helped get me started and showed me the ropes. Best of all, I managed to do my own kinds of creative financing to make my deals work–so my money was not directly at risk.

The hard part? The beginning. Thinking I couldn't do this without having a substantial bankroll to invest–then, facing my fear and anxiety, finding the answers to my dilemmas and, finally, being able to go ahead with my first deal. Obviously, I'm glad I found the courage to start–because I now know that I would have been a lot less rich without it!

In this chapter, then, let me tell you a little bit about myself and how I came to be a real estate mogul (LOL). Perhaps you'll see how you can do likewise!

Coming to Canada and Building a Life

My parents brought me to Canada when I was fourteen years old–
and I immediately began working at a series of odd jobs. For example,
I worked at a gas station as a cashier, I worked in a farm for a day or two
with my mom, I shoveled snow out of driveways, and I delivered the
Toronto Star newspaper with my brother. I still remember the thrill of
collection day–when I would go to all the delivery homes to collect the
newspaper subscription fees. Now, getting that money wasn't the real
thrill–no, that came from being able to buy a box of KFC chicken after
I was done!

My first experience in real estate came about when I was a teenager.
My father began his own business as a Conveyancer (someone who
searches property titles), and I began working summers helping him. I
got to learn more about the legal aspect of property ownership. As an
adult, I went to work for a law firm, and I've been at the same one for
the past 18 years; my employment there gave me even more exposure
as to how real estate business was done. Still, during all that time, I
had never thought of doing any actual investing in real estate-up until
about six years ago. That's when I felt I *had* to.

Why? Because my husband and I had split up–leaving me a single
mom–and responsible for my and my children's future. I had to think
about how to make that future a secure one–and I knew I would need
some extra income to help my teenage children attend university. So
… I began to look at real estate as the way to make that happen.

I started by offering second mortgages to people who didn't qualify for conventional loans. I borrowed on my own line of credit at
around 6% and lent that money at around 10%-14%, meaning, if I lent
$100,000, I would be making $4000 to $8000 in extra interest. One of
those arrangements went very wrong, though, and I got badly burned
on it. Obviously, I didn't want to go on with that plan.

One day at the law firm where I worked, however, a client came in
and mentioned to me that she was buying a property in Cornwall, Ontario, where real estate, at the time, was really very affordable. That got
me thinking–maybe this was a better way to go.

She invited me to her real estate club, and I began attending meetings with her. It was at one of these meetings that I first met Sunil. I learned a lot from participating in these gatherings, and it made me think to myself, "You know what? I can do this."

My first investment was a home I purchased at a tax sale for only $5,000. To prepare for this, I took a tax sale course, so I understood the process. Yes, the home only cost five grand–but it required ten times that much in work–about $50,000 worth. I used my Home Depot card and other credit to get the job done. So, yes, I was on the hook for all that money–but after the work was completed, I was able to get the home appraised and refinanced to the tune of $72,000. All the money I borrowed was instantly paid back–and still made a very good profit! I own that house to this day, and the tenant currently pays me $790 a month rent–and also pays for all the utility expenses.

That inspired me to do more. I put in a lot of offers at one time–about 30!–and finally got a six-plex for about $106,000, which was a very good price for that large a property. To this day, it nets me about $1000 a month, after all expenses. At the time, however, I was terrified of this huge investment–not necessarily because it was huge money, but because I did not have the money, so I had to be able to present it to the investor–in this case my family. I borrowed the down payment from my family and arranged a Vendor Take-Back mortgage for the balance. Numbers would be running through my head constantly; I found myself sleeping next to a calculator and a notepad because I would wake up in the middle of the night, anxious to double-check some of my arithmetic on the property–and needed the right tools to do that. I have since paid back the loan from my family, but the investment continues to pay off to this day.

Winning at the Numbers Game

The calculator has become my best friend during these last few years of investing. If I have a talent when it comes to real estate, it's this–I can listen to the numbers involved in a deal and I can see, instantly in my head, if it's worth doing (or, at the very least, investigating).

I carry the calculator with me at all times just to make sure I can check out any potential deal I might run across, but I've developed a kind of "investing intuition" that leads me to deals that will work. For instance, if someone were to say to me, "You can buy a single family home for $500,000 and rent it for $2500 a month," I would answer right away, "It's not worth it" and that would be the end of it.

I have been a member of Sunil's Private Investment Club since its inception, and that has also helped me through all my investment adventures. This is an elite group of people who are interested in the same things as me, and we pool our resources to find and execute the best deals.

It is true that experience is the best teacher–which is maybe why the last deal I made was my best one so far. I bought a Power of Sale home, one sold by the bank when the owner defaults on the mortgage, for $275,000–it was a five-unit building located about twenty minutes from my house.

How did I find it? Well, let me give you a tip–don't be shy, and don't be afraid to ask people if they know of anything, because I talk to anybody and everybody to find out if they know of any real estate opportunities in which I might be interested. In this case, I was talking to a mortgage manager of a bank and asked him, "Don't you get any Power of Sale properties?" And he said, "Yes, we do. As a matter of fact, I have one right now." Later, he emailed me the information.

I went to look at it with my real estate agent–and found out there was a retaining wall issue on the property. The bank got a quote for the repair, which was quite costly–between 68 and 92 thousand dollars. I asked the bank to take that amount off the cost of the property, and I would take care of the issue myself. We bought it for $275,000–what it might have sold for, say, twenty years ago.

After the purchase went through, we needed to take care of the retaining wall. Well, my contacts at the law firm come in handy for other purposes too–and I was able to find a contractor that would make the repairs for about 70% of the price the bank was quoted. In addition to that, three of the five units needed cosmetic work done to make them suitable for tenants–so my joint venture partner and I did that work ourselves on the weekend–with a lot of elbow grease.

That's right–I forgot to mention that I had a JV partner on this deal. This was someone who wanted to get into real estate investing–and who also provided all the money for the purchase and repair of the fiveplex after I found the deal. And he was glad he did–because, when all was said and done, the property was reappraised after our repairs and remodeling at $750,000!!! Our total cost, including repairs? A little over three hundred and forty thousand dollars. Profit? About $410,000.

Don't you think that's a pretty good return on investment?

My partner and I ended up parting ways on this property, however–he wanted to sell it right away and take the immediate profit. I refinanced it to the full price and bought him out. He made his return–and is now interested in doing more "fix and flips." As for me, I hung on to the property myself–and, even after making the monthly mortgage payment, I'm still making a profit from my new tenants.

To sum up–I put no money in this investment, yet I now own it 100%, and I'm making roughly $1500 a month on that property, plus I have a couple hundred thousand dollars in equity in the home.

Do you have to be rich to be a successful real estate investor? I'm living proof that you do NOT!

Moving Forward with Success

Now, you might think that, if I'm able to realize these kinds of returns, I should be thinking about finally leaving the law firm and doing this full time.

Well, I really love my job, and I'm happy to do real estate as a side venture. Eventually, if I do end up owning enough properties, I may switch over full time, but I'm certainly in no rush. While some people want to rack up the numbers, buying twenty or thirty properties a year, I'm comfortable going at my pace and handling what I want to handle at the moment. I also like to keep my properties and continue to make positive cash flow every month, while their value hopefully appreciates over the long term.

Best of all, even though I own all these properties, they don't require a lot of my time-I only spend about three to four hours a week on them (and because I love to work on them, I don't mind that time at all!). That means there is virtually no conflict with my "day job" hours.

To tell you the truth, because my job *is* related to real estate, I end up making a lot of contacts. For instance, I found out about an estate sale through the law firm; the father had died, and his children wanted to sell his house ASAP. I connected them with an investor friend of mine who bought it for around $267,000 with a short-term loan and, two months later, it was appraised at $350,000 after some minor work was done to improve it. She got it refinanced for $280,000, and that means the short-term loan was immediately paid off, so she basically did the deal for free and picked up almost $70,000 in equity.

I love real estate investing because it's challenging-and it's so much fun to think about what you might be able to accomplish with your next deal. After I started buying properties, I never looked at the newspaper I used to deliver the same way again-I go through the homes advertised for sale, my mental calculator kicks into high gear, and I try to find something with which I can create a lot of profit.

Again, I don't have a lot of savings or other financial resources. I've financed all my deals with equity from my other properties, lines of credit, money from JV partners and so forth-and I've always found the means to get the ball rolling. As a spiritual person, I always find that when I am in need of something in my life, it comes my way in one form or another, if I am open to it-and this principle even extends to when I need money for a deal that I know is going to turn out great!

Why *Not* Invest?

One of my favorite quotes is from the inspirational author, Kobi Yamada: "Sometimes you just have to take the leap and build your wings on the way down."

A huge obstacle to those who want to try real estate investing is what's called "analysis paralysis." They continually read and learn and go to seminars-and yet, they never seem to "take the leap" and actually do a deal.

If you have done your homework, take that leap–and it will all work out. You may make a mistake–I've made them myself (remember my second mortgage debacle), but you know what? You learn from those mistakes.

The important thing is to keep a positive attitude–don't dwell on improbable negatives. Just do it.

If you are a woman, you definitely shouldn't let that hold you back. The more you talk to people, the more they'll put you down or warn you off trying something like this. I went through that, as do a lot of Indian women like myself. I remember when I started, when I was driving seven hours looking at properties, my family would say, "What are you doing? This is crazy!"

Now, what do they say? Well, they don't *say*, they *ask*: "Did you make any new deals? How much did you make?" That makes me smile.

The other thing you must develop is patience and persistence. There was another deal I had a JV partner on–and it took five months to negotiate. During that tense time, more than once, my partner said, "You know what? I can't deal with this any longer." Even my real estate agent thought we should give up. I said, "Be patient, be patient." And by the way, this was my last deal–the one I told you about, where we took the value of the home up to $750,000. I think it was well worth the wait!

If you are ready to leap and build wings too–or if you have a deal that you don't know what to do with–feel free to contact me at **sadhanasabharwal@hotmail.com,** and we can work together to help you fly. Come and get mentored by me one-on-one.

Here's to *your* financial freedom–cheers!

About Sadhana Sadharwal

Sadhana Sadharwal is a single mother with three sons, a full-time law clerk and an enthusiastic real estate investor. Her motto is, "When the student is ready, a teacher will appear."

Over the past four years of investing in real estate, Sadhana has acquired eighteen different properties, including single family homes, duplexes, fourplexes, a fiveplex, a sixplex, and most recently eight-unit buildings. She enjoys positive cash flow from all her properties and looks forward to investing in more.

Sadhana's specialty is buying undervalued properties that need work, fixing them up, and then refinancing them in order to get the newly-gained equity out of the property; she then continues as owner in order to rent them out to tenants, who provide her with an ongoing positive return on her investment.

Sadhana has built up her portfolio of properties through what she calls "recycling" her money and also by creative financing strategies, including traditional bank financing, lines of credit, financing from private lenders, borrowing from family, credit cards, as well as joint venture partners who provide initial funds for down payments.

Sadhana, whose name means "meditation," is a native of India who came to Canada with her family at the age of fourteen. She is a spiritual person who believes in nurturing relationships and helping others attain their goals. Sadhana is happy to assist anyone who wishes to invest in real estate or would be interested in one-on-one coaching or joint ventures with her; she can be reached at

sadhanasabharwal@hotmail.com

BUSINESS INTELLIGENCE THE KEY TO PROSPERITY

By Michael Adoranti

"If you can't measure it, you can't manage it!"
—*W. E. Deming*

What separates the greatest entrepreneurs from the rest of the population? For most of these individuals, it starts with a dream of creating something new—original— something that will add value to the world. That sounds wonderful, doesn't it? But does it really happen this way?

Humanity's capacity to dream is perhaps one of its most powerful, if not enduring qualities. For anyone daring to brave the challenges that come with successfully running a business, the ability to visualize and focus on what matters is imperative. Everything else should follow. Sadly, that is typically not what happens.

Every year, statistics reveal how many new businesses fail within the first 6 months . . . 1 year . . . 5 years and so on. There is no doubt each of these businesses started with an awesome idea and someone's dream. So, what happened along the way? More importantly—why?

According to *Forbes* magazine, there are many reasons why businesses fail. Here are some of the most common:

- Lack of Leadership
- Toxic Company Culture
- Lack of Vision
- Lack of Innovation
- Poor Branding
- No Market Role
- Lack of Execution
- Poor Professional Advice
- Lack of Capital
- Inability to Attract and Retain Talent
- Poor Management
- Competitive Awareness
- Lack of Sales
- Obsolescence or Market Changes

If you look at this list, two questions should come to mind. 1. Who hijacked the leaders? 2. What happened to the company processes that demand performance measurements?

Clearly, the right hand had no idea what the left was doing. That's not to say that all failed businesses suffer from all of the above reasons at once. But it's a shame: All of these reasons could have been prevented and were *always* the responsibility of the leaders. Have you ever noticed that most successful companies always boast how they are in touch with their Business Intelligence (BI) and how, without it, they would not be able to hold their current market position? Is this something new, born of the "Digital Age," or has it always been a key to success?

It All Starts As a Cry for Improved Quality

All businesses want to improve what they can offer as it justifies a substantial increase in revenue. The trick, however, has always been to limit the amount of quality producing innovation and drive for the most profit. Prior to the 1940s, most large businesses in North America focused primarily on sell … sell … sell—regardless of working conditions or management practices. All focus was put on producing in mass quantities, cheaply. Essentially, everyone was working hard to meet quotas. As humans, though, we have physical limitations, and this type of business mentality can achieve only so much before it plateaus.

At this time, in order to continue to grow and expand, businesses needed to make significant management changes; they just had no idea what these changes would entail.

In the 1920s, a man who would bring a profound change to business management and leadership was starting his journey to becoming a "colossus to modern management thinking."[1]

As a child, William Edwards Deming was an ideal student. It was no surprise that in 1917, he set out to raise his academic prowess by attending the University of Wyoming. During the 1920s and 1930s, he would acquire various degrees in the fields of math and physics. By the mid-1930s, he became responsible for mathematics and statistics courses offered at USDA's graduate program. This solid foundation of education demonstrated that Deming specialized in problem-solving techniques; however, it was also during this same time that Deming had the good fortune of meeting leading pioneers in Statistics and Quality Control. So what happened next? Do you even have to ask? Deming's mind excelled at solving real-world problems through mathematics (e.g., modelling physical systems through complex equations). When you add statistics into the mix, though, you get the opportunity to pull in live data, which can reduce the modelling aspect, making it less abstract and more concrete.

Now take it one step further. Apply what was just stated into the world of business quality control, and what you get is termed Statistical Process Control (SPC). Imagine that you can now take existing business processes and mathematically solve their existing problems. This doesn't mean that the factory workers are getting better hammers and screwdrivers. Not at all. *It means that you get the chance to model and analyze how management is leading the operations and make decisions based on these results.*

In 1939, Deming was hired by the U.S. Census Bureau. The population was growing dramatically, and the old method of an absolute count was rapidly becoming a costly endeavour—not to mention the dropping accuracy in the results caused by individuals who did not respond and/or respond correctly.

The solution was clear. Applying a sampling technique to a known segment of any region's population and calculating the results for the whole was a far more accurate and cost-effective strategy. True to his cause, however, Deming carried it even further. He analyzed the punch cards being collected by the census inspectors, along with management's approach to leading them, and discovered more discrepancies. He was able to determine which inspectors were "Out of Control" and needed further training. The payoff was a substantial increase in clerical productivity and significant cash savings in producing the census.[2]

In 1947, General MacArthur engaged Deming to advise on sampling techniques to be used in post-war Japan to ascertain, among other things, the amount of new housing required for the surviving homeless population. This was the first step in bringing about what was later called the Japanese post-war economic miracle of 1950. Deming was successful in sharing his knowledge of sampling the population to produce a census while stressing the importance of SPC. What he did not realize was that he was so successful in delivering his message that in 1950, the Union of Japanese Scientists and Engineers (JUSE) formally invited him to teach workers, plant managers and interested engineers his quality control methods. The idea was to design a product, test it, use the lessons learned to change it, and repeat the process until you have a superior product. Remember it's not just the finished product that becomes high quality, but the management and quality processes that also evolve. This, in turn, increases productivity and market share while decreasing expenses.

The rest is economic history. Japan rose from the devastation of WWII, and within 10 years, was able to capture certain markets the world over. [3]

Now, let's jump forward a bit. In 1981, Ford Motor Company's sales were declining. Between 1979 and 1982, Ford had incurred $3 billion in losses. Clearly, the once-successful techniques used by management were no longer adequate to keep the company profitable. A solution was needed and fast. Ford recruited Deming to help jump-start a quality movement. Not surprisingly, Deming did not criticize how the cars were being made, but rather how the production was being managed. He told Ford that management actions were responsible for 85 percent of all problems in developing better cars. The major issues were found in the company's culture and the way its managers operated. Ford needed to change the way it approached automobile production, and this largely included the manner in which key measurements were being made and used to control and predict the trends for future business decision making. By 1986, Ford had become one of the most profitable American auto companies.

If you can't measure it, you can't manage it!

How does this relate to current business? The stories above show a trend that successful businesses typically follow. Management Leadership and Control and Quality Processes have to evolve continually with the changing market to ensure survivability and sustainability. Sampling a company's products and/or services through statistical analysis and providing the results to the executive decision makers is necessary. This critical information will allow them to make the next series of strategic decisions. What has changed is the "jungle." The tools that management has traditionally used to control and predict business have evolved along with the market. Advances in database technology has allowed businesses to store vast quantities of data on a daily basis–so much data, in fact, that if the manner in which data was analyzed in the 80s were used today, any business would literally need a standing army of analysts just to read it, let alone extract any valuable information from it. Of course, with database advancement, we also have computers that have the capacity to process large quantities of data. So, while the approach of using the data statistically is still the right way to proceed, the challenge is how to do it in today's digital age and stay ahead of the pack.

A New Era

Consider that in the last 10 years in which IT solutions have enabled businesses to actively monitor, track and process routine business activities, the internet has further allowed us to access this data at high speed. Sounds great—so great, in fact, that many businesses outsource IT solutions as a method of controlling operating costs.

Is something still missing? Of course it is. IT solution companies never made the claim that they would actually analyze the data, let alone extract any meaningful message from it. People may now have massive quantities of data available at their fingertips, but who will draw any meaningful conclusions from it? IT has allowed us practically to automate data gathering, but that is as far as it goes.

Automate the Business Management Process

The next logical step is to take this data and automate the business management processes that use it. How can you achieve this? Simply put, in the same time frame that IT solutions have become available, the use of balanced scoreboards, portals and dashboards have also come into general use.

For the most part, businesses have directed analysts to create these boards on a periodic basis for reporting (monthly, quarterly, etc.). These boards contain the extracted performance results from the database, or in simple terms, this is the business intelligence. But how is this automated?

Many companies produce software tools that can perform business analytics. You can purchase any of these tools. They come in a variety of complexity and capabilities, not to mention a stiff price tag. No matter what the sales pitch is, however, it is common knowledge that many of these enterprise-level analytics tools are often rigid and not very customizable, and let's not forget the often less-than-stellar tech support that comes with them.

What you really need is an analyst that has the right talent and skill set to surf your database in a timely manner, extract the relevant data, perform the required analysis, and produce highly accurate and rock-solid boards that specifically pertain to your unique business management process. Ideally, this individual will make innovative use of in-house software tools to automate the above tasks without the need of expensive high-end tools. Clearly, this individual possesses the skills of an analyst; however, he or she needs to be capable of much more. You may have noticed a new term pop up in industry describing this type of person. We like to call them "Data Miners."

What are Data Miners?

Data miners are individuals who possess a strong knowledge of database design and how it is administered. They are responsible for collecting data, analyzing it from different types of perspectives, and drawing conclusions. These conclusions are often used to cut expenses, increase revenues, and make other important business decisions. Data miners are typically well versed with a company's business management processes and work closely with executives to determine which Key Performance Indicators (KPI) should be measured and how the information should be captured on the boards. Keep in mind that a data miner is not responsible for determining which KPIs are right for your business; that's up to the executive team. Data miners will assist by being able to predict the usefulness and outcome of the selection.

Balanced Scoreboards, Portals and Dashboards

The use of balanced scoreboards, portals and dashboards through software and the internet is similar to what Deming was teaching businesses to do all along. You need to foster the right business culture through continuous improvement of the business management process. Your database and the boards provide you with business intelligence derived from the data analysis, which in many cases includes sampling techniques.

With a data miner automating your business management process, all that remains is the selection of which KPIs to measure and which board to use. The following provides a general guideline to selecting a reporting board:

Dashboards: These boards are often used by floor managers or foremen to directly measure the output of a production and/or service department. You can expect to see measurements that show counted quantities of different items produced or services rendered, percentage complete of specified daily goals, measurement of sales and so on. These measures represent the lowest common denominator in the overall project.

Portals: These boards are often used by the different levels of middle management. The theory behind portals is that many middle managers control and oversee operations of several or many departments. The portal, in many cases, summarizes the dashboard results of all the relevant departments involved in a specified project. The summaries are then further analyzed to draw a conclusion as to the actual overall status of a specified project. Hence, these boards will illustrate measurements of project performance as a whole.

Balanced Scoreboards: The intended audience for these boards tends to be the president, CEO and/or executives. These individuals oversee all projects being conducted by the company. Whether you are reporting good or bad news, they want only the executive summary with key highlights over some predefined top-level KPIs. Only in extreme cases will they request lower-level data to see what's going on, which would be simply to provide them with the relevant portal data. Keep in mind the data selected to be visible in the Balanced Scoreboards is the most critical. Business leaders rely on its accuracy to be able to predict and control future business strategic decisions and market position.

10 Key Benefits of Reporting With Boards

1. Increased Visibility: Dashboards allow you instant access to all aspects of your business, which will allow users to make more informed and accurate management decisions with confidence.

2. Reduce Repetition and Excessive Costs: When consolidating and standardizing your information, performance dashboards can eliminate the need for redundant data that can ultimately undermine a single version of business information. Further, a single performance dashboard can help businesses reduce or eliminate numerous independent reporting systems, spread marts, data marts and warehouses.

3. Cross-company Product and/or Service Performance Improvements: W. E. Deming made it clear, "If you can't measure it, you can't manage it." Automated reporting boards allow you to measure your performance throughout your organization quickly and effectively, which in turn, can lead to continuous process improvement.

4. Empower Users: Performance dashboards allow users to access their information themselves, reducing and/or eliminating their reliance on the IT department in order to create customized reports. Business managers can further take advantage of guided analysis and layered delivery of information, as well as structured navigation paths, which make it easier and more efficient to analyze and act on this information.

5. Time Management: With the automation doing the heavy lifting, all levels of management have more time to spend on what really matters instead of having to log into numerous systems, running the reports and having to assimilate all the data to understand the overall business performance. Precious hours can be gained each month.

6. Users Can Act Quickly: Not only do performance dashboards help cut down on hours of work, but these dashboards also provide actionable information, meaning the information can be used quickly in order to capitalize on new opportunities or help customers who need immediate attention.

7. Measure Business Performance against Your Plan: Successful businesses always start a project with a planned schedule and budget, but that represents only half the victory. The other half is closely measuring your actuals, comparing them to your planned data, and making sure the project is performing to your company's expectations. A well-designed board can do this for you.

8. Consistent Business Information: Performance dashboards integrate and consolidate information using consistent and recognizable definitions, rules and metrics, which allow all users to see the same information.

9. Employee Performance Improvements: When employees know their performance is being judged in a dashboard and can see their performance results, they innately start to improve their work ethic and output.

10. Always in the "Know": Performance dashboards provide management with relevant and timely information that can help executives and managers avoid any surprises. Unforeseen issues can be eliminated before they affect bottom-line results.

Take Action—Now

Is your business achieving the goals and objectives that you have set? Do you have the market position you planned for? Is the competition moving in regardless of what actions you take? If you don't know what is happening in your business at the push of a button, you don't know enough. It's not just about having the latest data at your fingertips. The data has to be accurate and unconditionally available. You never know when the mother lode of opportunities will come calling. What you do know is that you need to be ready to ACT.

About Michael

Michael Adoranti is a Program Management Professional certified with the Program Management Institute (PMI), the world's leading professional association for program management. Michael is an innovative, results-oriented System/Software Engineer, Author, Conference Speaker, Mentor, and Successful Entrepreneur who has made a career of thinking outside the box. Michael's goal is to help leaders achieve their business goals faster and easier than they ever imagined by providing them with creative technological solutions to decrypt the overwhelming ocean of data in corporations across the country. Engaged in Naval Engineering Programs with Canada and the United States for over two decades, Michael understands how sensitive your data is and how your business intelligence is key for your business to prosper. Michael is a leading expert in **training and developing your team** to create customizable balanced scoreboards, portals and dashboards allowing business executives and managers the ability to make powerful and enlightened decisions to propel their businesses to the next level.

A Special Gift for your journey toward Prosperity

Michael has developed the *"Business Leader's Compass to Utopia"*, a practical guide for helping business leaders across North America determine what kind of Balanced Scoreboard, Portal and/or Dashboard is a perfect fit for their business needs. The book sells for $97, but for a very limited time, Michael is offering his readers a digital version for Free.

To get your gift, go to www.businesscompass.michaeladoranti.com

For more information on Michael Adoranti Programs and Solutions, go to www.michaeladoranti.com or email:
ClientSuccess@MichaelAdoranti.com

POWER OF THREE M'S

By Sockalingam PrabaHARAN

Your Master key to Success

What is the power of three M's? I would define it as the science of achieving success in your life. Until I understood the real power of the three M's, I didn't realize many successes, but when I realized it, I discovered my gold mine. Once you have a clear understanding of each of them, you will find yourself in a different universe.

One question always echoed in my mind: In this world, everyone gets equal opportunities and resources, so why does one person achieve success and others fail? I figured out the reason after reading several books. My conclusion is that if you realize the power of three M's, success is yours.

I came to Canada in my early 20's. I had $ 1,000.00 left in my pocket to start my life. There was no one to guide me and no clue of what to do next.

In a few days all my savings were gone and I was left with no cash to pay the rent. One of my friends, Ramesh, gave me his room and stayed with his friend Nishan.

I was on the balcony looking at the park and watching the people. I noticed the heavy traffic and busy people in the road, and my mind started saying, "Everyone has something to do except me. This country gives opportunities to everyone, but when am I going to find mine?" Then I asked myself, "Do I have to go in search of opportunity or will it come to me by itself?"

The next day, I decided to search for the opportunities. Since I was interested in finance, I decided to knock on every bank's doors to know what employment opportunities they have for new comers. I took leaflets from banks and started to read in order to understand the Canadian credit system, legal system and Taxations. In the meantime, I was desperately looking for my first job to satisfy my financial needs. Finally, through a youth support program, I got to work as a UPC Coordinator at Zellers for 12 weeks as a co-op student. I worked hard and got a permanent job.

While I was working there, I helped them with store activities, updating the store's software system. All the people working with me believed that I was an expert in computers, and because of their encouragement, I decided to apply for jobs in the IT department.

My wife had a diploma in computers, and she decided to do the Microsoft Certified System Engineer course. One day I went to drop my wife in the class, and I happened to meet the institute teacher, Mr. Jeffery, who brought about a change in my life. He made me realize the importance of having a mentor in my life.

I applied for a couple of internal jobs. After few rejections, I got a temporary job for 12 weeks. In order to make it a full time job, I decided to pursue a course. Since I didn't have enough money and time for a degree, I studied computer courses. I studied well with Mr. Jeffrey's mentorship. He gave me confidence and made me trust myself, and I completed my first Microsoft Professional certification. He rewarded me by returning my course and exam fees. Finally I successfully completed the Microsoft Certified System Engineering course.

As a result, my confidence level went higher. Within six months, my job turned permanent. I became a full-time Technology Analyst. I worked there for eight years until they gave me a layoff.

While I was working there, I created my own networking lab. On the other side, my inner mind kept telling me to find a career in finance, so I started attending seminars and searching for a mentor in the field. I badly wanted to become financially independent so that I could choose to work.

Many people who become financially free choose one of following fields:

1) Real estate

2) Stock marketing

3) Own businesses

4) Internet-based businesses

I decided to choose real estate, so I bought a property and rented the basement and one room upstairs. This helped me pay off my mortgages and gave some income. After 3 years, I bought another house. I realized that property is one of the greatest investments and liked the idea that my mortgages were being paid off by someone else. In addition, the appreciation of the properties' value increased, making my assets increase. After this I started buying one property every year.

In 2008, when I was laid off, my manager asked me what I was going to do after that. I told him that I was going to go to Florida with my family. I knew I was not depending on my pay cheques. So i was able to tell him with confidence. Every time the equity in my investment increased, I stood up with more and more confidence.

I started PrabaHARAN Wealth Institute in 2013. I educate my clients to become wealthy through Real estate and the Canadian Credit system, including how you can maximize your potential through the Canadian credit system by knowing the power of using other people's money for your financial success.

From the past 25 years of my journey, I would like to share the key ingredients for achieving financial successes. After spending thousands of dollars for many seminars, books and mentorships, I figured out that these key ingredients created my own power to teach and motivate people.

The power of three M's

1) **M**indset

2) **M**entor

3) **M**aster Mind Group

These are the Three keys to access to your success.

Mind set:

You must have a mindset that is set up for success. The mindset pulls you towards your goal. Most of the time you know what to do to achieve your goal, but your mindset becomes an obstacle to achieving it. It is necessary to set your mind to support your efforts.

Years back when I started buying properties, I made my mind to have property valued at $1.000.000,00. When I reached $1.000.000,00 I made my mind to add "0" to it and made it $10.000.000,00 then my mind started to work towards this goal.

When it comes to mind set, here are few things you should consider.

1. Learn to get over things quickly.
In your life you may get disappointments. For example, you desperately needed money and asked your best friend, but he refused. You applied for your dream job, but you weren't selected. A long-time relationship ended. You applied for a bank loan, but got canceled in the last minute. These issues are very common. You have to get over these issues quickly. Otherwise these disappointments will hold you back from progressing.

2. Accept the fact you become what you are thinking about.
It is true that you become what you think about most of the time. If you keep telling yourself your goals, you tend to take actions towards achieving them without your knowledge. All these depend on your mind set. The perception of a particular thing has very high value. A glass of water can be viewed as half empty or half full. If you believe that you will get your dream job, you automatically achieve it, so believe yourself and the goals.

3. Focus on what works for you.
Everyone in the world has a list of what *is* working for them and what is *not* working for them. Focus on things that work for you. Since time is a major factor for success, spend more time towards what works for you in your life, and you will see the results very quickly. You don't feel the tiredness when your mind is really into it.

4. Avoid negative people when you can.
Most of the time, it is difficult to avoid people, even though they are

your family members. At least try to avoid negative people until you see real success and gain confidence. Don't let anyone steal your dream. Don't ever compromise on your goals. For example, imagine someone who keeps calling you every day and complaining about life. He complains about the cold summer, hot winter, traffic and so on. Would you answer his phone call next time? The answer is "no" for certain.

5. Feed your mind with good things on daily basis.

Now the next question is "How do you feed your mind?" The best way to feed your mind is by reading positive books, watching video clips of famous people that are motivating and by attending free seminars. When I started my life in Canada. There are lot of free seminars to attend. The internet has all the resources. People who are conducting seminars have something to sell at the end of the day. People should learn to pay for the values they get. You cannot get free stuff all the time. If things are available for free, we don't value them much and fail to learn from them. I had a habit. If I receive a value from a seminar, I make sure that I enroll for the seminar conducted by the same person in the future.

6. Train your mind to face failure and falling down.

Failures are not results. They teach you how *not* to do a task to achieve success. They are actually the best mentors in your path towards success, so learn from them and don't try avoid them completely.

"Failures are master piece of of your success"
- *PrabaHARAN*

7. Teach your mind not to give up. Human minds are unstable.

They easily become tired of seeing failures and disappointments and tend to give up. Make sure that this doesn't happen. Every one of us must be able to control our mind rather than it controlling us, so make sure that you set your mind in such a way that it keeps persevering.

Set goals and review them daily.

"Download your goals to your subconscious mind. Miracles will happen automatically."
- *PrabaHARAN*

This is the most important essential activity for achieving success in life. When you fail to plan it, success cannot be achieved at all. Planning alone is not enough. More than that, one has to review it daily. There is no use planning a goal and allowing it to rust. Share your goals with your best friend. By doing so, you are telling the world that you have a target to achieve, and your friend will make sure that you achieve it by reminding you about it every now and then.

Mentor:

Who is a mentor? What is his actual job? How can he help me in progressing in my field? A mentor is a successful person in your field or a motivating personality who has already established his success in the same field you are try to prove yourself. His life history becomes a guide for you. Sometimes people ask me why they need a mentor when we can do most of the stuff, and my answer would be there is no use of doing this when you don't know the proper way of achieving success. He is the person who is going to guide and direct you when you get stuck in your journey. If he has a walking stick, then he can verify his destination with it, and it prevents him from falling down. Similarly, mentors can guide you with the direction and prevent you from falling.

"The person without a mentor is like a blind person walking without a white walking stick"
- *PrabaHARAN*

Now you get convinced with the fact that a mentor is important, but another question arises in everyone's mind when they decide to follow a mentor. How much do we need to spend on a mentor? Mentors can be costly, but sometimes their guidance is available for free as well. Most importantly, mentors need not be a person. It could be some form that represents your mentor's personality, for instance a book, their seminars, etc. Before you pay for the mentor, start by reading books written by them. This does not cost you much.

"You should have enough information and value the opportunity."
- *PrabaHARAN*

Once I didn't have enough money to pay for the books. I couldn't afford amount when I was working for basic pay, but my mind set was to read a book every day. I cut short my lunch time at my work to save the time and then walked to the nearby book store to read as much I can. There I started reading financial and self-motivating books. Most of the stores had a place for reading books before buying it. Every time I read a book and found something useful in it, then I paid for it and bought the book. So when I buy a book, I am certain that it will be very useful to me in one way or the other. It is not necessary that all the information in the book be applicable in your life. Apply the information that is useful to you and you like. You can be sure that the information will work for you because your mentor has already applied and achieved success in the same field.

You can't choose a mentor just by reading a few books. After reading so many books, I chose a few mentors to follow. They were the people who had already achieved things I wanted to achieve in my life, so I copied and pasted their success procedures into my life and achieved the results I wanted to. If you have any doubts in your mind about your mentor, you cannot follow his or her principles. Even now I follow the habit of reading at least a book every month. Just read 10 pages a day so that you can finish it early.

I have mentors who do not even know that I am following them. By following them, I have gained many financial benefits without having to pay for their mentorship.

If you have a mentors and follow them sincerely, then you know everything about them and their principles of success in your field. Concepts of your mentors get aligned with your thoughts, and you may find and attend the free seminars and workshops conducted by your mentors.

When you keep tracking your mentors, you not only learn their success formulas, but also the mistakes they made that earned them failures. Therefore their experiences become lessons for you, and you don't repeat them. Make sure you have mentors guiding you directly or indirectly.

Master Mind Group

The third important ingredient for success is Master Mind Group.

What is Master Mind group?

A Master Mind Group is nothing but the association of two or more like-minded people. They get together to encourage one another to achieve their goals and dreams. They offer a lot of programs such as brainstorming, training, education, peer accountability and similar motivational activities. They also help you to improve your personal and business skills, thus helping members to achieve success.

It is like an energy drink that boosts your depressed mind. Every week we meet to energize ourselves. Every week we experience mood swings. There are always ups and downs in our day-to-day activity. Every time our energy goes low, we need a place to go and boost us. Master Mind Group is the place that helps to achieve this.

Besides this there is always an accountability partner you can talk to. If you are feeling down, you can call him/her, and that person can restore your energy with their positive words.

To become a leader, a great person or financially successful person, you must join a mastermind group and visit every week without fail. You can either create a master mind group or join an existing one. All the information regarding these groups is available online. Almost every millionaire and billionaire is in a mastermind group.

The idea of a mastermind group came from the book *Think and Grow Rich*, written in 1937 by Napoleon Hill. Napoleon Hill defined the Master Mind Group principle as "The coordination of knowledge and effort of two or more people who work towards a definite purpose in the spirit of harmony." This book talks about 13 principles for success for all of these groups.

To create a mastermind group, talk to your co-workers or to people whom you do business with. Gather people and form a network. Then, whenever a mastermind member has an issue, the members brainstorm on the problem and come up with a solution. It is not a coaching center or a regular class or a networking group. It's a place where you get advice, feedback and support on the issues that are bothering you.

I personally have achieved many things through the mastermind group. Sometimes big ideas rise within seconds. My accountability partners played an important role in my huge success, so I would highly recommend each and every one of you to become a member of one of these groups.

Thinking + Talking = Zero (0) results

Thinking+ talking+ action = Success

You may send hours of reading books, spend lots of money for seminars and mentorship, but unless you put in action towards your goal, your success is far away.

When you have the mindset to achieve success in your field, find a mentor for yourself. When you smell success with marvelous mentorship and strong mindset, join a Mastermind group to keep you active each and every day. If you are in this track, you need not go in search of success. Success will automatically knock on your doors.

Wishing you the best of luck.

About Sockalingam Prabaharan

Sockalingam Prabaharan is one of the leading voices of real estate, financial consulting and wealth-building professionals in Toronto.

He is the founder and CEO of PrabaHARAN Wealth Institute, a real estate training and mentorship company in Markham. He is a licensed real estate agent and a financial advisor/insurance broker.

Initially he started his career in the IT field. He successfully completed his Microsoft Certified System Engineer in 2000. He invested the money he allocated to spend for his university into real estate and bought his first property at the age of 27. Then he traced run-down properties and rented those after repair. He earned his real estate license in 2004.

From his youth he had a strong interest in finance management. This led him to get his insurance license in 2007, and he became a Financial and Insurance Advisor.

Apart from his investments he wished to buy his dream house.
In 2008, he achieved it by buying a huge, newly built property in Markham. As soon as he moved to the new house, he was laid off from the company because of globalization, but he didn't lose hope because of the financial independence he gained through his real estate investments.

Having always had the desire to learn, he attended numerous seminars to learn from top realtors. He also participated in "The learning Annex-The Real Estate & Wealth Expo," which influenced his real estate career greatly. He was impressed with the teachings of Donald Trump, Tony Robbins and David Bach and was also mentored by Raymond Aron, Frank Cobin and Sunil Tulsiani, mentors guidance and hard work he became financially independent at when he was at age of 38.

He expanded his business in all the areas by helping his friends and family. He established himself as a successful real estate sales representative and financial advisor in Canadian Society.

THE NUMBERS GAME: 25 MUST-KNOW TIPS TO MAKE THE CRA AND IRS YOUR REAL ESTATE INVESTING PARTNERS

By Sangita Tulsiani
Income Tax Specialist and Real Estate Investor

Put two Canadian strangers into a room and they'll undoubtedly start talking about the weather . . . and eventually, they'll talk about taxes. Taxes are as Canadian as Tim Horton's. We love our country, but most Canadians feel the inevitable tax burden. And real estate investors feel it even more.

Whether you invest in Canada or the US, you'll celebrate your investing income until that first tax bill comes due. But there's no reason to feel animosity toward the Canada Revenue Agency (CRA) or the Internal Revenue Service (IRS). Although their job is to tax us, and make sure we pay, there are ways to improve your investing power and legally put more money in your pocket. Here are 25 sure-fire tips to make both the CRA and the IRS your real estate investing partners.

Tip #1: Be "tax aware"

Taxes won't pay themselves and ignoring them won't make them go away. Make it a point to educate yourself about the taxes you need to pay— from the Provincial Sales Tax (PST) and Harmonized Sales Tax (HST) to federal and provincial corporate and personal income taxes and any taxes you pay when you invest in another country.

Yes, there are a lot of taxes. But taxes are a part of any business, so don't ignore them. Learn what they are and how they are calculated, and stay on top of their prompt payment to the appropriate agency. Both the CRA and IRS will penalize you if you are late—and they don't mess around. Some penalties are harsh, but if you work with an accountant who is experienced in real estate investing or in your type of business, they'll help you to figure out how little taxes to pay and when.

Tip #2: Tax deductions from expenses

You'll incur expenses as you invest in real estate— that's true of any business. And you have the right to deduct all applicable business expenses you have incurred, so keep all your receipts. Be aware, however, that sometimes these expenses can exceed your actual income— which is completely normal in some years, especially if you are just starting out. So here's what you need to know: Even if your expenses exceed your income, you cannot increase losses in the case of your home office expenses. However, you can carry home office expenses forward and apply them to another year.

Tip #3: Take advantage of capital gains

Capital gains are earned from the sale of an asset. We tax-savvy accountants love them because they are taxed at a lower rate. In Canada, capital gains are taxed at only 50 percent of the gain. In the US, there's an attractive capital gains rate as well (although it is slightly more complex to understand.) I recommend you find a knowledgeable accountant who understands both Canadian and US taxes—someone who knows the rules, but will also try and find you the best possible outcome within these rules.

Tip #4: Start with a proprietorship

As an accountant who specializes in real estate investing, I'm frequently asked by investors, "Should I incorporate now or get started quickly as a proprietorship?" Although each person's situation is different, I often recommend you start out as a sole proprietor (it's faster and cheaper to start) and then later, incorporate when your business picks up. Incorporating can not only be expensive and time consuming, but it also comes with a whole new set of tax rules and guidelines. So if you can manage as a sole proprietor, I would suggest you do.

Tip #5: Incorporate when your business picks up

A corporation may take some effort to start and run, but incorporating also comes with many advantages:

When you earn income in your corporation, but leave it in the company or invest it, you pay the corporate tax rate, which is lower than being a sole proprietor.

Money earned by corporation shareholders as dividends is taxed at a more attractive rate than money earned as income.

The corporation allows for an easier transfer for estate planning, or if you choose to pass on your business to your children. It further allows for such things as the necessity to break up the company because of a failed marriage. When the corporation is sold, you are allowed up to $750,000 as tax free income. This is called the Lifetime Capital Gains Exemption on the sale of Qualified Small Business Corporation (QSBC) shares. This tax-savings rule was put in place as an economic incentive to help raise the level of investment in small businesses in Canada. There are two US corporate structures available to Canadians: The Limited Liability Corporation (LLC) and the C-Corp.(you might have heard of S-corp., which is a corporate structure not available to Canadians).

Each of these two structures, the LLC and the C-Corp., have their own advantages. For example, LLCs are fairly simple to set up and losses can offset personal income. C-Corps. take more work to set up and they require more complex structure; their losses are carried forward and applied to future profit. Your accountant and lawyer can help you understand and choose the right corporate structure for you.

Tip #6: Know what expenses you can deduct as rental income

Rental income is essentially income earned by an investor who holds a property for a period of time and earns rental income from that property. Rental income allows you to deduct many expenses you will face as a property owner. Here are a few of the highlights, :

Appliances used in your rental property, as well as the building, fittings, and fixtures(these can be claimed as depreciation)

Advertising costs, Bank charges

Gardening and lawn care

Repairs and maintenance

Home office costs

Insurance premiums

Inspection fees

Mortgage and related costs interest

Accounting or legal fees

Loan and credit cards interest

Property management fees

Travel

Utilities

The interest you pay when financing your vehicle (if you use the vehicle as part of your business)

Membership to real estate clubs for learning better ways to invest.

If you plan to write off these expenses, you must make sure you keep good records and have receipts for all of your payouts. If you plan to claim travel expenses, make sure you maintain accurate travel logs. You can either keep track of the exact kilometres you drive strictly for investing purposes (the detailed method), which can include any meetings, showings purchases etc. and then multiply that by the allowable rate per/km your province allows, or you keep a record of your mileage at the beginning of the year and then again at the end (the simplified method). Determine the percentage of use for business-related activities i.e. maybe you use your car 50 percent of the time for business. Calculate your mileage based on 50 percent.

When filling out your tax papers, rental income is reported on form T776 in Canada.

Bonus tip: Rental income is added to your personal income, which can increase your eligible RRSP contribution room!

Tip #7: Know what expenses you can deduct as business income

If your properties do not have renters for very long, or if you flip real estate instead of renting it out, the CRA considers that to be business income instead of rental income.

You still get some great deductions, too, including:

Advertising expenses (that you might use to attract sellers, buyers, and joint venture partners)

Business insurance

Interest on business loans

Wages and benefits

Group term life and health insurance premiums

Meals and entertainment (100 percent for your staff and up to 50 percent for clients)

Your business phone and cell phone

A home office

Vehicle Depreciation

Website

Courses you take to become educated about real estate investing.

. . . And more. Your accountant can help you find even more deductions, which you can report against your business income on form T2125.

Tip #8: Get the right paperwork to invest in the US

There are so many great reasons to invest in the US— including really low property prices. But it's not as simple as finding a property and buying it. You need the right paperwork, including an Individual Taxpayer Identification Number (ITIN), which is a United States tax processing number issued by the Internal Revenue Service (IRS) to foreign investors.

Tip #9: Investing in the US means paying taxes twice?

As a Canadian investing in the US, you will need to have your Tax Specialist fill out a US tax return as well as Canadian return.

Here's how it works: You'll pay tax to the IRS on your income and then you need to file your Canadian tax return and claim the foreign tax credit (which means you'll only pay the difference between what you paid the IRS and what you would pay if you paid it all to the CRA.) So, you really are not paying taxes twice, just paying taxes on the total amount of income you made.

Be aware that you may also need to do a state return for the particular state your rental property is located in, although this only applies to some states, and U.S. state taxes can range from 0 percent to 11 Percent.

Tip #10: Know the best way to report US rental income

If you own rental property in the US, you have a choice of two ways to report this income for tax purposes. You can report your gross rental income or your net rental income. Which one is right for you? That depends on your situation. Talk to an accountant who is experienced in US real estate taxation to help you.

Tip #11 File your US return on time

Canadians who need to file a US tax return must do so by April 15 of the year following the tax year. If you fail to file on time, the IRS charges penalties and interest. The IRS may also disallow the deductions associated with the property, which means taxable income will increase.

Tip #12: Borrow smart

Borrowing money can be good for business! If you borrow money to make a business or real estate investment, your interest on borrowed money is 100% deductible. In a roundabout way, you end up increasing your "take-home" income while reducing the financial impact the loan's interest has on your business! It's as close as you can get to borrowing money for free! And who doesn't want to take advantage of that?

Tip #13: Disclose your foreign property net worth

If you hold foreign real estate investments with a combined net worth of over $100,000 in Canada, you need to complete the foreign property disclosure form, T1135. Failure to do this will result in a penalty of $2500.00, plus interest of course.

Tip #14: Know your style of investment

When an investor is sitting across from me, this is one of the questions I ask in our first meeting: What style of investing do you do? The style of investing will influence what kind of taxes you pay.

So know your style. Are you a long-term investor? A flipper? What is your risk tolerance? Are you actively involved in property management? Do you use a property management company? This information helps your accountant to better determine what strategy to take and what tax savings rules they can use to your advantage.

For example, a flipper who flips every 6 months is considered by tax agencies to be running a business and therefore earns business income. Someone who rents out their investment property for several years and/or has a property management company is considered to be earning rental income. This influences whether or not you are entitled to capital gains on the real estate (the flipper would not be entitled to this but the rental investor would be).

Tip #15 Know the transfer tax rules and rates

Provinces charge a transfer tax for a real estate seller to transfer property to a real estate buyer. Buyers typically pay this transfer tax. To find out how much the transfer tax you need to pay contact your local Government taxation office. .

Tip #16 Take advantage of income splitting

If you accept all income, it can put you in a higher tax bracket. But if you employ income-splitting methods so that your family earns some of that income, it can help keep you out of higher tax brackets. Income splitting methods include: Owning properties jointly with your family members and paying your family a wage for doing work (for example, you can hire your teenage children to mow the lawn of your rental property.) If you plan on paying a salary to family members, however, make sure the salary is reasonable and in line with average income for the services they perform. You do not have to pay CPP contributions for children under the age of 18. You may need to discuss EI deductions with your tax adviser as this may be to both yours and your family member's advantage in some cases. It is also good for minors to file tax returns so they can begin to build up RRSP contribution allowances based on their salary, even with no taxable income for the year. They can then use this for future income tax deductions.

Note: Income splitting can be a fairly advanced skill and is risky if not done properly.

Tip #17 Report all income —even Internet income

If you earn an income through an Internet business, CRA has announced additional disclosure requirements. This includes any income earned from:

One or more websites

Shopping carts

Auctions or online marketplaces

Advertising, affiliate programs, etc.

If you earn income through the Internet, be sure to let your accountant know so it can be reported accurately.

Tip #18: Keep proper records

Consider your accountant as your business partner who will get you all the tax deductions you are entitled to. In the end, this helps you to keep more of the money you earned through your investments. But your accountant can only be as effective as your record-keeping. I always recommend to my clients that they use a computer program or hire a bookkeeper to help them maintain good records.

Bonus tip: Keep your records for at least 6 years from the date of assessment. Even if you do not have to attach certain supporting documents to your return, or if you are filing your return electronically, you are required to keep these items in case the tax agencies decide to audit you down the road… and in many cases, they will. The CRA specifically can request documentation (like cancelled cheques or bank statements) as proof of any deduction or credit you claim.

Tip #19: Work with an expert

You don't grab a screwdriver when you need to hammer a nail. Both are essential tools for your toolbox but each one has their own unique purpose. In the same way, there are many different types of accountants so make sure you're working with someone who is familiar with real estate investing and actually does real estate taxes.

Build a good relationship with your accountant.

Keep them up-to-date on your business' activities.

Don't keep them at arm's length. Think of them as a business partner whose only job is help you make more money. A good real estate investing accountant can help you to structure your business, and stay within legal boundaries.

Tip # 20: Family loans

For investment purposes, you can lend money to family members in a lower tax bracket. You must, however, charge interest on this loan based on CRA's interest rate at the time the loan is given. As the lender, you must collect the interest by January 30 of the following year. The borrower (your family member) on the other hand, can deduct the interest paid when he or she prepares his/her income tax return. As the lender, you are required to pay tax on the interest payments you receive. So, depending on the investment yield, you could receive a good tax savings. This is something you will need to discuss with a tax professional.

Tip # 21 Donations

You may want to consider donating publicly-traded securities with accrued capital gains to a registered charitable organization instead of donating cash. There is no tax associated with unrealized capital gains if you donate listed shares to a charitable organization. As a bonus, the charity would also receive a larger amount than it would have if you were to have simply sold the shares and then donated the resulting proceeds, after paying tax on the capital gain. The charity will provide you with a donation tax receipt, (a tax credit) for the full market value of the shares, and you do not pay any capital gains tax on this sale.

Tip # 22 Issue shares of your company to your partner or children

This is essentially another form of income splitting that would be reported on Line 120 Dividends from Canadian Corporation.

The advantage of issuing company shares to your family members is to transfer assets to low-income family members, which also helps them to earn income. This rule may apply whenever you transfer a property. Not surprisingly, there are rules you will have to consider.

If you give property to your spouse or children, any capital gains from the transferred assets will be attributed to you.

If you give property to a minor (a son, daughter, niece or nephew under the age of 18), any income from the funds will be attributed to you, but the capital gains from the property will be taxed to the child.

Tip # 23 Business investment losses

Any unrepaid money that you loaned to a family corporation may qualify as a business investment loss. This can be a bit complicated, so ask your accountant about this and whether you qualify.

Tip # 24 Northern Residents Deduction

For those of you who live in a particular northern zone, you may qualify for this tax deduction. As well, there is a taxable benefit if you travel to this particular zone. As such, you may be able to deduct all or a part of this from your total income. This includes travel for you and your family for 2 trips. Your tax-savvy accountant can give you more information on this particular deduction.

Tip # 25 Contribute to a spousal RRSP

As a higher income-earning spouse, you can contribute to a spousal RRSP in the name of your lower income-earning partner. The advantage of this is that the spouse with the higher income can use the RRSP deduction to reduce their income tax paid, while the lower tax bracket spouse will pay income tax on the RRSP withdrawals sometime in the future.

The bottom line is that there are so many reasons to invest in real estate, and tax savings will be only a small portion of the scenario. So, find a good real estate investing accountant to help you to structure your business, maximize your profits, and stay within the legal boundaries. The last thing you want is to be audited and fined—as well as have to pay back any tax savings you made, with interest. If you are part of a RE group, ask other members for a recommendation.

About Sangita Tulsiani

Did you know that 90 percent of all businesses pay too much tax? Sangita Tulsiani knows. She's been in the tax industry since 1995. She has studied accounting, bookkeeping, and taxation for Canadian real estate investing scenarios and honed her skills at large and small accounting firms.

Today, she's a highly sought-after accountant who specializes in helping real estate investors legally keep more of their money in their own pockets and out of the hands of the Canada Revenue Agency or the Internal Revenue Service. It's no wonder that she has more than 300 *returning*, loyal clients from all over Canada who trust her to help them make more money and who seek her out year after year to complete their taxes.

For a limited time, readers can get a complimentary 20 minute tax consultation absolutely FREE, simply by calling 905-915-3399.